I0558713

Praise for Heartfulness

"This book has an excellent collection of essays on Islamic spiritual practices that will benefit a wide audience. I commend the editor for enriching the field of Islamic Psychology."

- AMBER HAQUE, PH.D. Program Director, Muslim Family Services, ICNA Relief, USA.

"Carrie York's edited volume Heartfulness is a groundbreaking work that reshapes the expanding field of Islamic psychology. The book makes a significant contribution by advancing research on Islamic mindfulness, meditation, prayer, and other psycho-spiritual practices and healing methods, positioning them appropriately within the realms of health, wellness, and complementary and alternative medicine (CAM). The innovative and profound concept of "heartfulness" greatly enriches the mindfulness landscape, which has been largely influenced by Indian and East Asian traditions up until now."

- MUHAMMAD U. FARUQUE, PH.D. Author of Sculpting the Self: Islam, Selfhood, and Human Flourishing

"This book presents important scholarship and experiential knowledge on the practice of mindfulness within the Islamic tradition from a variety of perspectives. Readers interested in Islamic spiritual practice, mindfulness traditions, and the psychological benefits of mindfulness will find this to an excellent resource"

- ANISAH BAGASRA, PH.D. Associate Professor of Psychology - Kennesaw State University

In the name of God,
the Most Gracious, the Most Merciful

HEARTFULNESS

---

*Islamic Spiritual
Practices for Health
and Well-being*

---

edited by
Carrie M. York, PhD

ALKARAM
PRESS

This book first published December 2024
Alkaram Press
Virginia, USA
Copyright © 2024 by Alkaram Press

Printed in the United States of America

FOR LINA

Table of Contents

Acknowledgements.. I

Preface II

Introduction
Carrie M. York, PhD...IV

CHAPTER 1
From Mindfulness to Heartfulness: A Sufi Islamic Perspective on Being and Spiritual Practice
Ghena Ismail, PsyD...1

CHAPTER 2
The Impact of Heartfulness on Health and Heredity via Epigenomic Regulation
Farah R. Zahir, PhD..23

CHAPTER 3
Islamic Practices as Psychotherapeutic Interventions
Zuhal Ağılkaya-Şahin, PhD...52

CHAPTER 4
Islamic Mindfulness and Recovery from Addiction
Sarah Huxtable Mohr, LCSW..............................84

CHAPTER 5
Easing Distress and Increasing Acceptance: Islamic Mindfulness for Patients Diagnosed with Cancer
Fyeqa I. Sheikh, PsyD..102

CHAPTER 6
Mindfulness Meditation for the Management of Chronic Pain: An Islamic Approach
Razia Bhatti-Ali, DClin, Psych 123

CHAPTER 7
Heart-Centered Mindfulness as a Tool for Self-Knowledge and Self-Improvement
Wadud Hassan and Maneeza Dawood, PhD.......................157

CHAPTER 8
The Centered Healing: Navigating Psychological Pain and Peace through Attachment and Detachment
Mahrukh Mustansar, PhD...171

About the Editor...191
About the Contributors...............................192

ACKNOWLEDGMENTS

————————— ••••• —————————

Putting together an edited volume requires the help of many individuals. I begin by acknowledging those who helped with this project.

First, I thank God for all things, especially in helping me to finally finish this book. My personal and professional life took many twists and turns during the period of time it was being put together. Through His grace, I've finally made it over the finish line - Alhamdulillah!

Next, I offer endless thanks to the chapter authors - this book would simply not exist without them offering their extremely important contributions: Dr. Ghena Ismail, Dr. Farah R. Zahir, Dr. Zuhal Ağılkaya-Şahin, Sarah Huxtable Mohr, Dr. Fyeqa I. Sheikh, Dr. Razia Bhatti-Ali, Dr. Maneeza Dawood, Wadud Hassan, and Dr. Mahrukh Mustansar.

I also extend an extra special thank you to Dr. Anisah Bagasra for her lifesaving editorial assistance in the final stages of the book's assembly. Thank you immensely as well to Raabia Haque who did the typesetting, cover design, and many other aspects of production. Thank you also to my dear friend and colleague Dr. Khalid Elzamzamy for reviewing the frontmatter and giving – as always – astute and important feedback, not to mention much needed encouragement and support for my work and to me personally over the past decade.

Lastly, I thank my family, friends, and loved ones for their ongoing love and support. I am especially grateful to and for my 13-year-old daughter Lina who is the light of my life and whose protection and success I pray for daily. Being a parent is one of the biggest spiritual practices a person could ever have. I am humbled by the gift of this beautiful child and am doing my absolute best to raise her.

In short, thank you everyone, for everything!

PREFACE

———— ••••• ————

Putting together an edited volume on spiritual practices and wellbeing is somewhat of a full-circle moment for me. It was though my personal experience with spiritual healing practices and modalities that I entered into my career as a psychologist some 20 years ago (for more on this see York, 2024). In the early years of my doctoral work (2005), I was very interested in reiki – a Japanese energy modality. I also experimented with modalities like holotropic breathwork, Metta (lovingkindness) meditation, and then later, for my doctoral dissertation (2009) I explored the Islamic modality of ruqya (Quranic healing) and its use on non-Muslims (York Al-Karam, 2012; 2015). At that time, all of my scholarship was positioned primarily within the context of transpersonal psychology and complementary and alternative medicine (CAM) and I often cited important work being done at the National Center for Complementary and Alternative Medicine (NCCAM) which is now called the National Center for Complementary and Integrative Health (NCCIH). NCCIH is the federal government's lead agency for scientific research on complementary and integrative health approaches and is one of the 27 institutes, centers, and offices that make up the National Institutes of Health within the US Department of Health and Human Services (NCCIH, 2024). The mere existence of such an institution, which was founded in 1998, and the fact that it has grown to the extent that the name has already been revised, gives insight into just how robust this field is.

Back in those early years, I used to look at the list of CAM modalities on the NCCIH website and think how unfortunate it was that Islamic modalities were nowhere on the menu. I also used to think that they had great potential to help non-Muslims. I argued that you didn't have to be Chinese to use and benefit from acupuncture nor did you have to be a Buddhist or Hindu to meditate or do yoga and benefit from those modalities either. Similarly, you didn't need to be Muslim to use or benefit from an Islamic spiritual practice or healing interventions but the only problem was

II

that unless you were Muslim, you probably had never heard of them (York Al-Karam, 2012; 2018; 2020; 2021). Since that time, it became my personal mission to put Islamic spiritual healing practices and modalities onto the proverbial menu. This book is one more effort I have made over the years towards that broader goal.

I would like to mention that this book comes out on the heels of another book I just edited entitled *The Way of Love: Towards an Islamic Psychology of Virtues and Character Development* (Alkaram Press, 2023). Both books are essentially on the same topic – Islamic spirituality. What's different are the scholarly domains and contexts in which each book is positioned. *The Way of Love* is about Islamic spirituality within the fields of positive psychology and scholarship on virtue and character development. *Heartfulness* is about Islamic spirituality within the context of the health, wellbeing, and CAM. It is my hope that the work presented in both books demonstrates how one particular topic – in this case Islamic spirituality – can have relevance to and indeed advance so many different domains and in so many different ways. I can't emphasize how vital it is that Islamic and Muslim perspectives be part of scientific and academic life in order to set and advance research agendas for these areas and beyond. The ways in which all of this can be done though are endless.

I feel immense gratitude for having this project as one of my professional deliverables. As with all things, I gave it my absolute best. Any benefit or usefulness in the work is from God. Any mistakes or shortcomings are entirely my own.

Carrie M. York, PhD
September 2024
Great Falls, Virginia. USA

INTRODUCTION

Mindfulness, meditation, yoga, prayer, and other psycho-spiritual practices for health and wellbeing have become ubiquitous in the west. In the past thirty years, an overwhelming amount of theoretical and applied research has explored the impact that these and other spiritual practices have had on a plethora of variables including stress, anxiety, depression, virtue development and even cancer. In short, the evidence suggests that spiritual practices help people in myriad ways.

Until now, the religious traditions taking up the bulk of real estate in the 'health and spirituality' movement have been Buddhism, as in the case of mindfulness and meditation, Hinduism, as in the case of yoga, and Christianity as in the case of prayer. A glaring absence is the second largest religious tradition in the world – Islam – yet it is full of such practices waiting to be explored. Of course, some work in these domains has begun. Publications do exist that examine Islamic spiritual practices and healing modalities, but they are often within the domains of religious studies or theology and generally sporadic. There doesn't seem to be a concerted effort that seeks to advance Islamic practices and methods within the health, wellbeing, and CAM domains specifically. The objective of this edited volume therefore is to examine Islamic spiritual practices and healing modalities within the context of health and wellbeing and to lay some groundwork to advance this line of scholarship.

In chapter 1, *From Mindfulness to Heartfulness: A Sufi Islamic Perspective on Being and Spiritual Practice,* Dr. Ghena Ismail highlights the primary place the faculty of the heart occupies in the Qur'an and prophetic hadith and gives an overview of heartfulness or mindfulness as understood by contemporary Muslim psychologists. She also discusses the purpose of contemplative practices in wisdom traditions and concludes by discussing the implications of a Sufi understanding of consciousness (heartfulness) not only to Muslim clients and practitioners but to anyone

INTRODUCTION

interested in a practice that represents more than just a stress management technique but rather a way of being and serving in the world.

In chapter 2, *The Impact of Heartfulness on Health and Heredity via Epigenomic Regulation,* Dr. Farah R. Zahir presents an Islamic cosmological basis for the impact of heartfulness and explains Islamic Ihsan practices and how they act to harmonize the individual with the cosmos. She introduces the rapidly advancing science of epigenomics and discusses how it offers a robust and rigorous means to empirically assess the ability of spiritual practices to control gene function. She also examines how breakthrough discovery epigenomic screens have shown that meditative exercises affect changes in genes involved in immune system functioning, stress response physiology, psychological states, and even cellular ageing. She also summarizes seminal studies and their connections to Islamic heartfulness methods.

In chapter 3, *Islamic Practices as Psychotherapeutic Interventions,* Dr. Zuhal Ağılkaya-Şahin examines the possibilities and benefits of Islamic practices such as tawakkul, duʿāʾ (prayer), and tafakkur in psychotherapy. She argues that tawakkul has religious, socio-psychological effects and can be applied to psychological concepts such as hope, trust, self-esteem, crisis, trauma, cognitive restructuring, behavioral change, and theories such as attribution, meaning, and locus of control. She also explores the psychological and psychotherapeutic effects of duʾa as it has been proven as efficient for coping, suggestion, catharsis as well as attachment, self-actualization, and meaning. Lastly, she examines tafakkur and suggests that like other practices, it can be elaborated within the frameworks of attachment theory, search for meaning, confrontation, responsibility, cognitive restructuring, and coping. She also examines ways forward in this area of theory and clinical application.

In chapter 4, *Islamic Mindfulness and Recovery from Addiction,* Sarah Huxtable Mohr, LCSW presents a review of the current research and commentary on mindfulness and addiction treatment. First, she does a brief literature review from the origins of mindfulness in Buddhism to its modern development as a secular behavioral health intervention and the subsequent increasing exploration of the topic by other faith traditions. This is followed by a closer look at mindfulness in addiction treatment specifically and why mindfulness is an effective solution for addiction. She further develops the literature on how Islamic mindfulness in particular can function in treatment and recovery, including the implications of the roots of mindfulness in Buddhism and how this pertains to its use in Islam. She concludes her chapter with a discussion on future directions for exploring the use of Islamic mindfulness in addiction treatment.

In chapter 5, *Easing Distress and Increasing Acceptance: Islamic Mindfulness for Patients Diagnosed with Cancer,* Dr. Fyeqa I. Sheikh examines the concept of mindfulness in Islam and its utility with people diagnosed with cancer. She begins by examining mindfulness and more specifically Mindfulness-Based Stress Reduction (MBSR). She then explores the Islamic concepts of muraqaba, muhasaba, and other practices and their use in cancer treatment today. Recommendations on ways forward in this line of research are also offered.

In chapter 6, *Mindfulness Meditation for the Management of Chronic Pain: An Islamic Approach,* Dr. Razia Bhatti-Ali delves into the benefits of incorporating Islamic mindfulness within the context of chronic pain management. She begins with an introduction to the growth of mindfulness and its applications in the Western world and explores the concept of mindfulness and its alignment with Islamic teachings found in the Quran and Sunnah. Her aim is to demonstrate how Islamic principles can integrate with mindfulness, creating a space where individuals may learn to accept pain and find meaning and purpose within the experience. The chapter ends with a practical dimension, offering exercises that integrate mindfulness and Islamic practices to serve as tangible tools, guiding individuals towards a holistic approach to well-being.

In chapter 7, *Heart-Centered Mindfulness as a Tool for Self-Knowledge and Self-Improvement,* Wadud Hassan and Dr. Maneeza Dawood explore a structured heart-centered mindfulness practice that was developed based on research on contemporary and Islamically–integrated mindfulness practices, as well as the principles of heart-centered mindfulness by Imam Al-Ghazali and inspired by the Quran. The program, a 6-week mindfulness masterclass, makes these practices accessible, manageable, and transformative for the general public. The authors also outline two key practices of the mindfulness program: cultivating the Presence of God (*hudhur*) and the Spiritual Body Scan (*muhasaba*). The chapter concludes with reflections on further avenues for research on heart-centered mindfulness and its integration into clinical practice.

In chapter 8, *The Centered Healing: Navigating Psychological Pain and Peace Through Attachment and Detachment,* Dr. Mahrukh Mustansar offers practical suggestions on navigating inner turmoil as well as the essence of the human soul and its journey through the tumultuous sea of life. She also discusses the path to safeguarding the heart (qalb) from sinking into despair and offers insights on how to resurface when it does. She also emphasizes in her chapter the inherent capacity of every heart to heal and the transformative potential embedded within each moment of adversity. The overarching goal of the chapter is to extend a lifeline of

INTRODUCTION

support to those grappling with their darkest hours, offering a roadmap towards healing, awakening, and rediscovering one's authentic self.

Discussion

The chapters presented in this edited volume demonstrate how vast this domain of scholarship can be. Breadth and diversity of topics aside, there are other points critical to a discussion about advancing the research and application of Islamic spiritual practices and healing interventions within the context of health and well-being.

First, philosophical worldview is a crucial starting point. Health, wellness/wellbeing, and CAM research is rooted in the contemporary philosophical norms of secularism and empiricism where research is relegated to what can be measured. Although there are some benefits to this approach, it's a completely different paradigm than an Islamic worldview. From an Islamic perspective, God exists, humans have a soul, God created everything in existence, and He is in control of all things. The primary purpose of such practices is not to obtain health, wellbeing, happiness, or healing. The primary purpose is to know and worship God. God is the goal. Outcomes of the practices like health, wellbeing, or stress reduction are byproducts. These distinct philosophical paradigms that underpin scientific or empirical research cannot be ignored.

Second, there is often the criticism that although empirical research suggests that many spiritual practices "work" in some way, the mechanism by which that happens is unclear. From an Islamic perspective, all healing is from God and He uses various tools to heal. Sometimes the tool is chemotherapy and sometimes it's prayer. Explaining the mechanism all depends on what worldview is being held by whoever is interpreting the data. Worldview matters and that is one reason more Islamic and Muslim perspectives are needed in all spheres of scientific and scholarly life. Nobody really knows how Tylenol and many other popular drugs work. Even Tylenol's information pamphlets states "the mechanism by which Tylenol works in unclear" and "Tylenol is *thought* to work by". Not knowing the precise or definitive mechanism should not be a reason to stop using a spiritual practice or intervention if the person doing so reports positive benefits. This highlights the importance of qualitative data and self-reports to broaden our understanding of such type of research. Health and well-being are qualitive experiences that cannot always be understood within the quantitative world of empirical research or clinical trials.

A third point needing to be mentioned is the use of Islamic spiritual practices and healing modalities on non-Muslims and within a western, non-Muslim context. As was stated previously, CAM modalities like mindfulness or yoga stem from Buddhism or Hinduism, but most people using or researching them in the west are not from those religious traditions and, for the most part, they have been secularized. This raises a criticism about such practices being culturally appropriated and taken from the broader spiritual traditions in which they are rooted. On the one hand, it is indeed important to understand practices from within their own paradigm. On the other hand, sharing an Islamic practice or healing intervention with a non-Muslim is a great opportunity to change perceptions and educate the public about Islam. It was, after all, sent to everyone, not just Muslims.

The point of Islam being sent to everyone touches upon the fourth and final point which is the advancement of the emerging field of Islamic psychology (IP) and discussions on how that field can also have relevance within non-Muslim contexts today. The field of IP is one in which scholarship on spiritual practices and interventions can also be positioned.

Ways Forward

This edited volume is a call to action to advance research on Islamic mindfulness, meditation, prayer, and other psycho-spiritual practices and healing modalities and to give them their rightful place within the health, wellness, and CAM domains and beyond. It is hoped that such scholarship will become part and parcel of this overall field and to maybe even one day make it onto the proverbial and actual NCCIH website menu.

In terms of ways forward, much of the work done so far (in this book and elsewhere) has covered topics and practices many Muslims are familiar with like salat, dhikr, duaa, tafakkur, muraqaba, and the like. This is a great starting point. However, there are so many more practices and interventions that exist within the tradition that would advance this field exponentially. One prime example is sending salutations on Prophet Mohammed. Muslims believe there is an incredible healing and beneficial effect on the person who does this. Another example is the whole body of knowledge known as Al-Tibb Al-Nabawi (Medicine of the Prophetic) as well as many Sufi healing methods that barely see the light of day in scientific literature. Examining these and other underexplored practices and intervention has endless potential and implications.

It is my hope that this edited volume provides a framework and rationale to advance such work. Given the state of our world today that is wrought with wars, environmental crises, discrimination, and many other types of circumstances and behaviors that are rooted in a corrupt human heart, Heartfulness practices might just be a viable, affordable, and much needed methodology to bringing world peace through the hearts and minds of those engaged in such practices – an extremely good reason to make this

INTRODUCTION

topic a priority in research agendas, funding, and policy within these and other domains.

References

National Center for Complementary and Integrative Health (2024). Retrieved on October 3rd, 2024 from https://www.nccih.nih.gov/about

York, C. (2012). *Islamic Healing and Wellness: Not Just for Muslims.* New You Middle East. Dubai, UAE (journal article).

York Al-Karam, C. (2015). Complementary and alternative treatments in psychology: An Islamic therapeutic modality. In C. York Al-Karam & A. Haque (Eds.). *Mental health and psychological practice in the United Arab Emirates.* New York: Palgrave Macmillan.

York Al-Karam, C. (2018). Islamic psychology: Towards a 21st century definition and conceptual framework. *Journal of Islamic Ethics, 2*(2018), 97–109.

York Al-Karam, C. (2020). Islamic psychology: Expanding beyond the clinic. *Journal of Islamic Faith and Practice, 3,* 111–120.

York Al-Karam, C. (2021). Islamic Psychology in the United States. In Haque and Rothman (Eds.), *Islamic Psychology Around the World* (pp. 308-323). International Association of Islamic Psychology.

York, C. (2023). *The Way of Love: Towards an Islamic Psychology of Virtues and Character Development.* Alkaram Press.

York, C. M. (2024). Living Islamic psychology: Portrait of a Muslim American psychologist. *Spirituality in Clinical Practice, 11*(1), 7682 https://doi.org/10.1037/scp0000349

CHAPTER 1

———— ••••• ————

From Mindfulness to Heartfulness:
A Sufi Islamic Perspective on Being
and Spiritual Practice

Ghena Ismail, Psy.D.

Introduction

Recently, the term 'heartfulness' started to be used not only in Islamic circles but also in mainstream psychological literature, reflecting a sentiment felt by many scholars regarding a nuance missing from current approaches to mindfulness. According to Jon Kabat-Zinn (2013), founder of mindfulness-based stress reduction, "when we speak of mindfulness, it is important to keep in mind that we equally mean heartfulness", adding that "... in Asian languages, the word for 'mind' and the word for 'heart' are usually the same." He elaborates, "... if you are not hearing or feeling the word heartfulness when you encounter or use the word mindfulness, you are in all likelihood missing its essence" (p. 26).

The emphasis on the heart is noted across different traditions, yet the delineation of the relationship between the mind and heart differs. Whereas in some traditions, the word for mind and heart may be interchangeably used, in Abrahamic traditions, a distinction is often made between the two terms. The distinction does not aim at separation but rather at denoting different types or levels of consciousness meant to culminate in a mode of knowing that is holistic, centering, and authentic (i.e., grounded in Divine love) as opposed to material or self-serving ends.

1

In this chapter, I shall highlight the primary place that the faculty of the heart occupies in the Qur'an. I will then provide an overview of contemporary approaches to Islamic psychology, paying special attention to heart-based interventions. Reference will be made to Sufi writings throughout the chapter to contextualize certain ideas. The Islamic contemplative practice will be discussed in the context of wisdom traditions which share an emphasis on the heart as an agent of knowing. I will end with discussing the implications of a Sufi Islamic understanding of consciousness (heartfulness) not only to Muslim clients and practitioners but to anyone interested in a practice that represents more than just a stress management technique but rather a way of being in the world. (For a commentary on the relationship between Sufism and Islam, see Ismail et al., 2023. Suffice it to note here that Sufism constitutes the inner or mystic tradition within Islam. Its impact on the Islamic civilization can be seen beyond the bounds of formal Sufi orders, in mainstream forms of Islamic practice, art and literature).

The Heart in the Qur'an and Prophetic Hadith

The term heart is mentioned (132) times in the Qur'an, along with several related notions, including "sadr," the human chest, "fou'ad," the inner in both the singular and plural forms, and "lubb," our innermost reality (Seker, 2012). These concepts reflect an understanding of human consciousness that has been described as *tawhidic* and multi-layered, pointing to the oneness of God and the multiple imprints and manifestations of His reality.

The Heart as the Seat of Consciousness

Qur'anically, the heart is not merely the seat of emotions and sentiments but rather the locus of experiential knowledge and holding Divine presence. "Do they not meditate earnestly on the Qur'an, or are there locks on the hearts?" (Q 47:24) represents the Qur'anic view of the heart as being endowed with the function of comprehending or contemplating reality. The Qur'an also says: "It is not the eyesights (*absar*) that are blind, but blind are the hearts (*qul̄ub*)" Q 22:46), highlighting the Islamic view of the heart as representing a mode of consciousness which transgresses the bounds of the empirical sphere.

Different States of the Heart

It is important to note herein that the literal meaning of the word heart in Arabic, qalb, means "to turn," which sheds light on the heart's inclination to constantly turn or change. In recognition of the turning and fluctuating nature of the heart, the heart has been described as having different states or types. Relatedly, it has been classified by scholars into different typological schemes. For the purpose of simplification, reference shall be made to the following three categories: (a) the healthy or sound heart, (b) the dead heart, and (c) the sick or defective heart.

Healthy or sound hearts, referred to in the Qur'an in terms of *'qalb saleem'* have been associated with being soft, compassionate, gentle, humble, sincere, discerning, and ultimately open to witnessing God's signs in the world. Dead hearts, in contrast, have been associated with being hard like a stone, lacking in humility, guided by personal whims and worldly pleasures, and sealed from the truth. As to sick or diseased hearts, they have been described as having mixed inclinations and/or frequently fluctuating between different states (Olatoye, 2013; Tarip & Abu Bakar, 2020). The Qur'an contains numerous warnings of the hardening of hearts. Consider the following words "Then your hearts hardened thereafter, being like stones or harder still" to the end of the verse [Q 2:74] (Dagli, 2017). Consider also the words "If only, when Our Might came upon them, they had humbled themselves. But rather their hearts hardened" to the end of the verse [Q 6:43] (Dakake, 2017).The relationship between humility and softening of the heart recurs throughout the Qur'an as in the following verse "Has not the time yet come for those who believe that their hearts should soften with humility and submit (to God to strive in His cause) in the face of God's remembrance (the Qur'an) and what has come down of the truth (the Divine teachings)?" (Q 57:16; Seker, 2012). The importance of having a humble heart is further denoted in the Prophet's saying: "The best of people are those most humble before God," and in his prayer, "I seek refuge in You … from a heart that is not humble (lā yakhsha')" (Wensinck 1936–1969, kh-sh-' as cited in Khalil, 2020). Genuine, as opposed to fake humility, may be regarded as a prerequisite for correctly assuming any act, without which there can be no true remedy for the heart. According to Khalil (2020), "humility is unique among virtues in that it is the only virtue of which one cannot claim possession without relinquishing the very possession itself" (p. 239).

Dhikr as the Chief Remedy for the Heart

Hearts have been likened to innermost jewels holding the deepest mysteries and truths of existence (Seker, 2012). They have also been likened to mirrors which may nonetheless rust if not polished and taken care of. As per the prophetic tradition, "For everything there is a polish, and the polish of the heart is the remembrance of Allah" (Geels, 1996). The Qur'an also says, "Verily, it is in 'dhikrullah' (the remembrance of God) that hearts shall find rest and contentment" (Q13:28). This verse points to the intimate relationship between two key Qur'anic themes, namely, qalb (the heart) and *dhikr* (remembrance of God). It also sheds light on the heart as the site for the remembrance of God through which inner tranquility may be realized.

Dhikr, in the broad Islamic sense, includes the recitation of the holy book of the Qur'an and also the formal prayers performed five times a day, which have a designated set of bodily movements. Dhikr, as specific to Sufi ritual conducted in Sufi circles, involves repetitive utterances of God's names (qualities) with the intention of establishing continual remembrance of Him (Chittick, 2008). It is a type of repetitive prayer that has been compared to the Jesus-prayer or prayer of the heart within Orthodox Christianity (Mayeur-Jaouen & Patrizi, 2017), Nembutsu within Japanese Buddhism, or Japa in Hinduism (Geels, 1996). Whereas dhikrullahhas been recounted as a heart-based intervention, it is important to highlight that it also constitutes the motive force for all interventions and acts. Any act that is done with an orientation towards God, and to the extent that God's presence is felt in it, may be considered an instance of dhikr.

Finally, the attitude with which remembrance is engaged is particularly significant. For remembrance to yield the desired fruit of the heart's softening, it should be carried out in awe and humility. Such an attitude is at once the prerequisite and fruit of remembrance (Seker, 2012).

The Relationship between Actions, Attitudes and the State of the Heart

In highlighting the cyclical relationship between the state of the heart and one's own attitudes and actions, the Qur'an says, "So, we seal the hearts of the transgressors (Q 10:74)". This means that it is the people themselves who have hardened their hearts against God's message, and it is through their own actions that God has sealed their hearts. Accordingly, the Medieval Muslim scholars described the impact of deeds and thoughts in terms of 'traces left upon the heart', 'marking of the self', or 'branding of the heart' (McGremor, 2021, p. 197). Actions include not only our observable but also our internal behaviors (Olatoye, 2013), in reference to one's intentions *(niyyāt)*. Dividing deeds into two kinds: inner deeds or deeds of the heart and deeds of the body or action is not uncommon in Sufi manuals and is meant to highlight the importance of bringing the inner and outer behaviors into harmony (Feuillebois-Pierunek, 2017). It also points to the very important relationship envisaged in Sufism between the inner (batin) and outer (Zahir) which is considered key to the Islamic tawhidic worldview. (See Hofer, 2016 for an explication of how the Sufi conceptualization of this relationship was key not only to Islamic philosophy and spirituality but also to other spiritualities in the Mediterranean including Judaism).

To safeguard the purity of our hearts and to keep them open to God's grace and mercy, we should observe our intentions as well as our thoughts and emotions. We should also strive to keep an inner attitude of humility and trust as opposed to defiance and despair, no matter the situation. "If only when Our chastisement came upon them, they had humbled themselves (*taḍarraʿū*). Instead, their hearts hardened, and Satan made all they used to do seem fair to them (Q 6:43)" (Khalil, 2020).

An Example from Gaza

To bring the concept of heartfulness alive it may be helpful to invoke testimonies from Gaza through which we encountered stories marked with courage, humility and acceptance [of God's will]. As they buried their own children and sometimes whole families, survivors pleaded for God's satisfaction amidst their pain. This does not mean that the survivors did not feel the pain caused by such difficult afflictions; it rather means that they were trying to accept the pain while remaining steadfast and true to their faith in God. The example of Khalid Nabhan known for his famous utterance of '*ruh al ruh*' (soul of my soul) in reference to Reem, his grand-daughter who was killed in November 2023 during the war on Gaza (Karadsheh et al., 2023), provides a most apt illustration of an attitude characterized with love, humility, and deep acceptance of God's will. As one listens to his account of the special bond he had with his granddaughter, one can neither miss the gravity of his loss nor the depth of his faith and reliance on God. In an interview in which he was asked whether he would leave Gaza, his response was:

سنبقى هنا.. بإذن الله سنبقى في هذا المكان

لأن الله عز وجل قال لنا أنه هو الله

أنسحك وأبكى وأنه هو أمات وأحيا

فإذا الله كتب لنا الحياة فمرحبا بالحياة

وإن كان الله عز وجل كتب لنا الموت فمرحبا بالموت ومرحبا بلقاء الله

سنبقى إلى أن يشاء الله وأن يحدث الله عز وجل بعد ذلك أمرا

We will remain here. God willing, we will remain in this place.

Because Allah most Glorious and Majestic said:

He is the Ultimate Source of laughter and tears

And the grantor of death and life

So, if God willed Life for us, then Life we shall welcome

And if He the most Glorious and Majestic willed death for us, then death

And the meeting with Him we shall embrace

We will remain here until God wills otherwise

And you don't know. Perhaps God will bring about change

Whereas such utterances about surrendering one's will to God are not uncommon among people of faith, it is perhaps the authenticity and gentleness with which Khalid uttered those words in the face of severe trials that touched the hearts of many individuals worldwide, crossing boundaries of race, ethnicity, and religion. Khalid's speech, marked with pain and love, seemed to embody the nobility of his character and the tenderness of his heart.

The following section provides an entry into heartfulness as understood by contemporary Muslim scholars and the methods therapists incorporate to cultivate awareness at the level of the heart. These include *dhikrullah* (i.e., the remembrance of God), cultivating noble character and healthy emotions, addressing different emotional and bodily states as potential entry points into the person's current state, discerning one's intentions, and understanding the role of the body in the context of dhikr and the overarching tawhidic worldview.

The Heart and Heartfulness in Contemporary Islamic Discourse

In his article on heartfulness, Rothman (2019, para. 1) posed the following questions: "How do we understand mindfulness from within the Islamic tradition?" and "Is there an Islamic version of mindfulness?" Of course, the answer to this is yes—that there is an Islamic version. He elaborates that Islamic mindfulness shares similar elements with secular mindfulness as understood in the West today, including cultivating awareness of one's thoughts and slowing down.

He pointes out, however, that from an Islamic perspective, being aware of one's thoughts is insufficient, as one needs to become conscious of what is beyond one's thoughts. Relatedly, one needs to understand not only with one's mind but also with one's heart, denoting a mode of knowing that transcends the bounds of the analytical mind and the individual self. He elaborates, "The key of why we would want to have self-awareness is only as a vehicle of opening up to a broader conscious awareness that leads to an awareness of God." Hence, an emphasis on the ultimate motivation or purpose behind mindfulness or awareness of one's thoughts is the knowledge and love of God. This stance echoes that of other Islamic psychologists. Consider Badri (2006, as cited in Ismail et al., 2021), who asserted that the ultimate purpose of mindfulness or meditation in Islam is to love and worship God.

In the following section, I will discuss the similarities and overlap between heartfulness (or Islamic mindfulness) and contemporary mindfulness highlighting the focus of the former on remembrance. I will then discuss the practice of drawing upon the example of the prophet to cultivate noble character and healthy emotions. The relationship between attending to one's emotions and facilitating heartfulness will be elucidated in a separate section. After that, I will offer a brief overview of the primary role of intentions in the Islamic spiritual life to conclude with a section on the role of the body in the Islamic worldview and the practice of dhikr.

Heartfulness—Beyond Noticing Internal Phenomena toward Dhikr

Mindfulness, in the commonly understood sense, is treated in Islamic literature as a doorway to witnessing and remembering God. Awareness of one's thoughts, bodily sensations, or emotions latent within one's subconscious is treated as a means to access tawhid (i.e., witnessing the Oneness of God and experiencing wholeness and emptiness within). We are complete with God, and we are empty every time we seek to experience life outside His bounds. Here, it is important to reiterate that tawhid in Islam is contingent on appreciating both the radical transcendence of God as well as His radical immanence. In other words, from an Islamic perspective, God is beyond all imagination and definition, and thus, it is not possible to completely grasp the nature of His reality; yet at the same time, God's traces or imprints may be felt within one's innermost soul or heart.

Cognitive awareness or paying attention to one's thoughts and accompanying bodily sensations and emotions, which will be discussed in a separate section, may contribute to stress reduction and noticing one's personal limitations and struggles in the hope of overcoming them. According to Muslim psychologists, however, to facilitate realizing the human potential in its fullness, cognitive, bodily, and/or emotional awareness should be embedded in an overall way of living and being that cultivates openness to God's gaze. The choice of the term 'heartfulness' by Muslim scholars (e.g., Rothman, 2018) is meant to bring attention to the importance of not stopping at the level of noticing one's thoughts and emotions but seeking to cultivate awareness of God's presence in our lives, within our own souls and hearts. Hence, the description of Islamic psychology (Isgandarova, 2019, as cited in Ismail et al., 2021) in terms of helping the client see through "the eyes of the heart" in addition to fulfilling the tasks of the modern psychotherapist. Seeing (or accessing the Real) through the faculty of the heart, has been described as a perceptual shift, a conversion of the gaze where the practitioner "sees the universe with new eyes, as if he were seeing it for the first time (Ferhat, 2020)." Heartfulness or tapping into the realities of the heart in Islamic psychology is, thus, not merely a mental exercise; it is rather an ongoing endeavor that requires the engagement of one's whole being such that one becomes a vessel or a mirror reflecting realities of a higher or more sublime order.

This is consistent with the Qur'anic perspective which emphasizes the heart as the locus of experiential knowledge and holding divine presence. Hence, the focus of Muslim psychologists is on introducing what they refer to as heart-based interventions or therapies. Rothman (2018) noted that one of the first tasks he undertook in orienting his clients toward an Islamic understanding of the self was to teach them how to center their awareness in their *qalb,* in their heart, and move away from the tendency to overidentify with the mind.

To prepare his clients for this task, and in a manner that appears initially akin to mainstream mindfulness techniques, Rothman (2018) teaches his patients that they are not their thoughts, inviting them to move away from the tendency to over-identify with their minds. He would then use visualization to help them bring their conscious awareness to the physical place in their body where their heart center is—in the chest. Rothman (2018) would then ask his patients to bow their heads to their chests and to imagine that they are relinquishing their overidentification with the mind's chatter, allowing the heart to take more of a center stage during this process. Lodi (2018) asserts that many Muslim clients find it useful to associate therapy with the heart, which is believed to be the center of consciousness (Ghazali and Yusuf, 2010, as cited in Lodi, 2018).

Pryor (2006, as cited in Ismail et al., 2021), in her turn, explains that in her work with women struggling with substance use, she "teaches them to quiet their minds by focusing on their breath and in their heart. The clients, then, would start to experience themselves in a way that is trying to be separate from "I'm just an addict," or "I'm a loser," or "I messed up my life." Consider, also, Helminski's (2016) emphasis on the importance of cultivating non-judgmental awareness of one's thoughts as key to the practice of heartfulness. The above descriptions point to obvious similarities between the heart-focused method and contemporary mindfulness practices. At the same time, there appears to be a consensus among Muslim and Sufi scholars and practitioners alike that mindfulness of one's thoughts and emotions is only a preparatory step to tap into the consciousness of the heart. Relatedly, it should be seen as part of a broader contemplative practice aimed at facilitating an understanding of the nature of reality (Helminski, 2016; Ismail et al., 2021). Here, presumably, lies a key difference between Islamic contemplative practice and contemporary applications of mindfulness.

Ultimately, Islamic psychology presumes that all methods, practices, and life events may be incorporated and contemplated to cultivate awareness of God's presence in our lives. As an extension to this principle, even one's sins may provide an opportunity to cultivate the remembrance of God. Rothman (2018) referred to repentance as the very act of turning our hearts to Divine presence instead of beating ourselves up for our misgivings noting the fluctuating nature of the heart while shedding light on the linguistic root of the Arabic word repentant, which is "to return," Rothman (2018) elaborated that the key idea in repentance is not to bring attention to the [wrongful] act but rather to the remembrance of God. He reiterated that *tawbah*, the Arabic term for repentance, is really about returning to one's true self. It is about recognizing our reliance on God and recentering our focus on the greater reality of our existence over the distractions within our *nafs* (self). These distractions may take the form of a preoccupation with worldly pleasures and also with one's wrongdoings. (Ismail et al., 2021).

Highlighting the inextricable relationship between *tawbah* and remembrance of God, Rothman (2018) asserted that *tawbah* should be invoked not only for major transgressions but even for more subtle things, such as simply forgetting God, which might happen not only during times of adversity but also during times of abundance and bliss (Khalil, 2020). Ultimately, tawbah may be a doorway to remembrance to the extent that it is accompanied with an attitude of reliance on the creator and humility before Him. The relevance of cultivating humility and overall nobility of character cannot be overstated and is conceived as key to Islamic psychology, ethics and related contemplative practice.

Drawing Upon the Example of the Prophet to Cultivate Noble Character and Healthy Emotions

A clear premise of Islamic psychology, philosophy, and spirituality lies in the notion that cultivating nobility of character is necessary for cultivating a healthy heart—one that is mindful of God's presence at all times. In her HEART Method (HEART being an acronym for Healthy Emotions Anchored in RasoolAllah's Teaching), Lodi (2018) drew upon the example of the prophet to cultivate noble character as well as a wise and healthy attitude toward one's emotions and grievances. Lodi (2018) explained that during the initial interview, she typically explored whether the Muslim client could relate positively to Prophet Mohammed as a spiritual exemplar. If the response was positive, she would help the client use this belief as a resource to facilitate his or her own resiliency.

Lodi (2018) would then cite the Prophet's prayer at *Al-Ta'if* to highlight his absolute awareness and reliance on God and how, in speaking to God, he acknowledged challenging emotions, reframed the situation in line with the bigger picture, and engaged in prosocial behaviors of compassion and forgiveness, thereby staying optimistic. This attitude of God consciousness combined with reliance and trust in God (*tawakkul*) buffered the prophet from feelings of despair. Lodi (2018) noted that a schema of compassion would also protect individuals from being consumed with the need for revenge and would help refocus them on problem-solving. One may add that an attitude of compassion may help individuals remain receptive to God's will and grace, and thus remain centered in their inner truth as opposed to dispersing their energy in fantasies about revenge. Finally, whereas the role of cognition in regulating emotions has been acknowledged by Muslim psychologists, there seems to be a growing emphasis on the role of the body in accessing emotional material blocking the heart.

Emotions, the Body and the Heart

Overall, there seems to be an understanding among Muslim psychologists that if left unaddressed, emotions could contribute to forming a crust over the heart, thus impeding its capacity to mirror realities of a higher order. Rothman and Coyle (2020) explain, "the emotional material stored within the qalb can be a deep, underlying source of imbalance or pathology within the total system of the person," noting that unaddressed emotional material may constitute "a block at the level of the qalb, covering over or impeding one's ability to open the heart to its natural potential to be in a state of peace and balance" (p. 13). Similar to varied streams within clinical psychology, emotions are evaluated in Islamic psychology in terms of their adaptive utility or their ability to propel instinctual survival" (Keshavarzi & Keshavarzi, 2021, p. 173). They are further evaluated in terms of their potential for facilitating spiritual connection. In Islamic psychology, emotions may serve as "important vehicles and motivating instruments for spiritual experiences and religious performance" (Keshavarzi & Keshavarzi, 2021, p. 175).

As noted above, whereas the role of cognition in regulating and orienting emotions has been acknowledged by Muslim psychologists, there seems to be a growing emphasis on the role of the body in accessing emotional material blocking the heart. In a qualitative study by Rothman and Coyle (2020), a few participants argued for embodiment as a core element of an Islamic psychotherapy, noting that accessing the body or bodily awareness may provide a gateway into the source of imbalance or pathology. One of the participants elaborated that she understood that trauma–based emotions become stored in the body. She referred to the *ayahs* (verses) in the Qur'an that say that on the Day of Judgment, when people are taken to account for their actions in this world, their own limbs will testify to how they have been used.

Rothman and Coyle (2020) comment that in some works of *tafsir* (Qur'anic exegeses), verses in which the limbs are said to testify to how they have been used point to a memory intrinsic to the body. Participants in their study reported that they actively sought to engage the bodily memory as it helped them more readily access emotional material that seemed to block individuals from being able to live within their fitrah state (Rothman & Coyle, 2020). In Islamic psychology, the concept of *fitrah* is commonly understood as "the innate nature of human beings that inclines them towards recognizing and submitting to the existence and oneness of Allah and adhering to moral and ethical values" (Haruna, 2023). Individuals hoping to realize the fullness of human potential should seek to live within their fitra state, which entails cultivating the intention of performing all acts and approaching all situations through the eyes of God and for the sake of God.

Intentions

Despite it being a cornerstone of Islamic teaching and its foundational connection to the heart, the theme of *niyya* (i.e., intention), according to Olatoye (2013) has not been given due attention in contemporary Islamic psychology. Drawing upon prophetic hadiths and Qur'anic verses, Olatoye (2013) highlighted the relationship between a sound heart and pure intentions, noting that the focus of Muslims in contemporary times seems to be generally on [outer] actions and beliefs with little regard for intention.

This has not been lost on contemporary Muslim psychologists. Highlighting the centrality of intention in Islamic theology, Sheikh (2018) pointed out that some schools of Islamic thought went as far as saying that intention was more important than action, mainly to illustrate the point that it is one's intention that determines the validity of one's action(s). In her turn, Assar (2017) wrote that "Muslims are encouraged to reflect on the intention behind their behaviors, for they know that their state of heart and intention is what God will judge" (p. 27). She cited the prophetic hadith, "Verily actions are by intentions, and for every person is what he intended" (p. 27). This means that if a seemingly spiritual act such as communal prayer was engaged to elicit praise rather than the satisfaction of God, one would reap the benefit one intended—in this case, it would be communal paise.

When you are in Love you are consumed with the Beloved. You are not busy watching if others are watching you being in Love. Otherwise, you would be a hypocrite. The holy Qur'an contains numerous allusions to the "heart" in the context of hypocrisy or *nifaq*. According to Ahmad (1999), a hypocrite is an insincere person who thinks he can get the best of both worlds by compromising with good and evil. He continued that the hypocrites or the half-hearted ones gradually lose their ability to discern between right and wrong and consequently incline towards moral depravity.

Discernment of one's intentions is thus key to understanding and orienting one's actions. Hence, the emphasis in Sufi treatises is on deeds of the heart being on a continuum with deeds of the body. As noted above, the differentiation between deeds of the heart and deeds of the body or action, in Sufi writings, is meant to highlight the importance of harmonizing the inner with the outer (Feuillebois-Pierunek, 2017), which is key to the tawhidic worldview.

The Body, Dhikr and the Tawhidic Worldview

The body was discussed in the literature on Islamic psychology, mainly in terms of its potential for accessing emotions that may not be readily accessed via rational reasoning alone (Rothman & Coyle, 2020). It was also discussed in the context of performing prayers and other rituals to actualize one's niyya [i.e. intention] and help establish a constancy and connection to the rope of Allah amidst the constant ups and downs of life (Rothman, 2018). In fact, the role of the body in actualizing niyya and its inextricable relationship to one's heart cannot be over-emphasized in Islam in general, and Sufism in particular, along with its practice of dhikr, key to realizing tawhid within. According to Sufis, while dhikr will likely occur initially at the stage of the tongue, it "should be performed with the 'intention of the heart;'" in the hope it may ultimately penetrate one's inmost being (Geels, 1996). It is relevant to point out herein that dhikr may be performed in a group or in solitude. When performed in a group, it typically involves rhythmic motoric movements associated with repetitive chants of *Allah*, or the formula of tawhid "*la ilaha illah Allah*" (i.e., There is no God but God). (Geels, 1996)

The whole ritual is laden with deep symbolism. Details of the ritual vary greatly between one Sufi group and another. Regardless of variations at the level of outward manifestation, dhikr is inspired by an overarching Sufi tawhidic framework. It is, relatedly, interwoven with an appreciation of the body as carrying a potential to hold and express realities of a higher order (Rosenfeld, 2013). This perspective is often lost in academic studies that examine dhikr from an external point of view, contingent on conceiving a duality between mind and body and a dichotomy between the subject and object of study (Geels, 1996).

Rosenfeld (2013) described the difficulty of grasping the role of the body in dhikr without participating in the ritual and the tawhidic worldview inspiring it. According to Rosenfeld (2013), scholars in Islam who have written about the body generally focused on the body in Islamic law, often overlooking the integrated view of the body, which embraces "the whole of oneself." Also overlooked is a key contribution by Sufism which pertains to the relationship between zahir (outer) and batin (inner), and the way these dimensions are reciprocally linked to the body (Hofer, 2016). Bodily based rituals are considered to be "the cause of further good, for outer acts create substantial inward change, making a transformative and permanent effect on the self" (Metcalf, 1984). Ultimately, the body in Islamic scholarship and especially in Sufi scholarship is not seen as a passive agent but rather as a reciprocal agent that may facilitate access to the divine within one's heart.

Concluding Remarks about Heartfulness in the Islamic Tawhidic Discourse

In conclusion, it appears that heartfulness or heart-based interventions constitute an attempt by Muslim psychologists to reclaim a contemplative heritage closely associated with cultivating noble character, good intentions and an overarching desire to be close to God. It is important to highlight here that the relationship between love and knowledge in Islam is perceived as inextricable for an aspect of what we seek to know (the Divine) is contained deeply within our inmost selves. This is beautifully depicted in the famous Persian poem of the Conference of the Birds by the Sufi poet Farid ud-Din Attar (d. 1229). It is also alluded to in the Hidden Treasure hadith often cited by Sufis "I was a Hidden Treasure and I sought/loved/desired to be Known so I created the world" to convey their understanding "of the ultimate motif of creation – being the desire by the Creator to be known/revealed through his creatures" (Ismail, 2023, p. 74). On the divine level, love can be called the motive force for God's creative activity. The human willingness to respond to this love constitutes realizing one's essence or one's authentic self. This is no easy task as denoted in the prophetic hadith 'Heaven and Earth are not able to encompass the True Lord, only the heart of the believer can encompass Him' (Hirtenstein, 2010; Petersen, 2013, as cited in Ismail, 2023). Eventually, "what God wants is our hearts, our love, and our efforts, as deficient as they are, rather than our so-called perfect souls. Hence, the Qur'anic verse: 'But only he (will prosper) who comes to Allah with a sound heart'" (Q 26:89) (Ismail, 2023, p. 74).

Again, this is not a simple task; it requires cultivating an 'adab' (i.e. mannerism) of being with God which involves recognizing in one's inmost being, what belongs to him or herself and what belongs to Him. In the Islamic worldview, the reality is that to us belong "poverty, weakness, incapacity, ignorance, and abject humility, while to Him belong affluence, strength, power, wisdom, and glory" (Abdul Rauf, 2008, p. 600). "To us belongs non-existence, to Him all-Being" (Abdul Rauf, 2008). Such deeply held recognition of one's neediness and faqr (i.e. poverty) towards God is so central to the spiritual path and its central practice of dhikr that faqr has been a far more common designation for Sufism than the world tasawwuf (i.e. the Arabic word for Sufism) itself (Chittick, 2008).

Another concept that is key to the Sufi tradition and of relevance to Islamic psychology in general and contemplative practice in particular that should be elaborated pertains to the dialectic of the heart and the ego. Travelers on the Sufi path are urged to differentiate between impulses that issue from the peripheral passional forces of the ego and the centering subtle energies within the heart (Ismail, 2023). Learning to notice one's thoughts and emotions and to see through the ruses of one's ego is a fundamental skill prompting the authority on Sufism Jalal al Din al Rumi to Qur'anically interpret the prototype of Pharaoh against the tendencies any individual may have in terms of inflicting injustice upon others and ultimately upon oneself. The pharaoh within as opposed to some external tyrant has been the primary concern of Sufi masters who sought to alert individuals to the pitfalls associated with making progress along the spiritual path (Latif, 2009). These pitfalls seem to include the many illusions and justifications our mind is capable of creating, with the chief illusion being that of autonomy. Here, it should be emphasized that self-mastery is key to psychospiritual development in Islamic psychology. That said, it should be tempered with humility, surrender and trust before God and amidst the turns and twists of life.

Ultimately, heartfulness seems to be an attempt by Muslim among other scholars to point to a mode of consciousness beyond the mind and to a mode of being beyond the ego. As such in the Islamic Sufi tradition, among other wisdom traditions, mindfulness in the contemporary sense is seen as a potential aid to a more comprehensive contemplative practice. This is in line with recent proposals to approach mindfulness as part of "a large ecosystem of ideas and potential actions" as a way to remind researchers that mindfulness was one among other interventions in the societies in which it originated. For instance, "Right Mindfulness is only one of eight Buddhist factors listed in the Noble Eightfold Path, a prescription for how to go about living one's life" (Galante & Van Dam 2024, Can Mindfulness and Public Health be Compared Head-to-Head section, para. 5).

Finally, heartfulness may be conceived as an ongoing endeavor that requires the engagement of one's whole being such that one becomes a mirror reflecting realities of a higher order. For that to occur, it is essential to de-clutter the inner space from transient thoughts and emotions and to see through one's ego so that God's qualities may shine through our being. It is equally important to immerse oneself in the beauty and rigor of God's word through taking time to reflect on His traces in His three books of creation: –1) Nature and its awesome workings, 2) the divine text, and 3) one's own soul. Such practices are meant to facilitate connectedness to the heart associated with Being beyond the individual ego.

Contemplative Practice in Wisdom Traditions

There seems to be a consensus that the contemporary understanding of mindfulness "has been substantially simplified and divorced from its origins" (Sun. 2014, p. 394). Tracing back the origins of the term 'Mindfulness' in the English language to the mid fourteenth century, Sun (2014) showed that the term existed long before it became associated with Buddhism and meditation, noting that it had been used in senses of remembrance, being full of care, being conscious or aware, or intending to do something. This emphasis on remembrance resonates with the use of the term 'dhikr' which means in Arabic remembrance, and which is used in Islamic Sufi literature to make reference to the remembrance of God through invoking His Name(s) and qualities. The holy book of the Qur'an is also referred to as 'dhikr' denoting its primary function of reminding human beings of the Divine word/reality. Along similar lines, mindfulness was seen as important "in supporting Christian ways of being, through maintaining a 'habitual' or 'continual' mindfulness of God's presence" (Sun, 2014, p. 395). It was also "closely intertwined with gratitude" and "paired with or described in terms that conveyed an affective quality of love, kindness, care and consideration for others" (Sun, 2014, p. 396). Mindfulness, therefore, not only supported religious life but also had "a distinct moral and affective quality with its largely other-oriented focus" Sun, 2014, p. 396).

The focus on moral qualities in Islamic and Christian contemplative practices resonates with Buddhist-based mindfulness embedded within the Noble Eightfold Path and the Islamic legacy of drawing upon the example of the prophet to cultivate noble character and healthy emotions. It is relevant to point out, herein, that despite empirical evidence showing that value–based actions are associated with improved mental health outcomes (Grégoire, 2021), traditional psychotherapy techniques typically overlooked the importance of identifying and committing to values. One notable exception is Acceptance and Commitment Therapy (ACT), a relatively recent third–wave intervention that bears the imprints of Buddhism and that is beginning to be examined in the context of Islamic and Christian faith-based therapies (Bhatti-Ali, 2024; Knabb, 2023; Tanhan, 2019). Connected to ethical practice is an emphasis in wisdom traditions on the importance of paying attention to one's inmost intentions associated with the faculty of the heart. The less likely one is to identify with one's transient thoughts and emotions the more open one may be to cultivating a mode of seeing with the eyes of the heart. Similarly to the Sufi Islamic tradition, contemplative practice in Christianity is not merely "an 'uncovering technique' whose ultimate goal is the integration and healing of the smaller (egoic) self. It is rather a direct and immediate encounter with a deeper relational ground, in which one begins to directly intuit the presence of a larger "I, which heals by relativising the small-self hegemony and bringing it into relationship with that deeper ground" (Bourgeault, 2016, p. 49). That deeper ground may be experienced as a relationship with a transcendent consciousness or the Buddha nature as in Buddhism, or with a loving God contained in Christ, the Holy Spirit and God the Father as in Christianity (Bourgeault, 2016); Trammel, 2017). It may also be experienced as a relationship with a God who is simultaneously transcendent (beyond all forms and definitions) and immanent (His presence is felt more closely than one's own jugular vein) as in the Qur'an. Regardless of the specific symbolisms or terminologies used, contemplative practice in wisdom traditions is said to occur "in the energetic field of love." (Bourgeault, 2016).

Conclusion, Implications, and Discussion

In highlighting the heart as the essence of the human being, special attention has been given in Islamic psychology and philosophy to (a) practices that acknowledge the heart as the seat of consciousness, (b) drawing upon the example of the prophet, for cultivating healthy emotions, (c) discernment of one's intentions, (d) appreciating the role of the body, and (e) realizing tawhid within as the ultimate purpose of life and the motivating factor for contemplative practice. The perspective of seeing with the eyes of the heart points to an emphasis on a mode of consciousness that cannot be accessed via rational reasoning or willful action alone. Such a perspective is not meant to foster a state of passivity, let alone sentimentality, but rather a mode of being that recognizes the intimate relationship between ethical action, contemplation and accessing realities of a higher order (Ferhat 2020). It is also meant to point to a mode of understanding reality in which loving, knowing and being are inextricably linked.

From this perspective, heartfulness may be understood as a practice embedded in a mode of seeing and being in the world that cannot be reduced to a stress management technique or an individualistic method aimed chiefly at de-identification with one's transient thoughts and emotions. Such application, which may be actually sufficient in some instances, should be regarded as a first step toward connecting to one's inmost self and ultimately realizing that the self belongs to God or "in relationship with a divine oneness" (Trammel, p. 367). Cultivating such a mode of consciousness or being is key not only to Islamic psychology but also to other traditions, including Christian and Buddhist psychologies (Trammel, 2017)

Whereas not all clients are open to spiritual explanations or interventions, many clients who are open to spirituality end up working, unfortunately, with clinicians who do not have the knowledge or training necessary for them to engage in therapies or conversations that draw on the rich existential framework guiding their clients' lives (Drew et al., 2021; Lee et al., 2019; Santiago, 2022; Vieten et al., 2016; Vieten et al., 2023). In light of the above, it is important that clinicians educate themselves about different wisdom traditions and that they take the time to explore the relevance of these traditions to their clients' lives and everyday practice. Appreciating areas of resonance between the clinician's own background - including the academic and the personal - and that of the client – may open up previously unexplored territories at the level of cosmic and intellectual conversational spaces or practical interventions.

As had been shown in this chapter, Islamic among other faith-based traditions, associate the heart with one's innermost values and intentions. As such, mindfulness or heartfulness practice may be understood as a doorway to learn about people's identities – who they are, what they value and what they aspire for deep within their hearts. Acceptance and Commitment Therapies which emphasize helping clients establish a link between daily behaviors and overarching values highlight how the question of values may be approached and operationalized in measurable and meaningful terms that remind clinicians and clients alike of the importance of differentiating goals from values (Fung, 2014). Through learning about the wisdom traditions' shared emphasis on meditative practices, values and intentions we, as clinicians, may become more attuned to possibilities of tapping into our clients' meaning systems helping them draw relevant connections between their everyday practices, goals, and aspirations.

Finally, the term 'heartfulness' potentially serves as an invitation for psychologists and clinicians to reflect on contemporary mindfulness-based practices in light of wisdom traditions including the Islamic Sufi tradition in which the technical aspects of contemplative practices (e.g. controlling one's thoughts, focused attention, paying attention to matters of posture and breathing) are treated as helpful, yet secondary to the ultimate life purpose of persevering in the remembrance of God (Chittick, 2008), connecting to essence, or understanding the nature of reality in terms best suited to characterize the client's worldview.

References

Abdul Rauf, I. F. (2008). Asceticism in Islam. *Asceticism Today, 57*(4), 591–602.

Ahmad, A. (1999). Pathology of the heart in the Qur'an: A metaphysico-psychological explanation. *Intellectual Discourse, 7*(1), 79-89.

Assar, M. (2017). *An Islamic psychological approach to psychotherapy* [Doctoral dissertation, The Chicago School of Professional Psychology]. ProQuest Dissertations Publishing.

Bhatti-Ali, (2024). *Integrating Acceptance and Commitment Therapy with Islamic psychotherapy for managing chronic pain*. Routledge.

Boehme, J. (1978) *The way to Christ*. P.C. Erb (Ed.) Mahwah NJ: Paulist Pres.

Bourgeault, C. (2016). From the egoic mind to the mind of the heart. The teaching and lived experience of the Christian contemplative path. *Journal of Consciousness Studies, 23*(1-2), 45-57.

Bourgeault, C. (2017, Jan. 31). The way of the heart. From the Christian esoteric tradition, a path beyond the mind. *Parabola*.

Chittick, W. (2008). Sufism: *A Beginner's Guide*. Oxford: Oneworld Publications.

Dagli, C. (2017). Chapter 2: The Cow *"Al-Baqarah"*. In S. H. Nasr (Ed.), *The study Quran: A new commentary and translation* (pp. 64-263). HarperOne.

Dakake, M. (2017). Chapter 6: The Cattle *"al- An'ām"*. In S. H. Nasr (Ed.), *The study Quran: A new commentary and translation* (pp. 626-736). HarperOne.

Drew, D., Banks, J, & Rigaud, J. (2021). Religion and spirituality in clinical practice: an exploration of comfort and discomfort among practitioners. *Journal of Religion and Spirituality in Social Work, 41*(34), 1-17. https://doi.org/10.1080/15426432.2021.1994099

Ferhat, L. (2020). Al-Ghazali's heart as a medium of light: Illumination and the soteriological process. *Journal of Islamic Ethics, 4*, 201–2022.

Feuillebois-Pierunek, E. (2017). ʿIzz al-Dīn Kāshānī and Abū al-Mafākhir Yahyā Bākharzī: Proper Sufi conduct (adab) through the Eyes of Two Persian Authors from Different Brotherhoods in the 13th–14th Century. In F. Chiabotti, E. Feuillebois-Pierunek, C. Mayeur-Jaouen, & L. Patrizi (Eds.), *Ethics and spirituality in Islam: Sufi adab* (pp. xx-xx). Brill.

Fung, K. (2014). Acceptance and Commitment Therapy: western adoption of Buddhist tenets. *Transcultural Psychiatry 2015, 52*(4) 561–576.

Galante, J., & Van Dam, N.J. (2024). Mind and the echo chamber: Mindfulness as a contemplative practice that can contribute to public health. *Mindfulness*. https://doi.org/10.1007/s12671-024-02343-4

Geels, A. (1996). A note on the psychology of Dhikr: The Halveti-Jerrahi order of dervishes in Istanbul. *International Journal for the Psychology of Religion, 6*(4), 229–251. https://doi.org/10.1207/s15327582ijpr0604_1

Grégoire, J. (2021). The relationship between value-based actions, psychological distress and well-being: A multilevel diary study. *Journal of Contextual Behavioral Science, 20,* 79–88.

Haruna, A. (2023). *Concept of fitrah in Islamic psychology.* International Students of Islamic Psychology.

https://www.isip.foundation/concept-of-fitrah-in-islamic-psychology/

Helminski, K. (2007). Adab: The Sufi art of conscious relationship. In W. Chittick (Ed.), *The inner journey: Views from the Islamic tradition* (pp. 93–98). Morning Light Press.

Helminski, S. K. (2016). *The foundations of heartfulness in Islam.* The Threshold Society. https://sufism.org/library/articles/the-foundations-of-heartfulness-in-islam

Hofer, N. (2016). Training the prophetic self: Adab and riyāḍa in Jewish Sufism. In F. Chiabotti, E. Feuillebois-Pierunek, C. Mayeur-Jaouen, & L. Patrizi (Eds.), *Ethics and Spirituality in Islam: Sufi adab* (pp. 325-355*).* Leiden, The Netherlands: Brill. doi: https://doi.org/10.1163/9789004335134

Isgandarova, N. (2019). Muraqaba as a mindfulness-based therapy in Islamic psychotherapy. *Journal of Religion and Health, 58*(3), 1146–1160. https://doi.org/10.1007/s10943-018-0695-y

Ismail, G., Shealy, C., & Nahas, Z. (2021). Psychotherapy through a Sufi Islamic lens: A dialectic of transcendence and acceptance. *Spirituality in Clinical Practice, 10*(3), 200–218. https://doi.org/10.1037/scp0000274

Ismail, G. (2023). Sufi ethical discourse: the relationship between self-transcendence, compassion and a beatific vision. *The Way of Love* (pp. 63-80). Al-Karam Institute Press.

Kabat-Zinn, J. (2013). *Full catastrophe living.* Bantam Books. https://ird.mcu.ac.th/wp-content/uploads/2021/07/Full-Catastrophe-Living-PDFDrive-.pdf

Karadsheh, A., Davey-Attlee, F., & Salman, A. (2023, November 29). 'I kissed her but she wouldn't wake up.': Grandfather grieves for 3-year-old granddaughter killed as she slept Gaza. *CNN.* https://edition.cnn.com/2023/11/29/middleeast/gaza-truce-israel-grandfather-returns-home-intl-hnk/index.html

Keshavarzi, H., & Keshavarzi, S. (2021). Emotionally oriented psychotherapy. In H. Keshavarzi, F. Khan, B. Ali, & R. Awaad (Eds.), *Applying Islamic principles to clinical mental health care: Introducing traditional Islamically integrated psychotherapy* (pp. 171–208). Routledge.

Khalil, A. (2020). Humility in Islamic contemplative ethics. *Journal of Islamic Ethics, 4*, 223–252.

Khan, F., Keshavarzi, H., & Rothman, A. (2021). The role of the TIIP therapist: Scope of practice and proposed competencies. In H. Keshavarzi, F. Khan, B. Ali, & R. Awaad (Eds.), *Applying Islamic principles to clinical mental health care: Introducing traditional Islamically integrated psychotherapy* (pp. 38–65). Routledge.

Knabb, J. J. (2023). *Faith-based ACT for Christian clients: An integrative treatment approach* (2nd ed.). Routledge.

Keane, R. (2018). The maladies of the nafs and their remedies: An analysis and translation [M.A. degree, The University of Georgia, Athens].

Latif, A. (2009). Qur'anic narrative and Sufi heremeneutics: Rumi's interpretations of Pharaoh's character [Doctoral dissertation, Stony Brook University, NY].

Lee, D., D., Goedeke, S., & Krägeloh, C., U. (2019). Spirituality and religion in clinical practice: the experiences of psychologists in the integration of spirituality and religion in therapy in Aotearoa New Zealand, Spirituality in Religion and Clinical Practice. *New Zealand Journal of Psychology (Online), 48*(2), 82-90.

Lodi, F. (2018). The HEART method: Health emotions anchored in RasoolAllah's teachings: Cognitive therapy using prophet Mohamed as a psychospiritual exemplar. In C. Y. Al-Karam

(Ed.), *Islamically integrated psychotherapy: Uniting faith and professional practice* (pp. 82–106). Templeton Press.

Mayeur-Jaouen, C., & Patrizi, L. (2017). Ethics and spirituality in Islam: Sufi Adab – An Introduction. In F. Chiabotti, E. Feuillebois-Pierunek, C. Mayeur-Jaouen, & L. Patrizi (Eds.). *Ethics and spirituality in Islam* (pp. 1-44). Leiden, The Netherlands: Brill. https://doi.org/10.1163/9789004335134

McGremor, R. (2021). Seeing is believing: sufi vision and the formation of the ethical subject. In B. Orfali, A. Khalil., & M. Rustom (Eds.). *Mysticism and ethics in Islam* (pp. 187-202). Beirut: American University of Beirut Press.

Metcalf, B.D. (1984). Islamic reform and Islamic women: Maulana Thanawi's jewelry of paradise. In B.D. Metcalf (Ed.), *Moral conduct and authority: the place of adab in South Asian Islam.* University of California Press.

Olatoye, R. M. (2013). Towards understanding the Islamic concept of the heart and its relationships with man's intention/actions. *European Scientific Journal, ESJ, 9*(19). https://doi.org/10.19044/esj.2013.v9n19p%p

Rosenfeld, L. (2013). *The body in remembrance: Dhikr in Moroccan sufism* [Doctoral dissertation, The University of North Carolina at Chapel Hill].

Rothman, A. (2018). An Islamic theoretical orientation to psychotherapy. In C. Y. Al-Karam (Ed.), *Islamically integrated psychotherapy: Uniting faith and professional practice* (pp. 36–64). Templeton Press.

Rothman, A. (2019). *Heartfulness.* Shifaa Integrative Counseling. http://www.shifaacounseling.com/blog/heartfulness

Rothman, A., & Coyle, A. (2020). Conceptualizing an Islamic psychotherapy: A grounded theory study. *Spirituality in Clinical Practice, 7*(3), 197–213. https://doi.org/10.1037/scp0000219

Seker, M. Y. (2012). A map of the divine subtle faculty: The concept of qalb (heart) in classical and contemporary Islamic scholarship [Doctoral dissertation, The Australian Catholic University].

Santiago, K. (2022). *Psychologists' Graduate Training Experience and Attitudes in Religion and Spirituality.* [Doctoral dissertation,

University of Denver Graduate School of Professional Psychology].

Sheikh, F. (2018). Marrying Islamic principles with Western psychotherapy for children and adolescents: Successes and challenges. In C. Y. Al-Karam (Ed.), Islamically integrated psychotherapy: Uniting faith and professional practice. Templeton Press.

Sun, J. (2014). Mindfulness in context: A historical discourse analysis. *Contemporary Buddhism, 15*(2), 394–415. http://dx.doi.org/10.1080/14639947.2014.978088

Tarip, I., & Abu Bakar, N. F. (2020). Al-Ghazali on the head, heart and hand tripartite, and its organisational implications. *International Journal of `Umranic Studies, 3*(2), 1–12.

Tanhan, A. (2019). Acceptance and Commitment Therapy with Ecological Systems Theory: Addressing Muslim Mental Health Issues and Wellbeing. *Journal of Positive Psychology and Wellbeing, 3*(2), 197-219.

Trammel, R. C. (2017). Tracing the roots of mindfulness: Transcendence in Buddhism and Christianity. *Journal of Religion & Spirituality in Social Work: Social Thought, 36*(3), 367–383. https://doi.org/10.1080/15426432.2017.1295822

Vieten, C., Scammell, S., Pierce, A., Pilato, R., Ammondson, I., Pargament, K. I., & Lukoff, D. (2016). Competencies for psychologists in the domains of religion and spirituality. *Spirituality in Clinical Practice, 3*(2), 92–114. https://doi.org/10.1037/scp0000078

Vieten, C., Oxhandler, H.K., Pearce, M., Fry, N., Tanega, C., & Pargament, K. (2023). Mental health professionals' perspectives on the relevance of religion and spirituality to mental health care. *BMC Psychology, 11*(1). DOI:10.1186/s40359-023-01466-y

CHAPTER 2

The Impact of Heartfulness on Health and Heredity via Epigenomic Regulation

Farah R. Zahir, PhD

Introduction

Spiritual training ensconced within the Islamic tradition includes a variety of practices based upon the example set by the Prophet Muhammed ﷺ (peace be upon him). The practices are numerous, highly varied, and cover every aspect of life. The corpus of practices can be said to affect the state of the heart, or *heartfulness*. Their goal is to harmonize the person's state of heart with a larger all-pervasive cosmology as understood by the Muslim tradition. The heart is considered the organ of connection with the One Divine, and therefore all Islamic spiritual practice focuses it. Harmonizing oneself with this One Divinity brings about a state of heart that is able to manifest its full Divinely ordained potential. This is the *raison d'être* of Islamic spiritual practice, termed the science of *Ihsan*.

This chapter first presents the Islamic cosmological basis for the impact of heartfulness, and then explains Islamic Ihsan practices and how they act to harmonize the individual with the cosmos. These include both mandatory and voluntary exercises. Among the mandatory, are famously: a) salat and b) fasting. Importantly, the Islamic tradition contains a plethora of voluntary spiritual practices designed to enhance heartfulness, such as dhikr (remembrance: repetitive intonation of spiritual formulae), and khalwa (retreat or spiritual seclusion: staying apart from society for a prolonged period, often while engaging in fasting and salat or dhikr).

These practices, by bringing about heartfulness, equate to optimal emotional and physical wellbeing in addition to the obvious spiritual wellbeing. The chapter next introduces the recently discovered and rapidly advancing science of epigenomics and discusses how it is offering a robust and rigorous means to empirically assess the ability of spiritual practices to control gene function. Breakthrough discovery epigenomic screens have shown that meditative exercises affect changes in genes involved in immune system functioning, stress response physiology, psychological states, and even cellular aging. Seminal studies are summarized and their connections to Islamic heartfulness methods probed.

Currently, experiential evidence for the prophylactic and therapeutic effects of *Ihsan* practices are abundant. Nevertheless, empirical mechanistic biological insights are still not well understood. However, epigenomics evidences a material mechanism for how the environment impacts genes, and thus is now offering a fascinating and potent lens capable of deciphering the physiological effects of Islamic spiritual practices upon bodily health and wellbeing. Despite only a handful of epigenomic studies conducted to–date on spiritual environmental influences, their findings already indicate that they can exert a powerful effect on human physiology.

Islamic Cosmology

Islamic cosmology can be defined as the science of how the Creator, creation, and the relationship between the Creator and creation, is understood in the Islamic tradition. Essential to this subject is the centrality of Islamic monotheism. Islamic monotheism itself is not simply an acceptance of there being one God, rather it is an all-encompassing concept that emphasizes that Divinity is complete and comprehensive.

The One Divinity therefore includes all things in it, animate and inanimate, static and dynamic. It is the creative and regenerative force, the source of all things, but is itself sourceless, the end and beginning of all, but itself without end and without beginning. This force is not divisible and cannot be separated from anything other than it. In other words, it is limitless yet expansive over all (the all here having no limit).

Thus, The One God as understood in the Islamic tradition is an all-encompassing, all-pervasive, active, vibrant, and alive force, from whom there is no separation between anything and itself. This One Divinity cannot be escaped and cannot fully be understood by any other than itself—as no created thing will ever equate to the Creator, and thus no mind can fully comprehend the One who made that mind. Thus, the One God is also all, and everything.

Given the above brief summation of Islamic monotheism, it is understood that the One God, though given the personal name Allah in the Islamic tradition, is not to be understood in the conventional sense of a Creator-God who may be personified. Indeed, Allah is genderless, and does not inhabit a given boundary.

Being limitless, Allah cannot be assigned a form. Furthermore, as nothing is removed from Allah, nothing can happen except under the direct agency and active force of Allah's doing. Hence, it is Allah that causes one to breathe, think, act, the sun to rise, the cycles of night and day, the workings of every minutia and maxima of ecology at any and every moment.

These fundamentals of Islamic monotheism comprise the tenets of *aqeeda* a word which may be interpreted to mean theology. The interested reader is referred to texts such as the Aqeeda Tahawiyyah that elaborate on the nature of Islamic monotheism and the fundamental beliefs that comprise Islamic theology (Jafar al-Tahawi, 900).

It can be understood from this succinct explanation about The Creator, that creation is ergo, intimately tied to The Creator or Allah. Thus, it is impossible to separate creation from the Creator. Nor can we consider the workings of the Creator as separate or divorced from the intimate presence and power of Allah Himself.

Here we note the use of the singular male pronoun when referring to the Creator is an unfortunate prop necessitated by the limitation inherent in the English language. This issue occurs in many other languages as well. It is not right to understand Allah as a male or as a female. However, the pronoun *it* can't be used because Allah is alive and indeed the definition of Life itself. As such, this necessary convention must be used. Given this, Islamic cosmology is not just the theological basis of the faith, but the whole of the effects of that theology in practice throughout the cosmos.

Importantly, the cosmos does not only mean the known universe but also includes other dimensions and realms, as well as the essence of the Divine being Himself. Therefore, Islamic cosmology is not just the understanding of who Allah is, but also of what and who Allah made, and how all of it works within the power of this all pervasive One Active Divinity.

Islamic cosmology, for example, defines and explains different dimensions of existence such as the *dhaat, ai'zzat, jabarut, malakut*, and *mulk* (Ifra'ah, 2022). There are further elaborations on entities that arise from the Creator which are not creation, such as *commandment* (Ifra'ah, 2022). The pre-eternity and semper-eternity of all knowledge as an attribute of the Creator, which by definition will take on the qualities of the Creator, and thus the Creator's knowledge is limitless and not bound by time–space constraints (in fact, the very nature of time itself as an entity is explained).

Therefore, from this concept it can be logically understood that all things that are to exist and happen, or existed and happened, including all the infinite possibilities for creation and commandment, are already known to Allah. Therefore, there exists destiny and predestination. Yet, the human being is capable of free choice, and thus bears responsibility for their actions and is thereby also able to affect their own destiny.

Islamic Cosmology elaborates on the complex relationship between the finite human being with the all-encompassing Divine destiny and predestination: the agency inherently given to the human-being, and the potential for fulfilling a person's destiny inherent in that person, and whether they will fulfill it, and the consequences either way. This has a direct and profound impact on the subject of heartfulness (*vide infra*). It also elaborates on the nature of human action as pertaining to the realm of the mulk (the universe or life on earth as it is customarily known), where time flows linearly to other realities (e.g. malakut) where time does not move linearly nor uniformly.

Having laid out some of the fundamentals of Islamic Cosmology, we next examine how these notions are found in the religion of Islam itself, via its main tripartite: Islam-Iman-Ihsan.

Islam-Iman-Ihsan

Islam as a religion is composed of three main branches: Islam, Iman, and Ihsan (Parrott, 2019; Usman dan Fodio, 1978). However, these three words can be used to mean the sum of all when used individually, but there is also a meaning specific to each. The word Islam specifically means the practices necessary to fulfil the religion, which are in the external domain. For example, fasting in the month of Ramadan, performing the five times a day mandatory ritualized worship-exercise termed *salat*, rules and methods pertaining to keeping the body clean, rules pertaining to how food and drink should be consumed, rules pertaining to how an income may be sought, and so on. The subject that delves deeply into this is called *fiqh* (jurisprudence).

Iman specifically refers to the internal beliefs the practitioner of Islam has adopted, such as there is Allah and no other deity, that Allah has sent scriptures to humanity, and divinely guided prophets, the existence of angels, and so on. Creedal beliefs are the focus of the above-mentioned subject of aqeeda.

The third is Ihsan. Ihsan is the most important as it is the objective of Islam and Iman, but it is also currently the least familiar. It has suffered massive erosion as a science due to centuries of neglect in the Muslim world.

Heartfulness falls under the scope of Ihsan. Ihsan as the prophet Muhammed ﷺ (peace be upon him) defined it in the famous Gabriel hadith (Muslim Ibn al-Ḥajjāj al-Qushayrī, 1955), is to "worship Allah as if you see Him, and if you see Him not, know that He sees you." In other words, it is to be in a state of complete consciousness of and harmony with the Divine presence (God-consciousness).

A person who can implement perfect Islam, upon perfect Iman, should achieve a state of perfect Ihsan. This is no small feat, and rarely found by even the most dedicated practitioner. The crux of the tradition is that the objective of practising Islam, upon entering Iman, is to attain Ihsan. Attaining a state of perfect God-consciousness means that one aligns oneself with the purpose of one's creation. One thus achieves complete harmony not only with the Creator, but with all the rest of creation, and other entities that arise from the Creator such as commandment (Ifra'ah, 2022).

In summary, the religion of Islam involves these three main components: to adopt a regimen of external behaviours and exercises (Islam), based upon a set of internal beliefs and convictions (Iman), so that one attains a state of being in harmony with the Divine (Ihsan). Not having these three completed, or an imbalance in any one component, can lead to serious harm to the person. At the very least it would mean not attaining the objective of the religion of Islam.

The Neglected Science of Ihsan: Living in a State Fully Conscious of and in Harmony with the Divine

The study of Ihsan, it being the most advanced or the higher-order science of the tripartite, was focused on predominantly in the early centuries of Islam. However, currently it has been vastly eroded for a variety of reasons. Nevertheless, remnants of the science and its methods are still extant in what is termed Sufism.

Sufism, though somewhat a fringe pursuit in post-World War II Muslim societies, was at one time practised by up to 80% of all Muslims (Buehler, 1998; Eaton, 1974; Murata, 2000; Nasr, 1972; Sells, 1996), though it may not have been termed that by those practitioners. This is because the practices that make up the bulk of Sufi ways today were part of a larger corpus of mainstream practices for attaining Ihsan in centuries past.

They were meant to train the soul-heart-mind-body axis to consciousness and harmony with the Divine.

To elaborate, early Muslim societies had a comprehensive understanding of the purpose of the Muslim way of life due to their proximity to the example set by the founder of the religion, the prophet Muhammed ﷺ and to those who closely emulated his lifestyle. They witnessed his state of always being in complete God-consciousness and therefore living a life on earth as God's vicegerent, or true servant, in complete harmony with the Divine in all things, and they understood this was the objective of the religion. In their assiduous following of his example, many of the early Muslims themselves reached very high states of Ihsan. And they in turn wrote of their experiences and formulated a science based on the prophetic example, which came to be understood as a means to attain Ihsan (Dwijayanti, 2015; Janssens, 2011; Mohamad et al., 2020).

The crux of the vast number of texts on the subject deal with how to train the heart to be in a state of witnessing Divinity at all times. They address advanced topics such as being able to recognize the different impulses that occur to one and being able to pinpoint the source of them. For example, Imam Al Ghazali's categorized the origin of thoughts as lordly, angelic, egoistic, or demonic (Abu Hamid al Ghazali, 2010). Others speak of the states the heart must witness as it climbs higher on the ladder of closeness to Divine presence (Ahmad Ibn Ajiba, 2012; Muhyiddin Ibn Arabi, 2009).

Yet others, such as the renowned knower of God, Rabia al Adawiyya, taught by virtue of their presence and state rather than by the medium of written scholarly works (Helminski, 2003; Smith, 1928). One of the earliest texts on the subject was penned by Abu Talib al Makki (died 996 CE) and is called "Qut al-qulub fi mu'amalat al-mahbub wa wasf tariq al-murid ila maqam al-tawhid." Succinctly translated this means "nourishment of the hearts" (Abu Talib Makki, 1978), which became a foundational text elaborated on by scores of later scholars (Nakamura, 1984).

As can be seen from the above, proponents of the science of Ihsan considered the heart to be the most important faculty when it comes to attaining this state of God-consciousness. Essentially, they considered human feeling as being more important than human thought. As will be elaborated in the next section, the Muslim organization of the human faculties-axis that comprise the whole person, is somewhat different to those found in other traditions. While different schools within the Muslim world differ in their precise organization, they all focus on the heart as the central organ or faculty.

Unfortunately, due to various forces of decay that set into the Muslim world in the past several centuries, present-day Muslims, for the most part, are unaware of the depth or the breath of the science of Ihsan, and how it ties into every other aspect of harmony with the cosmos and even with how essential it is in relation to Islam and Iman. Many Muslims still carry out practices that are relics derived from Ihsan methods, yet they often do not know that this is the case, nor the purposes and benefits of the practice.

For example, some Muslims still gather at specific days during a 40-day interval after a Muslim dies to read the Quran upon that departed soul—a practice with deep and lasting benefits for the community, as well as deeply helping the process of grieving, and importantly, having cosmological connotations for the soul of the departed as it journeys in other dimensions. Sadly though, as knowledge of the cosmological basis underpinning the practice is not commonly known, so is this tradition dying out. A notable contrast is the assiduous maintenance of Ihsan practices by those who belong to well organized Sufi orders (Buehler, 1998; Trimingham, 1971). A discussion of the Sufi orders is out of the scope of this chapter, however their importance in preserving and maintaining key aspects of the science of Ihsan is noteworthy.

Ruh-Qalb-Aql-Jism (Soul/Spirit-Heart-Brain/Intellect-Body)

One may find variation among the schools of Ihsan-science in how they define the faculties and axes that comprise a human being, though they all emphasize the centrality of the heart. For the purposes of this chapter, I will use a specific organization (Ifra'ah, 2022). Here, the human being is defined as composed of four essential entities: heart, soul (or spirit), body and mind.

In Islamic Cosmology, each of the four entities mentioned is understood to be existing in more than one reality at the same time. To explain, the heart of the human being can be said to have an existence in the Universe (what is termed the *mulk* in Ihsan-science) as it is composed of energy and matter.

However, the heart also exists in realities that permeate the known universe but are not of it, such as the angelic dimension, termed the *malakut* in Ihsan-science. The Malakut is a reality that is composed of primarily spirit—there is no energy or matter as understood by empirical science there. Yet, the notion of space, and faculties such as seeing, hearing, moving, and so on, are present in the malakut. Time, however, works very differently in the malakut, as it does not flow linearly nor uniformly there.

Other dimensions that extend beyond the malakut, such as the *a'izzat'* and *jabarut'* for example, which are more complex and beyond the scope of this chapter, are recognized by Islamic cosmology. There are seven of these dimensions or realities, each greater and permeating the ones below it. They are termed the *seven heavens.*

To return to the composition of the human being, each of the four components has an existence in all seven realities (Ifra'ah, 2022). Thus, it is essential to have this cosmological understanding to correctly grasp what is meant by the heart-body-intellect-soul quartet, according to Ihsan-science.

Importantly, the sum four together make up a human being, or the self (*nafs* in Arabic). There are other acceptable categorizations that may define these terms, especially the nafs, slightly differently. To summarize, according to the method I am using, the human being or individual person is a nafs, and that nafs is composed of the four essential entities named above. Each is next briefly described in the context of its existence in the mulk and the malakut.

Heart (Qalb): Its seat is the physical heart, and it has a connection to the physical heart, but the faculty referred to here is the spiritual heart. It also contains an intelligence, which, in Ihsan-science, is termed *heart-intellect*. The heart is able to understand and comprehend the mulk, as well as penetrate into the malakut when that faculty is developed. It is the spiritual heart that connects the body and the mind to the soul. Interestingly, recently it was discovered that the physical human heart does contain neuronal tissue (Ardell & Armour, 2016), suggesting an as yet-unearthed scientific basis for the Ihsan understanding of the heart-intellect.

Body (Jism): The corporeal body which can be understood as the biological human body. This too has a malakuti reality, but typically the physical body is what is focussed on by this term. The human body is the entity present in the mulk and its function is to house the heart, soul or spirit, and mind.

Brain-Intellect-Mind (Aql): Its seat is the brain, and it has a connection to the physical brain, but the faculty referred to here is more the ability to reason or the rational intellect. The mind is considered the organ whose purpose it is to study and understand the mulk. However, it cannot penetrate into nor comprehend the malakut.

Soul or Spirt (Ruh): Its seat is the lungs or the chest. It has a connection to this area of the body but of the four composites, the ruh is the most otherworldly. It is the faculty most able to penetrate into dimensions that are beyond the mulk. Not only can it penetrate into the malakut and travel in it as well as comprehend it, it can also penetrate to realms beyond that, such as the a'izzat and jabarut (Ifra'ah, 2022).

The heart is able to communicate with the ruh. Thus, the signals that come from heaven via the ruh are translated by the heart to the mind and rest of the body. This allows the human being with all four faculties functioning in correct alignment and harmony (especially the heart and ruh) to be able to live on earth in a Divinely guided manner, always connected to heavenly realities, also thereby translating those realities to human communities, societies, and to Earthly ecosystems (Figure 1).

Nurturing, nourishing, developing, and maintaining the ruh and the qalb are the focus of the science of Ihsan. It is critical to realize that for a wholesome, healthy human existence, a person must have all four of these entities—heart, body, mind, and soul—in a state of good health. Indeed, wellness in the body, which is the most entrenched in the mulk, depends a great deal on the health of the entities above it (Figure 1), and likewise the same for the other entities; the health of the mind depends on the health of the heart and the ruh, the health of the heart in turn depends on the health of the ruh.

Importantly, the heart is the center connecting the Malakuti dimension and those dimensions beyond it via the ruh, to the earthly dimensions of the body and mind. Thus, training the heart is the basis for unlocking the secrets of the ruh, as well as bringing about harmony of the mind and body with the greater cosmos. The heart, and therefore heartfulness, is the key and crux of it all.

Heartfulness and its Practices: Mandatory and Voluntary

This book no doubt provides several complimentary perspectives on heartfulness and how it may be achieved. For the purpose of the treatise, I present here, I will define it as *achieving a heart that is present with the Divine in all things at all times.*

To achieve such a state, it is necessary to have a ruh that is in alignment with the Divine, one that is nurtured and healthy. Further a "heart present with the Divine" is the gateway for spiritual energy to be channelled into the mind and the body. Thus, the key to alignment of the human being with all the realities or dimensions of existence, is the heart. Islamic cosmology has always recognized this significance. Ihsan scholars often note that the very biological arrangement of the heart, protected by two lungs on either side and the spine behind as well as the rib cage all around is a testament to how precious the heart is.

The arguments and treatises presented in this chapter are based upon the foundational entities of the religion of Islam, and therefore of Ihsan, which are the Quranic text and the prophetic example. Therefore, the basis for all the methods by which heartfulness is achieved in Islamic cosmology derives from Quranic principles. The Quran gives primal information about how to achieve heartfulness in many places, one such verse is below:

ٱلَّذِينَ ءَامَنُوا۟ وَتَطۡمَئِنُّ قُلُوبُهُم بِذِكۡرِ ٱللَّهِ ۗ أَلَا بِذِكۡرِ ٱللَّهِ تَطۡمَئِنُّ ٱلۡقُلُوبُ

Those who believe and complete (make it fulfilled/contented) their heart with the dhikr (remembrance) of Allah. Verily by the dhikr of Allah are hearts fulfilled. (Quran 13:28)

In short, heartfulness is achieved by the remembrance of Allah. Remembrance or dhikr is a vast concept in Ihsan and can encompass every aspect of a believer's life given the right intention or *niyyat. Dhikr is to be in a continuous state of remembrance of the Divine and in alignment with the working of the Divine will.* This is achieved using a variety of techniques, but they are all centered upon one's intention. Constantly watching over one's intention and aligning it with remembrance of the Divine can be said to be the purpose of the entire science of Ihsan, and indeed that of the religion of Islam itself. All aspects of what is encompassed by dhikr cannot be elaborated here, but the interested reader is referred to these books (Leaman, 2022; Tallal Alie Turfe, 2016; Usman dan Fodio, 1978).

For this chapter, I will categorize specific dhikr practices as mandatory or voluntary and explain how they relate to achieving heartfulness. Mandatory dhikr comprises all obligatory acts of worship and other obligated practices in Islam: the pillars of the practices of the religion, namely: (a) the five-times-daily ritual worship (salat); (b) fasting in the month of Ramadan—an intensive spiritual bootcamp the Muslim undertakes once a year for a whole month, along with voluntary extra-acts of dhikr highly encouraged in Ramadan such as chanting or reciting the entirety of the Quran, spending long hours in the night in additional salat, and seclusion and intense worship during the last 10 days of the month; (c) paying a charity-tax on one's wealth as an act of purification of the wealth once a year (zakat); and (d) the intense dhikr experience of the once-in-a-lifetime hajj pilgrimage—which is a complete immersion in renouncing the world to walk toward presence with the Divine.

When discussing voluntary dhikr, we move more into the science and methods of Ihsan. It is this science that elaborates on and gives formulations for constantly training one's heart to be in a state of heartfulness even when not engaged in mandatory worship rituals. There are innumerable methods that the practitioner may follow. Indeed, a famous Sufi aphorism states that, *"there are as many paths to Allah as there are breaths."*

Summarizing them all is impossible, but some that are considered to be most important and widely prevalent are: (a) dhikr proper—repetitive chanting aloud or silently, of formulations of the Divine name Allah, or other names of the Divine, or other specific spiritual litanies; (b) dhikr majlis—doing the same as above but in a group setting, often with a leader who will oversee the spiritual state of the members, and this may be accompanied by bodily movement and music; (c) khalwa—a guided seclusion where the practitioner will meditate alone, spending time in intense dhikr—often accompanied by not sleeping at night and very little consumption of food or drink; (d) rihla—spiritual wayfaring—travel undertaken with a spiritual guide that is meant as a means to train the aspirant to be in a constant state of heartfulness, no matter what one faces in life.

To summarize, both mandatory and voluntary dhikr is simply a means to achieve heartfulness. And heartfulness is the gateway to align the body-mind-heart-spirit axis, so that the full spiritual energies of the spirit are realized and thereafter channeled to the rest of the human being's consciousness via the heart, which in turn enlivens and rejuvenates the body.

Needless to say, these acts have powerful health benefits in both therapeutic and prophylactic ways. And indeed, extraneous to the point of whether a person is aiming to achieve heartfulness or become a Muhsin (a person who has achieved Ihsan) or not, these methods have been used for centuries as healing practices for both Muslims and non-Muslims by aficionados of the science. We will now delve deeper into the possible methods by which heartfulness can bring about biological change and thus healing and wellbeing. We do this via discussing its potential impacts on the recently emerging field of study termed *epigenomics*.

Epigenomic Modulation by Heartfulness Practices: Introduction to Epigenomics

Epigenomics is the science that deals with how the environment (macro and micro) impacts genomic functioning (Jaenisch & Bird, 2003; Tammen et al., 2013). This is conducted via examining the arrangements of certain chemical molecules that sit on top of (hence the Greek root *epi* which means exactly that) the DNA sequence that forms genes (Hirst & Marra, 2010; Wang & Chang, 2018). The attachment or de-attachment of the molecules has a direct impact on how the gene functions—whether it will be turned on, turned off, or how fast it will be transcribed (meaning how fast the gene is read, yielding a product).

There are four main epigenomic processes: DNA methylation and hydroxymethylation, histone modification, chromatin remodeling, and RNA interference (Jaenisch & Bird, 2003; Tammen et al., 2013; Yasin & Zahir, 2020; Zahir & Brown, 2011). To situate the reader, these main processes are summarized below. However, it must be noted that the field of epigenomics is complex (Non, 2021; Topart et al., 2020; L. Zhang et al., 2020; W. Zhang et al., 2020) and covers a diverse and vast array of biological phenomena that is still being unearthed (Mubarak & Zahir, 2022).

DNA methylation and hydroxymethylation refer to the addition of methyl or hydroxymethyl groups to the DNA backbone. These groups are added or removed at specific base positions along the DNA, according to environmental signals (Jaenisch & Bird, 2003; Tammen et al., 2013). Their addition or removal and the number and position of the added or removed molecules have a direct and indirect influence on whether genes are activated or not, and even the extent of transcription of an active gene. Not only do they influence the gene they are located on, but also critically, can influence genes further away, and even on different chromosomes, via chromatin remodeling (described below).

Histone modification refers to a more complex form of controlling how genes function via modification of the amino acid tails of histone proteins around which the DNA double helix is wound. There are a range of molecules that may bind the histone tails, such as methyl, acetyl, and phosphoryl groups among others (Tammen et al., 2013; Yasin & Zahir, 2020; Y. Zhang et al., 2021).

However, the concept remains the same—the number and position of the present or non-present molecule groups have a direct and indirect impact on how the genes are read. This is due to a mesmerizingly complex and beautiful symphony of chemical bonding that takes place depending on the number and type of added molecules, which ultimately acts to prevent or expose the gene (DNA) to transcription machinery (i.e., to being read or activated).

Chromatin remodeling, in turn, refers to a higher level of complexity that acts in concert with the aforementioned DNA and histone modifications (Yasin & Zahir, 2020; Zahir & Brown, 2011). In this process, cellular machinery will read the latter two arrangements and act with several factors to turn off or on whole swaths of chromosomal material (Cairns, 2005; Clapier & Cairns, 2009), therefore having the ability to impact several genes at once (Figure 2). Chromatin remodeling is thus a higher order epigenomic mark that is involved in macro level DNA organization and functioning (Clapier & Cairns, 2009), but nevertheless may also influence single gene activity.

RNA interference (RNAi) is yet another type of epigenomic regulation that is somewhat different to the above three, and some may not class it as a strictly epigenomic mechanism. However, its purpose is to exert environmental control upon genic functioning and hence it is discussed as an epigenomic mechanism.

34

In this process, genes that are transcribed but not translated will act to regulate transcripts of the same gene or other genes by causing their degradation prior to translation (Downward, 2004; Stallwood, 2005; Whangbo & Hunter, 2008). In other words, this mechanism does not allow the gene, even if read, to result in an active product. Though recently discovered, RNAi has proven to be a highly versatile modulator capable of exerting very fine control over gene expression. Its activity is also sensitive to environmental signals (Whangbo & Hunter, 2008).

The above four are by no means exhaustive, and merely encapsulate the major epigenomic processes thus known. It cannot be stressed enough that epigenomics is a science that is in its infancy and as more extensive investigations are carried out, other methodologies may come to light.

In fact, the related phenomenon of epitranscriptomics is already gaining traction. Epitranscriptomics details how certain molecules attach to the RNA transcript (rather than the DNA itself) and then influence its translation (Cayir et al., 2020; Meyer & Jaffrey, 2014) and is found to be especially predominant in the brain (Mubarak & Zahir, 2022). These arrangements are also influenced by the environment and open yet another window into our understanding of the complex ways the environment controls gene function (Cayir et al., 2020). However, we will limit ourselves to only epigenomics here.

Environmental Influences on the Epigenome and Epigenomic Inheritance

These four main epigenomic mechanisms are essential to our discourse, as they describe a biological method for how environment can impact genomic functioning. In other words, the discovery and exploration of epigenomics has led to the understanding that the old adage: "you are your genes," is not necessarily true at all. Indeed, via epigenomics, we are able to dissect the precise method by which a given macro-environmental influence, such as diet for example, can directly impact gene expression profiles.

Epigenomic changes induced by diet have now become established sufficiently to give rise to a sub-specialization: nutritional epigenetics/genomics (Niculescu, 2012). In fact, not only diet, but a whole plethora of micro and macro environmental factors are hypothesized to impact gene function epigenomically, everything from exposure to tobacco smoke, to stress levels, to sleep patterns, to emotional wellbeing, has been linked to epigenomics (Kanherkar et al., 2014). Critically, these environment-induced epigenomic signatures can lead to gene functional changes that become inherited (Bastaki et al., 2020; Bošković & Rando,

2018; Varela et al., 2022). For an excellent review see (Bošković & Rando, 2018).

Another offshoot of epigenomic investigations is the resurgence of interest in Lamarkian evolution. Lamark, in opposition to Darwin, proposed that evolution occurs due to environmental influences, including behaviours (Jablonka & Lamb, 1995). While scoffed at the time, his theories, so long buried under the shadow of the more popular Darwinian evolution, are now being looked at anew.

The idea is that a person's lifestyle, their exercise habits, eating habits and so on, will impact not only their health, but that of their progeny. In other words, their lifestyle choices lead to inherited epigenetic signatures. This idea has spurred a new interest in the epigenomic impacts of behaviour, especially with respect to traditional lifestyle and medical practices. The Lamarkian evolutionary model is also noteworthy as the notion that one's environment plays a role in one's spiritual connection to the Divine is understood from the following hadith:

The Prophet Muhammed (upon whom be peace) said, "No babe is born but upon Fitra. It is his parents who make him a Jew or a Christian or a Polytheist."

Reported by Abu Huraira, in Sahih Muslim (book 46, hadith 37)

The *fitra* in the above hadith refers to the primordial state in which every human being is created. It is a concept uniquely explained by the Islamic tradition, and it well captures the meaning of the human being with a correctly calibrated spirt/soul-heart-mind-body axis *(vide supra)*. This concept is also termed the *completed self* or *nafs ul mutma'innah* in Arabic. Thus, as Lamark proposes the environment alters one's physiology, it may also be extrapolated that one's spiritual practices might impact the evolution of one's consciousness, or in other words whether an individual is able to maintain and grow in the state of the original fitra or conversely, if neglected, result in those faculties diminishing within them. It is telling that the wording of the above hadith draws attention to a person being born upon the fitra specifically rather than using the term Muslim, emphasizing that being in a true fitra state is a level purer and more primordial than simply following a religion.

The emergence of the field of epigenomics also heralded renewed interest in complementary and alternative forms of medicine such as Traditional Chinese Medicine, Ayurveda, Unani, and Siddha. Referred to as Eastern Medical Systems (EMS), they have always focussed on the wholistic nature of man and held that a person's environment is critical to their wellbeing. As epigenomics was able to show empirically how environment directly controls genes, and as costs for heretofore exorbitantly expensive epigenomics assays (experimental systems that are able to read the precise epigenomic profile in an individual or given tissue or site) have been plummeting, there is currently a burgeoning interest in studying the epigenomics of everything EMS included (Hsieh et al., 2011, 2013; Kanherkar et al., 2017; Weng & Goel, 2022).

Recent Scientific Discoveries on the Epigenomics of Spirituality

Studies into how the spiritual environment may impact the genome (via epigenomics) are still few, as this is a new science, and efforts thus far have focused on the low-hanging fruit which are tangible environmental modulators. However, as the costs for epigenomic assays continue to reduce, a concordant increase in the number of studies that will investigate spiritual epigenomics is expected. There have been several studies showing how stress impacts the epigenome negatively (Gapp et al., 2016; Schiele & Domschke, 2018; Sheerin et al., 2021; Szyf, 2019; Torres-Berrío et al., 2019) and studies to date show that interventions such as exercising (McGee & Hargreaves, 2019), yoga (Bisht et al., 2020; Bisht & Dada, 2019) or meditation (Kaliman, 2019) can lead to improved epigenomics signatures. Selected seminal studies are briefly overviewed next.

Using robust next generation sequencing epigenomic assays, it was shown (Kaliman et al., 2014) that mindfulness-based meditation practice can bring about a definitively improved epigenomic signature versus a comparative non-meditation-based relaxation practice. Kaliman et al., subjected a test cohort and a control cohort to an eight-hour mindfulness-based meditation and an eight-hour leisure activity respectively. Blood samples taken from both cohorts before and after the intervention showed histone modification changes throughout the genome, which impacted the expression of genes involved with inflammation, among others.

Another study conducted by Chaix et al. (2017), on the same samples showed genome-wide differentially methylated regions in the test cohort following the intervention, but not in the control group. They identified 61 differentially methylated regions that included genes involved in immune response, inflammation, and aging with the subjects exposed to the mindfulness intervention showing reduced inflammation and aging metrics, as well as improved immune response gene activation signatures, compared to the controls.

These data clearly demonstrate the impact of a contemplative practice on the epigenome versus a non-contemplative leisure activity. To ensure the meditation intervention was carried out correctly, individuals with long-term experience of meditation (up to 30 years) were selected for the above studies. It is remarkable that in these genome-wide screens, the gene expression changes were focussed on metabolic pathways associated with chronic health and wellbeing impacts, such as inflammation and immune response (O'Donovan et al., 2012; Segerstrom & Miller, 2004; Slavich, 2015).

Advancing the epigenomic investigation into meditative contemplative practices, a paper recently published (Álvarez-López et al., 2022) reports testing participants at a month-long meditation retreat versus a control group of experienced meditators, but who did not participate in the retreat. In this case, blood samples were taken from retreat participants at day 2 and day 21, and the same was done from the control cohort. The data showed changes in expression levels for a targeted set of genes, finding reduced inflammation-related gene expression in the test cohort, indicating the positive health impact of the meditation retreat exposure. This study indicates that even for individuals who incorporate contemplative practice habits, an intensive spiritual, contemplative, and meditative retreat can further enhance physiological outcomes.

These studies are at the vanguard of reports unearthing facets of the still obscured area of how contemplative spiritual practices influence physiology. I have presented just three pertinent research findings, yet several more exist and have been reviewed (i.e., Venditti et al., 2020; Zahir, 2022). As the number and type of studies increase, it could be expected that these findings will be further expanded and elaborated on in terms of spiritual-physiological process. Thus far, they clearly indicate that epigenomic effects arising from spiritual practices are possible, and also suggest they are potent.

Expected Epigenomic Outcomes from Islamic Ihsan Practices

While, to our knowledge, robust epigenomics assays specific to Ihsan practices are not yet reported, there is significant literature showing altered health metrics using other physiological measurement scales (Zahir, 2022). For example, see Chamsi-Pasha and Chamsi-Pasha (2021) for a systematic review of health benefits reported due to salat and Ghiasi and Keramat (2018) for a systematic review of the impact of listening to Quranic recitation on anxiety.

However, several of the processes involved in meditation methods employed in the above studies (Álvarez-López et al., 2022; Chaix et al., 2017; Kaliman et al., 2014) are inherent in Islamic dhikr based meditative forms. Techniques used by the mindfulness-based meditation are found in the Ihsan equivalents: muraqaba (mindfulness), mushahada (observation), tasawwar (imagination), tafakkur (contemplation of creation), tadabbur (contemplation of the Divine), and muhasaba (self-assessment). These are as central to the practice of mindfulness-based meditation as they are to Ihsan science (Isgandarova, 2019).

Further, a khalwa is essentially an intensive meditation focussed seclusion which is similar to the intense retreat intervention studied (Álvarez-López et al., 2022). Thus, it is an entirely feasible hypothesis that Ihsan practices such as muraqaba, khalwa (meditation retreat), dhikr (meditation with chanting of specific spiritual mantras) and so on, will likewise induce significant genome-wide epigenomic alterations. A case in point is the already proven epigenomic alterations brought about by fasting (Hidalgo et al., 2014; Yong-Quan Ng et al., 2022), which is essentially the main practice during the mandatory Muslim fast in Ramadan.

Heart Tissue, Heartfulness and the Epigenome

This brings us to an interesting question: Do Ihsan-heartfulness practices directly influence the cardiac tissue, and does that affect the state of heartfulness? It is known that epigenomic regulation is essential to the development of cardiac tissue and that it also plays an essential role in cardiac disease and recovery (Rajan et al., 2021; Robinson et al., 2021; Rommel & Hein, 2020). In the science of Ihsan, the physical heart is considered to be the seat of the spiritual heart. Thus, there is a potential correspondence between the condition of the physical cardiac tissue and the spiritual states brought about by heartfulness practices.

Unfortunately, the likelihood of adequately answering this intriguing question is very low, as undertaking such a study would require access to actual cardiac tissue from a study participant—which of course is a near impossibility, unless conducted in an adequate model system. Nevertheless, it is entirely plausible that epigenomic alterations in cardiac tissue may be engineered by Ihsan practices, which in turn impact levels of consciousness experienced by the practitioner, either by directly impacting the physiology of the heart or by affecting the body via the heart's functioning.

Conclusion

In this chapter I have introduced Islamic cosmology and explained how the science of Ihsan aligns the human being to the expansive and complete Divine cosmos. Further, by overviewing two broad areas, Islamic Ihsan practices that are meant to affect the state of the heart, and the science of epigenomics which explains a mechanism by which the environment can impact physiology and heredity, I present the thesis that Ihsan heartfulness practices are able to affect not only health and wellbeing, but also human evolution via epigenomic profile alteration.

The first in-depth robust genome-epigenome screens for spiritual practices have shown that the function of key genes involved in a wide range of physiological pathways can be significantly impacted by epigenomic alternations induced by the spiritual intervention. This leads to the suggestion that Ihsan practices might also have similar epigenomic impacts. Supporting this hypothesis are the proven and varied physiological measurements already recorded by empirical studies for Ihsan practices (reviewed by Zahir, 2022). Therefore, it is expected that Ihsan practices may affect physiology via epigenomic alteration of key genes as well. In fact, pathophysiological links between Ihsan-heartfulness induced biometric changes and epigenomic pathways are already proposed to act via the stress-response pathway, the hypothalamus-pituitary axis, and endocrine system (Zahir, 2022).

Importantly, epigenomic alterations are known to be transmissible. That is, they are inherited, and therefore can lead to evolution. At the beginning of this chapter, we explained how the traditional Muslim lifestyle involved a constant regimen of both mandatory and voluntary heartfulness practices. Indeed, the entire *raison d'etre* of the Muslim life is to enter a higher state of consciousness of the Divine, which is done primarily via the vehicle of the spiritual heart, itself intimately connected to the physical heart.

This brings up the point that generations of assiduous practices of Ihsan-heartfulness can theoretically lead to the evolving of higher states of consciousness, as progressively contributory epigenomic profiles are laid out and transmitted through the generations. Conversely, the opposite is also possible; generations of individuals whose lifestyle is devoid of heartfulness practices may lead to subsequent generations with increasingly detrimental epigenomic profiling, that devolves their inherent biological ability to attain higher orders of consciousness. It is already proven that trauma can cause epigenomic profiles that are then inherited by the grandchildren of those who suffered the trauma, leading to detrimental health metrics (often manifested in mental health issues; see Lehrner & Yehuda, 2018; Youssef et al., 2018), making this assertion all the more plausible.

In the Islamic cosmological soul-spirit-heart-mind-body axis (Figure 1), the key nexus between the ruh or spirit-soul which is otherworldly (or heavenly, i.e., from the Divine essence), and the mind and body which is worldly and corporeal, is the heart. If the heart is harmed, or not nourished as it requires (and by nourishment it is meant spiritual nourishment), this leads to deficiencies in the mind and body, and stifles the ruh or spirit-soul from attaining the heavenly heights it is capable of reaching.

Therefore, cultivation of heartfulness by Ihsan practices is not only essential for the correct alignment and working of the spirt-soul-heart-mind-body axis, which is the basis for bodily, emotional, and spiritual wellbeing, but it also may lead to the evolution of consciousness in humans as a species. It follows, then, that the neglect of the same may cause a regression of the ability of the human being to reach a consciousness in tune with the rest of the cosmos.

Looking Forward

There are two aspects to how this field can move forward: One is to revive the depth and breadth of the science of Ihsan in Muslim societies, as well as introduce it to non-Muslims, because both can benefit from it; The other is to harness the potency of rigorous inquiry inherent in current epigenomic profiling assays to deeply probe and unearth the biological and psychological mechanisms by which Ihsan practices affect health and well-being.

This will, in turn, lead to better and wider usage of Ihsan practices in health care and wellness settings. A recent overview (Zahir, 2022) of Islamic Ihsan practices deployed in healthcare settings (formal and non-formal) in countries ranging from Iran to Saudi Arabia, India, Indonesia, and Malaysia found that they were able to help patients suffering from heart disease, kidney dysfunction, various mental illnesses and psychoses, as well as drug and opioid addictions.

Importantly, where studies included non-Muslim participants, there was no difference in positive outcome among the subjects, regardless of whether they were Muslim or non-Muslim (Zahir, 2022). These preliminary data were gathered from the few scientific studies reported in the English language to date. It is expected that the data existing on the health benefits of Ihsan practices documented in the traditional academia of the Muslim world (particularly extant in centuries-old texts in Persian, Urdu, and Arabic languages across the Muslim world; Ansary, 2022; Haīdara, 2010; Hunwick, 2003; Nadwi, 2003) would be highly beneficial to enhance our knowledge on this subject. An urgent need therefore exists for such texts to be accessed and translated into the modern international language, which is English. Concomitantly, it is necessary to increase rigorous empirical scientific studies on Ihsan practices to better understand how they impact and influence physiology, as well as broader health and wellbeing, at not just the individual but also the communal level.

As alluded to earlier in this chapter, the Islamic science of Ihsan has suffered from centuries of neglect in recent times. The reasons for this are complex and nuanced. However, we may broadly say that the long period of colonization of Muslim nations from its western (modern day Morocco and Algeria) to eastern (modern day Indonesia) extent by various European powers from approximately the 17th to mid-20th century CE led to a diminishing of the scholars of Ihsan. As Ihsan is the highest-order science among the Islam-Iman-Ihsan tripartite, as is the norm during occupations, it became the first to be lost and degraded. Despite this, much of its deeper knowledge has survived, usually in remote places of the world (Haīdara, 2010; Hunwick, 2003).

In recent decades we are fortunate to be witnessing a revival of Ihsan teachings across the globe. Furthermore, they are now being rapidly translated into English and made accessible to the western academic framework (Carle, 2019; York Al-Karam, 2018; York & Awan, 2023). In this regard, the term heartfulness is particularly cogent. As it perfectly encapsulates the crux and core of the teachings of the science of Ihsan. A deeper and wider understanding of what it means to have and increase heartfulness will greatly enrich human societies everywhere. Therefore, there is a pressing need to further our studies in not only Ihsan science but also conduct more epigenomics research in the field. The study of Ihsan is an endeavour that has great potential to unearth vital findings that can benefit societies globally and across religious affiliations.

References

Abu Hamid al Ghazali. (2010). *The Marvels of the Heart*. Fons Vitae.

Abu Talib Makki. (1978). *Qut Al-Qulub Fi Mu'Amalat Al-Mahbub*. Dar Al-Fikr li Al-Tibaah.

Ahmad Ibn Ajiba. (2012). *The Book of Ascension to the Essential Truths of Sufism*. Fons Vitae.

Álvarez-López, M. J., Conklin, Q. A., Cosín-Tomás, M., Shields, G. S., King, B. G., Zanesco, A. P., Kaliman, P., & Saron, C. D. (2022). Changes in the expression of inflammatory and epigenetic-modulatory genes after an intensive meditation retreat. *Comprehensive Psychoneuroendocrinology*, *11*, 100152. https://doi.org/10.1016/J.CPNEC.2022.100152

Ansary, S. I. (2022). Major centres of Arabic and Islamic studies in India. *International Journal of Health Sciences*, 3590–3602. https://doi.org/10.53730/ijhs.v6nS1.5505

Ardell, J. L., & Armour, J. A. (2016). Neurocardiology: Structure-Based Function. In *Comprehensive Physiology* (pp. 1635–1653). Wiley. https://doi.org/10.1002/cphy.c150046

Arthur F. Buehler. (1998). Sufi Heirs of the Prophet: The Indian Naqshbandiyya and the Rise of the Mediating Sufi Shaykh. University of South Carolina Press.

Bastaki, K. N., Alwan, S., & Zahir, F. R. (2020). Maternal Prenatal Exposures in Pregnancy and Autism Spectrum Disorder: An Insight into the Epigenetics of Drugs and Diet as Key Environmental Influences (pp. 143–162). https://doi.org/10.1007/978-3-030-30402-7_5

Bisht, S., Banu, S., Srivastava, S., Pathak, R. U., Kumar, R., Dada, R., & Mishra, R. K. (2020). Sperm methylome alterations following yoga-based lifestyle intervention in patients of primary male infertility: A pilot study. *Andrologia*, *52*(4). https://doi.org/10.1111/and.13551

Bisht, S., & Dada, R. (2019). Yoga: Impact on sperm genome and epigenome-clinical consequences. *ANNALS OF NEUROSCIENCES*, *26*. https://doi.org/10.5214/ans.0972.7531.260202

Bošković, A., & Rando, O. J. (2018). Transgenerational Epigenetic Inheritance. *Annual Review of Genetics*, *52*(1), 21–41. https://doi.org/10.1146/annurev-genet-120417-031404

Cairns, B. R. (2005). Chromatin remodeling complexes: strength in diversity, precision through specialization. *Current Opinion in Genetics & Development*, *15*(2), 185–190. https://doi.org/10.1016/j.gde.2005.01.003

Camille Adams Helminski. (2003). *Women of Sufism: A Hidden Treasure* . Shambhala.

Carle, R. (2019). Islamically Integrated Psychotherapy. *Journal of Religion and Health, 58*(1), 358–360. https://doi.org/10.1007/s10943-018-0724-x

Cayir, A., Byun, H.-M., & Barrow, T. M. (2020). Environmental epitranscriptomics. *Environmental Research, 189,* 109885. https://doi.org/10.1016/j.envres.2020.109885

Chaix, R., Alvarez-López, M. J., Fagny, M., Lemee, L., Regnault, B., Davidson, R. J., Lutz, A., & Kaliman, P. (2017). Epigenetic clock analysis in long-term meditators. *Psychoneuroendocrinology, 85,* 210–214. https://doi.org/10.1016/J.PSYNEUEN.2017.08.016

Chamsi-Pasha, M., & Chamsi-Pasha, H. (2021). A review of the literature on the health benefits of Salat (Islamic prayer). *The Medical Journal of Malaysia, 76*(1), 93–97.

Clapier, C. R., & Cairns, B. R. (2009). The biology of chromatin remodeling complexes. *Annual Review of Biochemistry, 78,* 273–304. https://doi.org/10.1146/annurev.biochem.77.062706.153223

Downward, J. (2004). RNA interference. *BMJ (Clinical Research Ed.), 328*(7450), 1245–1248. https://doi.org/10.1136/bmj.328.7450.1245

Dwijayanti, B. (2015). Tazkiyatun Nafs in Classical and modern Islamic Tradition Qur'anic Worldview. *Teosofia: Indonesian Journal of Islamic Mysticism, 4*(2), 109–122. https://doi.org/10.21580/tos.v4i2.1718

Eaton, R. M. (1974). Sufi Folk Literature and the Expansion of Indian Islam. *History of Religions, 14*(2), 117–127. https://doi.org/10.1086/462718

Gapp, K., Bohacek, J., Grossmann, J., Brunner, A. M., Manuella, F., Nanni, P., & Mansuy, I. M. (2016). Potential of Environmental Enrichment to Prevent Transgenerational Effects of Paternal Trauma. *Neuropsychopharmacology, 41,* 2749–2758. https://doi.org/10.1038/npp.2016.87

Ghiasi, A., & Keramat, A. (2018). The effect of listening to holy quran recitation on anxiety: A systematic review. *Iranian Journal of Nursing and Midwifery Research, 23*(6), 411. https://doi.org/10.4103/ijnmr.IJNMR_173_17

Haïdara, A. K. (2010). An Overview of The Major Manuscript Libraries in Timbuktu. In *The Trans-Saharan Book Trade* (pp. 241–264). BRILL. https://doi.org/10.1163/ej.9789004187429.i-424.46

Hidalgo, B., Irvin, M. R., Sha, J., Zhi, D., Aslibekyan, S., Absher, D., Tiwari, H. K., Kabagambe, E. K., Ordovas, J. M., & Arnett, D. K.

(2014). Epigenome-Wide Association Study of Fasting Measures of Glucose, Insulin, and HOMA-IR in the Genetics of Lipid Lowering Drugs and Diet Network Study. *Diabetes*, *63*(2), 801–807. https://doi.org/10.2337/db13-1100

Hirst, M., & Marra, M. A. (2010). Next generation sequencing based approaches to epigenomics. *Briefings in Functional Genomics*, *9*(5–6), 455–465. https://doi.org/10.1093/bfgp/elq035

Hsieh, H.-Y., Chiu, P.-H., & Wang, S.-C. (2011). Epigenetics in Traditional Chinese Pharmacy: A Bioinformatic Study at Pharmacopoeia Scale. *Evidence-Based Complementary and Alternative Medicine*, *2011*, 1–10. https://doi.org/10.1093/ecam/neq050

Hsieh, H.-Y., Chiu, P.-H., & Wang, S.-C. (2013). Histone modifications and traditional Chinese medicinals. *BMC Complementary and Alternative Medicine*, *13*(1), 115. https://doi.org/10.1186/1472-6882-13-115

Hunwick, J. (2003). The Timbuktu Manuscript Tradition. *TINABANTU: Journal of Advanced Studies of African Society*, *1*(2). https://doi.org/10.14426/tbu.v1i2.1643

Ifra'ah. (2022). The Original Revelations from the Knowledge of the Cosmos (1st ed.). Ras al Haq Publications.

Isgandarova, N. (2019). Muraqaba as a Mindfulness-Based Therapy in Islamic Psychotherapy. *Journal of Religion and Health*, *58*, 1146–1160. https://doi.org/10.1007/s10943-018-0695-y

Jablonka, E., & Lamb, M. (1995). *Epigenetic Inheritance and Evolution*. Oxford University Press.

Jaenisch, R., & Bird, A. (2003). Epigenetic regulation of gene expression: how the genome integrates intrinsic and environmental signals. *Nature Genetics*, *33* *Suppl*, 245–254. https://doi.org/10.1038/ng1089

Jafar al-Tahawi. (900). Al Aqeeda Al Tahawiya. Bayan al Sunnah wa al Jama'a. Imam al-Tahawi's Creed of Islam.

Janssens, J. (2011). Al-Ghazālī between Philosophy (Falsafa) and Sufism (Taṣawwuf): His Complex Attitude in the Marvels of the Heart ("Ajā'ib al-Qalb) of the Iḥyā" 'Ulūm al-Dīn. *The Muslim World*, *101*(4), 614–632. https://doi.org/10.1111/j.1478-1913.2011.01375.x

Kaliman, P. (2019). Epigenetics and meditation. *Current Opinion in Psychology*, *28*, 76–80. https://doi.org/10.1016/j.copsyc.2018.11.010

Kaliman, P., Álvarez-López, M. J., Cosín-Tomás, M., Rosenkranz, M. A., Lutz, A., & Davidson, R. J. (2014). Rapid changes in histone deacetylases and inflammatory gene expression in expert meditators. *Psychoneuroendocrinology*, *40*(1), 96–107. https://doi.org/10.1016/J.PSYNEUEN.2013.11.004

Kanherkar, R. R., Bhatia-Dey, N., & Csoka, A. B. (2014). Epigenetics across the human lifespan. *Frontiers in Cell and Developmental Biology*, 2. https://doi.org/10.3389/fcell.2014.00049

Kanherkar, R. R., Stair, S. E., Bhatia-Dey, N., Mills, P. J., Chopra, D., & Csoka, A. B. (2017). Epigenetic Mechanisms of Integrative Medicine. *Evidence-Based Complementary and Alternative Medicine*, *2017*, 1–19. https://doi.org/10.1155/2017/4365429

Leaman, O. (Ed.). (2022). Routledge handbook of Islamic Ritual and Practice. Taylor and Francis.

Lehrner, A., & Yehuda, R. (2018). Cultural trauma and epigenetic inheritance. *Development and Psychopathology*, *30*(5), 1763–1777. https://doi.org/10.1017/S0954579418001153

Margaret Smith. (1928). The life and teachings of Rabia Al-Adawiyya Al-Qaysiyya of Basra, together with some account of the place of the women saints in Islam. School of Oriental and African Studies (University of London).

McGee, S. L., & Hargreaves, M. (2019). Epigenetics and Exercise. *Trends in Endocrinology & Metabolism*, *30*(9), 636–645. https://doi.org/10.1016/j.tem.2019.06.002

Meyer, K. D., & Jaffrey, S. R. (2014). The dynamic epitranscriptome: N6-methyladenosine and gene expression control. *Nature Reviews. Molecular Cell Biology*, *15*(5), 313–326. https://doi.org/10.1038/nrm3785

Michael A. Sells. (1996). Early Islamic Mysticism: Sufi, Qur'an, Miraj, Poetic and Theological Writings. Paulist Press.

Mohamad, A. D., Osman, K., & Mokhtar, A. I. (2020). Spirituality in Maqasid for the Empowerment of Human Well-Being. *International Journal of Business and Social Science*, *11*(10). https://doi.org/10.30845/ijbss.v11n10p6

Mubarak, G., & Zahir, F. R. (2022). Recent Major Transcriptomics and Epitranscriptomics Contributions toward Personalized and Precision Medicine. *Journal of Personalized Medicine*, *12*(2). https://doi.org/10.3390/jpm12020199

Muhyiddin Ibn Arabi. (2009). *The Four Pillars of Spiritual Transformation*. Anqa Publishing.

Muslim Ibn al-Ḥajjāj al-Qushayrī. (1955). Ṣaḥīḥ Muslim: kitab al-Iman bab ma'rifah al-Iman wal-Islam wal-Qadr wa 'alamat al-sa'ah - 1:36#8. Dār Iḥyā' al-Kutub al-'Arabīyah.

Nadwi, M. A. (2003). Review: The Development of Exegesis in Early Islam: The Authenticity of Muslim Literature from the Formative

Period * Herbert Berg: The Development of Exegesis in Early Islam: The Authenticity of Muslim Literature from the Formative Period. *Journal of Islamic Studies*, *14*(3), 370–377. https://doi.org/10.1093/jis/14.3.370

Nakamura, K. (1984). Makki and Ghazali on mystical practices. *Orient*, *20*, 83–91. https://doi.org/10.5356/orient1960.20.83

Niculescu, M. D. (2012). Nutritional Epigenetics. *ILAR Journal*, *53*(3–4), 270–278. https://doi.org/10.1093/ilar.53.3-4.270

Non, A. L. (2021). Social epigenomics: are we at an impasse? *Epigenomics*, *13*(21), 1747–1759. https://doi.org/10.2217/epi-2020-0136

Parrott, J. (2019). Islām, Īmān, Iḥsān: Climbing the Spiritual Mountain. In *Yaqeen Institute for Islamic Research*. Yaqeen Institute for Islamic Research.

O'Donovan, A., Tomiyama, A. J., Lin, J., Puterman, E., Adler, N. E., Kemeny, M., Wolkowitz, O. M., Blackburn, E. H., & Epel, E. S. (2012). Stress appraisals and cellular aging: A key role for anticipatory threat in the relationship between psychological stress and telomere length. *Brain, Behavior, and Immunity*, *26*(4), 573–579. https://doi.org/10.1016/j.bbi.2012.01.007

Rajan, K. S., Ramasamy, S., Garikipati, V. N. S., & Suvekbala, V. (2021). The cardiac methylome: A hidden layer of RNA modifications to regulate gene expression. *Journal of Molecular and Cellular Cardiology*, *152*, 40–51. https://doi.org/10.1016/J.YJMCC.2020.11.011

Robinson, E. L., Anene-Nzelu, C. G., Rosa-Garrido, M., & Foo, R. S. Y. (2021). Cardiac epigenetics: Driving signals to the cardiac epigenome in development and disease. *Journal of Molecular and Cellular Cardiology*, *151*, 88. https://doi.org/10.1016/j.yjmcc.2020.11.005

Rommel, C., & Hein, L. (2020). Four Dimensions of the Cardiac Myocyte Epigenome: from Fetal to Adult Heart. *Current Cardiology Reports*, *22*(5), 26. https://doi.org/10.1007/s11886-020-01280-7

Sachiko Murata. (2000). *Chinese gleams of Sufi Light*. State University of New York.

Schiele, M. A., & Domschke, K. (2018). Epigenetics at the crossroads between genes, environment and resilience in anxiety disorders. *Genes, Brain and Behavior*, *17*, 1–15. https://doi.org/10.1111/gbb.12423

Segerstrom, S. C., & Miller, G. E. (2004). Psychological Stress and the Human Immune System: A Meta-Analytic Study of 30 Years of Inquiry. *Psychological Bulletin*, *130*(4), 601–630. https://doi.org/10.1037/0033-2909.130.4.601

Seyyed Hossein Nasr. (1972). *Sufi Essays*. George Allen& Unwin Ltd.

Sheerin, C. M., Lancaster, E. E., York, T. P., Walker, J., Kmett Danielson, C., & Amstadter, A. B. (2021). Epigenome-Wide Study of Posttraumatic Stress Disorder Symptom Severity in a Treatment-Seeking Adolescent Sample HHS Public Access. *J Trauma Stress*, *34*(3), 607–615. https://doi.org/10.1002/jts.22655

Slavich, G. M. (2015). Understanding inflammation, its regulation, and relevance for health: A top scientific and public priority. *Brain, Behavior, and Immunity*, *45*, 13–14. https://doi.org/10.1016/j.bbi.2014.10.012

Stallwood, Y. (2005). RNA interference. *Pharmacogenomics*, *6*(1), 13–16. https://doi.org/10.1517/14622416.6.1.13

Szyf, M. (2019). The epigenetics of perinatal stress. *DIALOGUES IN CLINICAL NEUROSCIENCE* •, *21*(4), 369–378. https://doi.org/10.31887/DCNS.2019.21.4/mszyf

Tallal Alie Turfe. (2016). *Remember Me and I will remember you*. iuniverse.

Tammen, S. A., Friso, S., & Choi, S.-W. (2013). Epigenetics: the link between nature and nurture. *Molecular Aspects of Medicine*, *34*(4), 753–764. https://doi.org/10.1016/j.mam.2012.07.018

Topart, C., Werner, E., & Arimondo, P. B. (2020). Wandering along the epigenetic timeline. *Clinical Epigenetics*, *12*(1), 97. https://doi.org/10.1186/s13148-020-00893-7

Torres-Berrío, A., Issler, O., Parise, E. M., & Nestler, E. J. (2019). Dialogues in Clinical Neuroscience Unraveling the epigenetic landscape of depression: focus on early life stress Unraveling the epigenetic landscape of depression: focus on early life stress. *DIALOGUES IN CLINICAL NEUROSCIENCE* •, *21*(4), 341–357. https://doi.org/10.31887/DCNS.2019.21.4/enestler

Trimingham, J.S. (1971). *The Sufi Orders in Islam*. Oxford University Press.

Usman dan Fodio, B. al-S. (1978). Handbook on Islam, Iman, Ihsan The Kitab 'usul Ad-deen (The Roots of the Life-transaction) and the Kitab 'ulum Al-mu'amala (The Sciences of Behaviour). Iqra Inc.

Varela, R. B., Cararo, J. H., Tye, S. J., Carvalho, A. F., Valvassori, S. S., Fries, G. R., & Quevedo, J. (2022). Contributions of epigenetic inheritance to the predisposition of major psychiatric disorders: Theoretical framework, evidence, and implications. *Neuroscience & Biobehavioral Reviews*, *135*, 104579. https://doi.org/10.1016/j.neubiorev.2022.104579

Venditti, S., Verdone, L., Reale, A., Vetriani, V., Caserta, M., & Zampieri, M. (2020). Molecules of Silence: Effects of Meditation on Gene

Expression and Epigenetics. *Frontiers in Psychology*, *11*. https://doi.org/10.3389/fpsyg.2020.01767

Wang, K. C., & Chang, H. Y. (2018). Epigenomics: Technologies and Applications. *Circulation Research*, *122*(9), 1191–1199. https://doi.org/10.1161/CIRCRESAHA.118.310998

Weng, W., & Goel, A. (2022). Curcumin and colorectal cancer: An update and current perspective on this natural medicine. *Seminars in Cancer Biology*, *80*, 73–86. https://doi.org/10.1016/j.semcancer.2020.02.011

Whangbo, J. S., & Hunter, C. P. (2008). Environmental RNA interference. *Trends in Genetics : TIG*, *24*(6), 297–305. https://doi.org/10.1016/j.tig.2008.03.007

Yasin, H., & Zahir, F. R. (2020). Chromodomain helicase DNA-binding proteins and neurodevelopmental disorders. *Journal of Translational Genetics and Genomics*. https://doi.org/10.20517/jtgg.2020.30

Yong-Quan Ng, G., Paul Lee Kok Sheng, D., Bae, H.-G., Wook Kang, S., Yang-Wei Fann, D., Park, J., Kim, J., Alli-Shaik, A., Lee, J., Kim, E., Park, S., Han, J.-W., Karamyan, V., Okun, E., Dheen, T., Prakash Hande, M., Vemuganti, R., Mallilankaraman, K., K Lim, L. H., … Vemuganti, R. (2022). *Integrative epigenomic and transcriptomic analyses reveal metabolic switching by intermittent fasting in brain*. https://doi.org/10.1007/s11357-022-00537-z

York, C. M., & Awan, H. (2023). Introduction to the special issue on Islamic spirituality in clinical contexts. *Spirituality in Clinical Practice*, *10*(1), 1–3. https://doi.org/10.1037/scp0000316

York Al-Karam, C. (2018). Islamic Psychology: Towards a 21st Century Definition and Conceptual Framework. *Journal of Islamic Ethics*, *2*(1–2), 97–109. https://doi.org/10.1163/24685542-12340020

Youssef, N., Lockwood, L., Su, S., Hao, G., & Rutten, B. (2018). The Effects of Trauma, with or without PTSD, on the Transgenerational DNA Methylation Alterations in Human Offsprings. *Brain Sciences*, *8*(5), 83. https://doi.org/10.3390/brainsci8050083

Zahir, F. R. (2022). Epigenomic impacts of meditative practices. *Epigenomics*, *14*(24), 1593–1608. https://doi.org/10.2217/epi-2022-0306

Zahir, F. R., & Brown, C. J. (2011). Epigenetic Impacts on Neurodevelopment: Pathophysiological Mechanisms and Genetic Modes of Action. *Pediatric Research*, *69*(5 Part 2), 92R-100R. https://doi.org/10.1203/PDR.0b013e318213565e

Zhang, L., Lu, Q., & Chang, C. (2020). Epigenetics in Health and Disease. *Advances in Experimental Medicine and Biology, 1253*, 3–55. https://doi.org/10.1007/978-981-15-3449-2_1

Zhang, W., Qu, J., Liu, G.-H., & Belmonte, J. C. I. (2020). The aging epigenome and its rejuvenation. *Nature Reviews. Molecular Cell Biology, 21*(3), 137–150. https://doi.org/10.1038/s41580-019-0204-5

Zhang, Y., Sun, Z., Jia, J., Du, T., Zhang, N., Tang, Y., Fang, Y., & Fang, D. (2021). Overview of Histone Modification. *Advances in Experimental Medicine and Biology, 1283*, 1–16. https://doi.org/10.1007/978-981-15-8104-5_1

CHAPTER 3

Islamic Practices as
Psychotherapeutic Interventions

Zuhal Ağılkaya-Şahin, PhD

Introduction

The purpose of this chapter is to demonstrate the possibilities and benefits of Islamic practices such as tawakkul, du'ā', and tafakkur for psychotherapy. Tawakkul has both religious effects and socio-psychological effects, and consequently can be applied to psychological concepts such as hope, trust, self-esteem, crisis, trauma, cognitive restructuring, behavioral change. Similarly, theories such as attribution, meaning, and locus of control are also applicable.

For example, trust in Allah can provide hope in times of despair. Religious explanations of tawakkul can show the psychotherapist and client how to practice that trust. By applying it, the client may find in Allah a secure attachment figure, redefine the locus of control, and increase self-esteem.

Du'ā' also has psychological and psychotherapeutic effects. It has been shown to be (Arıcı, 2005; Doğan, 1994; Fatemi, 2018; Güzel, 2009; Seyhan, 2019) efficient for coping, suggestion, catharsis, and so on. In the psychoanalytic sense, for example, prayer has a cathartic effect; in behaviorism, it can provide behavioral change; in cognitivism, correct/restructure maladaptive thoughts and beliefs; in existentialism, death, fear, and meaning also find their reflection in du'ā'. In addition, attachment, self-actualization, meaning, and coping can be also addressed in relation to duʻāʼ.

The final Islamic practice is tafakkur. There is little research on the psychological effects and therapeutic use of tafakkur. Suggestions for the performance of it and its psychological benefits could help fill this gap. Like previous practices, tafakkur can be elaborated within the frameworks of attachment theory, search for meaning, confrontation, responsibility, cognitive restructuring, and coping.

The increasing academic interest in psychology and religion paved the way for the integration of religious and spiritual practices or rituals into psychology and psychotherapy by the early 2000s. Literature emerged on topics such as the impact of religiosity and spirituality on mental health, the integration of religious and spiritual practices into psychotherapy, the contribution of psychology of religious and spirituality research to academic and clinical psychology, and the derivation of religious psychologies (e.g., theistic psychology, Islamic psychology; Ağılkaya Şahin, 2020a).

When religious and spiritual practices or rituals were accepted as psychotherapeutic tools, critical issues for clinical application developed. According to the ethical principle "to benefit those with whom they work" (https://www.apa.org/ethics/code) counselors must be attentive to the needs and desires of the counselee. This also requires inclusion of the counselee's spiritual and religious lifeworld.

Research shows that counselees need and want their spirituality and religiosity to be integrated into therapy (Ağılkaya Şahin, 2018, 2020a). A psychotherapeutic atmosphere and relationship that is open to spiritual and religious experiences and needs will also bring forth opportunities and possibilities for integrating related practices into the therapeutic process.

There are numerous guidelines in the literature on how and when to integrate such practices into therapy (Ağılkaya Şahin, 2018, 2020a). A psychotherapist who has some knowledge of the counselee's religious tradition and is trained to integrate spiritual and religious themes into therapy might prefer to use them as psychotherapeutic interventions, since secular psychotherapeutic methods do not consist of interventions that address the counselee's spiritual and religious dimension (Richards & Bergin, 2004b).

However, it is the counselee's own choice and decision to use either secular or religious practices. To decide, the counselor or therapist should be able to use the counselee's religious language, which in turn would show a respectful and nonjudgmental attitude toward the counselee's religious or spiritual side. After weighing these factors, the counselor can decide what intervention techniques the client needs and wants and at what time and in what context they should be used (Genia, 2000; Haug, 1998; Miller, 2003).

The functionality of general religious practices and Islamic practices, in particular, for psychotherapy is well documented theoretically and empirically (Aboul-Enein, 2016; Bonelli, 2018b; Doğan, 1994; Genia, 2000; Haque, 1997; Haque & Keshavarzi, 2014; Henry, 2015; Karaca & Acar, 2016, 2019; Lines, 2006; O'Grady & Bartz, 2012; Pfeifer, 2018; Rassool, 2016; Richards & Bergin, 2004b; Utsch, 2018a, 2018b, 2018c). This literature addresses religious practices such as prayer, such as duʿāʾ, as a coping strategy (Canda, 1990; Kelly, 1990; Miller, 2003; Tan, 2000), reading sacred scripture as a means to eliminate maladaptive thoughts (Aboul-Enein, 2016; Richards & Bergin, 2005), grief work from a psychodynamic perspective, or tawbah (i.e., repentance) as behavioral change (Bonelli, 2018b; Ellenberger, 1994; Haque, 1997).

Research demonstrates that these and other religious practices provide clients with hope and strength to cope, recover, and change. According to Richards and Bergin (2004b), this is why these practices have survived to the present day, because they express and provide a response to people's deepest needs, concerns, and problems. Empirical studies have also demonstrated the healing potential of spiritual or religious practices such as duʿāʾ, tawbah, dhikr, and meditation (Doğan, 1994; Güldaş, 2021; Richards & Bergin, 2004b; Seyhan, 2013; Walsh & Shapiro, 2006; Wilson, 2009; Vasegh, 2009; Yapıcı, 2007;).

The healing potential is explained as a change in worldview, improvement in identity perception, removal of feelings of shame, and change in values from material to spiritual ones. Sincere change and transformation of values and beliefs lead to healthier behaviors and a reduction in psychological and physiological symptoms and problems. Therefore, Richards and Bergin (2004a) recognize religious and spiritual practices as interventions that promote physical and mental health.

Regarding Islamic practices, Karim (1984) wrote "The Islamic rituals will no longer be regarded as mere rituals but play a vital role in the mental stability of the individual" (p. 40). He made an effort some 40 years ago to develop Islamic interventions and techniques based on their direct psychological benefits. Since then, Muslim psychologists have sought to develop or improve exclusively Islamic psychotherapeutic interventions (for examples, see Ahmed & Amer, 2012; Dwairy, 2006; Keshavarzi & Haque, 2013; Keshavarzi et al., 2021; Rassool, 2016; Rothman, 2022; York Al-Karam, 2018).

Here the works of Keshavarzi et al. (2021) and Rothman (2022) are notable examples that seek to develop unique Islamically integrated psychotherapies based on a sound theoretical and conceptual framework. In addition to these specific examples, there is an extensive body of literature that emphasizes the importance and benefits of approaching clients with their religious sources, incorporating their religious practices, and integrating their religious rituals into the counseling process (Ağılkaya Şahin, 2018, 2019; Aten, et al., 2012; Richards & Bergin, 2004a). In this chapter, the possibilities and benefits of Islamic practices, such as tawakkul, du'ā', and tafakkur, as psychotherapeutic intervention techniques are highlighted by relating them to mainstream psychological theories and concepts.

Tawakkul

Tawakkul is a religious term that describes the state of submission to and trust in Allah and His will, recognizing Him as the guarantor and trusting only in Him for provision (rizq) and deeds (Çağrıcı, 2012). At the heart of tawakkul is firm faith ('īmān). This 'īmān, and consequently tawakkul, denotes the affirmation and acceptance that Allah is the Creator and Owner of everything (Çağrıcı, 2012; Karataş & Baloğlu, 2019).

Another aspect of tawakkul is submission to Allah. Acceptance of Allah as the Creator and Builder of everything requires submission and contentment (riḍā) with His will and decree (Quran 4:132). However, this kind of submission does not make the individual passive; showing riḍā does not mean remaining lazy, or incautious, but motivates proactive behavior, endeavor, and effort to use all available means (Çağrıcı, 2012; Karataş & Baloğlu, 2019).

After all personal efforts have failed to achieve the desired result, tawakkul evolves and the individual stops blaming themselves or the circumstances, maintains pessimism, and recovers from breaking down (Çağrıcı, 2012). Thus, the individual recognizes that they must make personal effort to achieve something but that nevertheless Allah is the Creator of the result. This implies a belief that things have another side, especially when efforts do not produce the desired result.

Studies suggest that tawakkul as a "cognitive and behavioral expression of the deep faith and trust in Allah" (Karataş & Baloğlu, 2019, p. 116), and it has religious, as well as socio-psychological aspects. Although some authors use tawakkul as a concept in counseling and therapy (e.g. Hamjah & Akhir, 2014; Lodi, 2018), other empirical studies have shown the mitigating effect of tawakkul for depression and anxiety, and its capacity to increase psychological resilience. Some have also suggested it for the treatment of OCD in particular (Lodi, 2018).

Still others have included tawakkul in their treatment plan and used it as a cognitive restructuring tool (Keshavarzi & Khan, 2018). In addition to psychological resilience, tawakkul has been found to be a resource in times of distress and despair, resolution processes, health and financial problems, and provided relief, peace, increased resilience, and acceptance of outcomes. Especially for religious people, tawakkul proved to be an important psychological support mechanism (Şahin, 2018). Karataş and Baloğlu (2019) consider tawakkul as a spiritual support system and positive coping mechanism, pointing to the functionality of tawakkul for feeling secure and coping with anxiety-related stress. Karataş and Baloğlu state that tawakkul serves to satisfy certain emotions and they list reflections of tawakkul in human psychology as follows: existential emotions—belief in the afterlife (akhira) versus fear of death; weakness—trust in a higher power; neediness—trust in a higher power for material and immaterial needs; search for meaning—discovery of the ultimate goal of life; loneliness—experiencing the protection of a merciful power.

The literature examined on tawakkul suggests that tawakkul can lead to cognitive, emotional, and behavioral changes. In the following, psychological effects of tawakkul, related psychological theories and concepts, and their implementation in psychotherapy as a resource are addressed.

Hope

Hope is an essential theme in the Islamic faith (see Ağılkaya Şahin, 2020b). The Quranic verse "He exclaimed, 'Who would despair of the mercy of their Lord except the misguided?'" (15:59) highlights the importance of hope for faith ('īmān) and the believer. The connection between tawakkul and hope is that tawakkul helps overcome feelings of despair. Despair, in turn is the primary emotion in suicide incidents. In times of distress, failure, loss, and pain, tawakkul can be a source of hope. For example, the Sūrah Yūsuf (12:83) relates how Prophet Yaqub, in all his despair, preserved his hope through tawakkul.

Since tawakkul is reliance on Allah for results, it can be considered hope in itself. Trusting in Allah after all personal efforts to achieve the desired goal can protect against the psychological damage of hopelessness. Providing hope and fostering existing hope are key functions of spiritual and psychological counseling. Counselors can apply the concept and act of tawakkul to inspire hope or eliminate hopelessness.

Trust

In psychology, trust is discussed in the context of theories of individual development, self-actualization, and attachment (Ainsworth, 1979; Bowlby, 1980; Erikson, 1993; Maslow, 1943). These theories have also been associated with religion (Hayta, 2006; Kirkpatrick, 1992). In an Islamic context, Allah is described in terms of the basic attributes of an attachment figure, such as being close, responsive, compassionate, and providing security and protection when needed (Bonab, et al., 2015; Marzband, et al., 2016).

By positing Allah as a secure attachment figure, Lodi (2018) finds similarities between taqwa, tawakkul, and attachment. The emphasis on trust in the definitions of tawakkul and its associated āyāt (e.g., Quran 65:3) indicate that those who bind themselves to Allah and trust Him, do not need any other protection. Thus, tawakkul fulfills a basic human need, the need for trust and security.

The fact that Allah protects those who seek shelter in Him (Quran 64:11) and loves such behavior (Quran 3:159) can also increase self-esteem (Dinç, 2017). With the help of tawakkul and trust, the psychotherapist can help the client overcome negative feelings such as loneliness, inability, fear, despair, etc. This is because finding a cognitive refuge reduces anxiety in people who have lost their sense of control and thus their psychological integrity (Tarhan, 2012).

Attribution Theory

Attribution theory is concerned with how people explain the reasons for their behaviors and events (Heider, 1958). People tend to attribute their behavior and the behavior of others, as well as the outcomes of events, to a particular reason. These reasons may be external or internal, such as character traits, motivations, attitudes, or situational circumstances. Religious people tend to use external attributions, such as God, when explaining the reasons for an event.

Attributing events to a specific reason provides a coherent worldview and a sense of control (Heider, 1958). Religions provide such patterns of explanation and meaning. In Islam, for example, belief in the afterlife (akhira), fate (qadar), trials (imtiḥān), punishment, atonement (kaffarah) for sins, and the belief that everything is in Allah's hands are such explanatory patterns. These kinds of beliefs can be reinforced by tawakkul, or trust in Allah's will for determining the causes and results of events.

Attributions arise from the individual's motivation to establish control. Attributing this control to Allah gives one a different sense of control, such as reliance on and submission to Allah does not eliminate personal control but conveys a sense of transpersonal control. Transferring a situation no longer under one's control to a higher and more powerful authority dissolves the feeling of being lost and lacking control. For example, the phrase "'In shā' Allāh" (if God wills), often used by Muslims, can be understood as an expression of tawakkul. Trust in and submission to Allah's will means believing that Allah knows best and does best. Because of this belief, psychological stressors and the pain they cause are understood within the framework of Allah's will (Al-Krenawi & Graham, 1999). Such a mental framework eliminates pain and anxiety (Amer & Jalal, 2012). Thus, faith, trust, submission—in short: tawakkul—can help solve adjustment problems and serve as a resource for coping with psychological problems caused by life events.

Self-esteem

According to my professional experience, low self-esteem or negative self-perception are encountered very often in psychotherapy and counseling. As mentioned in the context of attribution theory, people tend to attribute situations to personal characteristics. While negative behaviors of others are attributed to personality traits, one's own behaviors are attributed to situational conditions or external reasons, and sometimes events are attributed to completely wrong reasons. Such fundamental attribution errors, as they are called in social psychology, serve to preserve self-esteem (Myers & Twenge, 2022).

However, when people make this mistake with themselves by attributing negative things to themselves, they may develop a negative self-perception and thus lower their self-esteem. An understanding of tawakkul, which assumes that only Allah decides all reasons and arrangements, can protect against such low self-esteem caused by attribution errors.

Tawakkul also removes the fears of failure (Şahin, 2018). This is because a believer will know that their efforts and preventions will only be effective by Allah's will. Leaving the outcome to Allah after taking all precautions, or having tawakkul, can therefore protect the individual from self-reproach and guilt when things fail. In psychotherapy, tawakkul can be an antidote to the feelings of guilt that diminish self-esteem. The psychotherapist might offer tawakkul to religious clients as an alternative way of thinking and acting on feelings of guilt, low self-esteem, and fear of failure.

Search for Meaning

Frankl (2006) defines the search for meaning as a primary human motivation. Numerous studies have demonstrated the role of religion and faith in this process (Emmons, 2000; Pargament, 1997a; Park, 2013; Seligman, 2002; Tacey, 2004; Wong, 2010; Yalom, 1980; Zinnbauer & Pargament, 2005). Just as tawakkul offers religious attributions to explain the reasons for what has happened, making sense of the causes and outcomes of events can also be fostered by tawakkul and have a therapeutic effect. Allah as al-Ḥakīm (the All Wise) is the one who acts with wisdom (hikma) and creates everything in its proper place in the most perfect and beautiful way. Believing this could give a sense of meaning that there is another, greater plan at work behind apparent things. Other names of Allah, such as al-Wakīl (the Trustee) or al-Qādir (the Powerful), and āyāt on tawakkul (e.g., Quran 9:51; 65:3) can be used to reinforce tawakkul. The desired behavioral and cognitive change in psychotherapy could be closely related to the meaning-making process. Consequently, a religious and spiritually sensitive psychotherapist can use the understanding of tawakkul as an additional resource.

Locus of Control

Locus of control is another social psychological theory that explains the problem-solving generalized expectancy of individuals (Rotter, 1966). The concept of locus of control describes how people perceive their levels of personal responsibility in certain situations. Depending on the perceived locus of control, which can be either internal or external, people attribute the outcomes of events either to their control, such as their efforts and abilities; or to external circumstances, such as, luck, fate, powerful others, things beyond their control.

Research findings report that people who attribute uncontrollable events to themselves have poorer mental health (Benassi et al., 1988; Gültekin, 2004; Thompson, 1999). In such cases, tawakkul can be a helpful tool in accepting uncontrollable events or advocating for controllable things. Since tawakkul emphasizes personal effort first while simultaneously relying on Allah for the rest, it could be useful in choosing a locus of control.

This kind of behavior is recommended in the Quran (2:159): "Once you make a decision, put your trust in Allah. Surely Allah loves those who trust in Him." Such an understanding can prevent one from being too hard on oneself, blaming oneself for failures, and worrying too much about the outcome or falling into passivity and avoiding any kind of behavioral change. By explaining and suggesting tawakkul, the psychotherapist can intervene in the decision-making process for a locus of control and thereby prevent or treat related psychological problems.

Crises and Traumas

Crises and traumas are situations in which the psychological balance of an individual is destroyed. Extraordinary life events can exhaust a person's coping abilities. All this leads to despair, incapacity, anxiety, guilt, anger, and disorganization. Religion and belief are effective coping strategies and serve as a resource when struggling with such emotions. Especially in times of crises, such as when one's potential is exhausted, one's known problem–solving skills are no longer sufficient, and the coping strategies previously employed no longer work.

This is when the thought and act of tawakkul can be life-saving. In traumatic cases that evoke guilt, anger, and hopelessness, victims of such circumstances feel weak and desperate toward the wrongdoer who has harmed them or their loved ones. This is where an omnipotent image of God can be a relief. Allah's attributes indicate His absolute greatness, power, and authority.

Therefore, it would be tawakkul to seek refuge in, relate to, and turn to God who possess such abilities to alleviate destructive emotions and behaviors in and after crises or traumas. The chance to take refuge in such a power when personal strengths and resources are destroyed or depleted may be a unique psychological resource. In coping with trauma, spiritual resources such as hope, trust, and tawakkul are critical (Dinç, 2017). As mentioned in the "Trust" section, confidence and tawakkul contribute to self-esteem; and feeling valuable is an indispensable resource in trauma (Dinç, 2017).

A higher power or belief in such a power can also strengthen people who exhibit burnout syndromes. If the psychotherapist explains tawakkul as "taking someone's burden, giving confidence and guarantee, relating to and trusting" and supports this with accompanying āyāt (e.g., Quran 3:160; 33:48; 58:10), a new perspective, coping strategy, resource for strength, hope, and self-worth can open up in therapy and for the client.

In summary, in addition to its religious meaning and importance, tawakkul can also be considered a spiritual resource that can be operationalized for cognitive restructuring. The psychological theories and concepts presented here are all open to empirical investigation and psychotherapeutic experience. Actually, tawakkul is a concept that contradicts mainstream psychology's image of the human being. In this image, the individual possesses all kinds of freedom, abilities, talents, potentials, and resources to cope, manage, and overcome life, make choices and decisions, succeed and flourish, and so on. This image is also reflected in Carl Rogers' client-centered approach, which asserts that only the client themselves know best what they need or what is best for them. The concept of tawakkul postulates just the opposite. Therefore, tawakkul should be treated with caution in psychotherapy and would perhaps be easier to apply in cultures and societies where an alternative to the Western psychology paradigm is needed.

Du'ā'

The Arabic word du'ā', means to call, to request, to ask for help, to supplicate (Cilacı, 1994) and is understood as a way of communicating with the transcendent being (in Islam, Allah) in whom a person believes (Köylü, 2003; Vergote, 1996). In this communication, a person expresses their wishes, complaints, confessions, or requests for forgiveness. The request for protection and security turns this communication into a relationship.

This relationship with the divine also evokes feelings of love, fear, and awe. It is a human characteristic to plead either out of fear or out of love. Considering the hierarchy between the one who prays and the one who is prayed to, this relationship and communication can be seen as one-sided, but for the one who turns to the divine, this relationship and communication is mutual.

This is because people tend to believe and hope that their prayers will be heard and accepted, otherwise no one would pray. Research shows that for people who pray, the meaning of du'ā' is to seek protection and help from the Creator (Doğan, 1994). Therefore, du'ā's include devotion and different emotions, depending on the type of prayer: love and awe in prayers for gratitude (shukur), fear in prayers for protection, remorse in prayers for forgiveness (tawbah), humility in prayers when asking for something.

In Islamic literature, du'ā' has meanings such as supplication to Allah, expressing needs and desires, asking for Allah's mercy, blessing, and help, worship (ibādah'), acknowledging Allah's oneness, showing respect and admitting one's weakness (Cilacı, 1994; Güzel, 2009). The Quran (25:77; 2:186; 3:38; 40:60) and Ḥadīth (Suyuti, 2012 [1876]; İbn Mace, 2012 [Dua 1]; Hanbel, 2003 [III, 477]) emphasize the importance of du'ā' and encourage believers to make du'ā'. Prophet Muhammad recommends working on desired things, keeping hope for the fulfillment of the prayer, and avoiding hopelessness (Canan, 1995).

The literature of both theology and psychology consists of numerous theoretical and empirical studies on du'ā'. The vast majority of these studies, which fall within the field of psychology of religion and spirituality, focus on the psychological and psychotherapeutic effects of personal prayer, revealing that praying acts as protection in times of fear and distress and reduces stress, sadness, feelings of guilt, and sinfulness

(Doğan, 1994; Güzel, 2009; Helminiak, 2001; Kirkpatrick, 1992; Pargament & Hahn, 1986). Moreover, Tekke and Watson (2017) noted that duʿāʾ is crucial for Muslim personality formation and therefore must be considered when describing Muslim personality.

Numerous researchers in medicine and psychiatry, for example, have shown that changes and reactions occur in the body and brain during praying (Cohen et al., 2000; Newberg et al., 2003; Sloan et al., 1999; Surwillo & Hobson, 1978). Quranic verses (14:41; 47:19; 59:10) and Ḥadīth (Ṣaḥīḥ Muslim 2732) urge believers to pray for each other. Modern medicine proves the medical effects of praying for others (Benson, 1996; Byrd, 1988; Roberts et al., 2009).

By stating that prayer is the mental and emotional relationship with the Creator, Carrel (1981) refers to the cognitive and emotional aspects of prayer. Doğan's (1994) research confirms that people tend to make duʿāʾ regardless of the expectations of their prayers being fulfilled, which shows that people value the psychological functions of duʿāʾ more. Consequently, prayer, or duʿāʾ is not only a religious practice but also has psychological and medical effects. Maybe this is why Matthews (cited in Sides, 1997) stated that "The medicine of the future is going to be prayer and Prozac" (p. 85).

Because of such psychological effects, there is the potential for its use in psychotherapeutic application. Within the psychoanalytic approach, prayer has a cathartic effect; in behaviorism, prayer is a means or reinforcer for behavioral change; the cognitive approach views prayer as a tool for correcting maladaptive thoughts and beliefs or restructuring cognitive processes; in existentialism, existential themes such as death, loneliness, and meaning find expression in prayer (Güzel, 2009).

Researchers (Frank, 1991; Kara, 2019; Seyhan, 2013; Tekke & Watson, 2017; Utsch, 2018b, c) emphasize the influence of worship in general and prayer in particular in the psychological treatment process. Helminiak (2001) explains the function of prayer in psychotherapy by stating that "the therapist can understand the processes in the human psyche and spirit through which prayer sustains hope and trust and can legitimately affirm prayer as a practice that advances the integration of the dynamic human spirit" (p. 175).

According to Wilson (2009), prayer can be used as a means of cognitive transformation. Through praying, individuals can perceive truths that they were previously unable to recognize and can correct misbeliefs. Consequently, prayer facilitates changes in thinking. However, prayer not only has cognitive effects, but also facilitates release from harmful emotions

(Wilson, 2009). Empirical findings suggest that clients who pray feel relief, their therapy and recovery process accelerate, and they feel closer to God (Abramowitz, 2001; Doğan, 1994; Finney & Malony, 2001; Koenig, 2005). These studies, conducted on Muslims, Christians, and Jews, show that religious affiliation has no influence on the psychological effects of prayer.

Aside from these benefits of prayer, the literature is divided on its use in psychotherapy. While some authors (e.g., Tan, 2007) endorse it, some others accept it only as an adjunct to therapy, and still others find it unprofessional and reject it altogether (e.g., Poole & Cook, 2011). Prayers may touch people deeply and elevate the therapy to other levels. The immediacy that results can enhance the relationship between client and therapist or violate the therapeutic rule of professional distance between them.

This concern is why some authors do not recommend praying together with the counselee (e.g., O'Grady & Bartz, 2012). However, Pfeifer (2018) cites case studies in which clients place a great deal of emphasis on prayer and expect the psychotherapist to pray for them or with them. In such cases, the therapeutic relationship between client and psychotherapist intensifies.

In light of these differing views, Poloma and Pendleton (1991) suggest six different ways of integrating prayers into therapy: (a) implement no prayer, (b) private prayers by client for self, (c) therapist prays for client outside of therapy, (d) therapist informs client of their prayers for them, (e) therapist prays for counselee in front of him/her, and (f) client and therapist pray together in therapy. In the following, the implementation of duʿāʾ in psychotherapy is addressed by relating it to certain psychological concepts and theories.

Hope

In duʿāʾ, people submit their concerns and situation to Allah, who is believed to be omnipotent. This belief raises the hope that their desires will be accepted and that their situation will be understood. This condition, in turn, can increase people's motivation to actively work for their desires. Therefore, through the hope it conveys, duʿāʾ is a spiritual energy that has a catalytic effect on therapy (Henry, 2015).

In the Quran, hope is mentioned along with awe and fear (32:16; 12:87), and the relationship with Allah requires a balance between the two. Moments or states of duʿāʾ are spaces where these poles of fear and hope are experienced. On the one hand, one fears Allah's infinite power, and yet on the other hand, one seeks protection in Him. By thematizing this emotion, the psychotherapist can explain that one can refer to Allah in any kind of emotional state and that duʿāʾ is a place and time in which all kinds of emotions one feels toward Allah can be expressed.

One of Allah's names—as-Samīʿ (the All Hearing)—reveals that Allah hears everything (Quran 31:28), and as al-Muǧīb (the Responsive One) He answers prayers (Quran 11:71), and as ar-Raḥmān (the Most Merciful) He shows mercy (Quran 42:25). As Bayram (2017) states: "The name al-Muǧīb is directly dedicated to those who make duʿāʾ. This means that our Rabb [Lord] preserved this name only for those who make duʿāʾ, thus guaranteeing them the answer to their duʿāʾs" (p. 46).

In the Sūrah Hūd (11:61) the name al-Muǧīb is preceded by the name al-Qarīb, the Near. This can mean that Allah is near in general (Quran 50:16) and that He is near to those who make duʿāʾ in particular. In all kinds of situations, even the worst, such knowledge—that Allah is near to those who pray and that He will hear them—can evoke tremendous hope, in addition to being a source of comfort. Informing the client in this way can activate alternative resources of hope and psychological strength.

Attachment and Trust

Duʿāʾ is an expression of trust in and commitment to Allah. Krauss et al. (2006) explain that duʿāʾ establishes a direct relationship with Allah for a Muslim. Bonab et al. (2013) explain Muslim identity through communication between Allah and the individual and that the individual designates Allah as the ideal attachment figure with whom they can maintain a faithful and loving relationship through duʿāʾ.

Therefore, duʿāʾ fulfills a human being's need to establish meaningful relationships. This relationship, in turn, helps to solve problems and overcome difficulties. The research findings (Tekke & Watson, 2017) confirm that duʿāʾ supports the emotional, motivational, behavioral, and attitudinal aspects of Muslim identity. The other research results mentioned above also show that communication, relationship, and closeness to Allah provide comfort, peace, and trust.

Behind these feelings is the belief that Allah sees and hears and protects one everywhere and every time. However, that Allah sees and hears one does not necessarily mean that He will always protect and save one. So, the counselor or therapist should be aware of this and pay attention to their formulation. It may be useful to reinforce such a belief if the client already has one, but the psychotherapist should refrain from inducing such a belief, as depending on the client's circumstances, they might object to it.

Especially in the case of traumatic events, this can be very risky. Therefore, the psychotherapist should first find out and understand the client's image of God and beliefs. And then, ideally, carefully, restructure the negative perceptions into positive ones. Here again the concept of tawakkul comes into play. It might be helpful to suggest trusting in Allah's mercy and power and making du'ā' for the best outcome that only He can provide, rather than insisting on a particular thing. "Pray as if everything depends on God, work as if everything depends on you" can apply to both du'ā' and tawakkul. This relationship between du'ā' and tawakkul can be kept in mind by the psychotherapist.

Self-Esteem and Self-Actualization

During du'ā', a personal and intimate relationship with Allah is established. In this relationship, the person experiences that they are addressed, have a designated authority to apply, are heard and seen, and will be answered. Although du'ā' is a personal, one-way call to Allah, these experiences make the relationship mutual. Receiving a response, in other words, being addressed by a higher power in this way, could increase self-esteem.[1]

Moreover, such a relationship would show that the person is accepted unconditionally, no matter what state they are in. The previously mentioned āyāt indicate this. Knowing that all the empathy, love, unconditional acceptance and regard shown by the psychotherapist because of their role, is first shown by Allah can have a unique impact on the client's self-esteem.

The special relationship established during du'ā' can also remedy the person's feelings of loneliness, abandonment, and despair. All the emotions, thoughts, confessions, regrets, and desires that cannot be revealed to others for fear of being judged find a language and a way of being transmitted directly to Allah as the supreme authority, the Creator and Owner of man, in the du'ā'. This sense of acceptance and being heard can heal damaged self-perception, as Ayten (2005) reports that the experiential dimension of religiosity is positively related to self-respect.

Additionally, the increase in self-esteem can lead the person to self-actualization (Arık, 1996). According to Haque and Mohamed (2009), worship in general supports potentials and self-actualization. Maslow (1970) emphasizes the role of religiosity in self-actualization and refers to self-actualizers as people "who walk in the path of God" (p. 169). Whereas strengths, potentials, competence, and abilities are relevant to self-actualization, incompetence, despair, and submission are relevant to du'ā'.

---

[1] Man was created as the khalīfah of Allah and was bestowed a superior order among all creation (Quran 2:30; 17:30). This fact should have a powerful impact on the self-worth of a Muslim.

How can du'ā' be related to self-actualization? Tekke and Watson (2017) explain these seemingly contradictory concepts by saying that the individual who is unaware of his weakness, powerlessness, and inability will not develop any effort or motivation to get rid of these negativities.

When asking Allah for help, these efforts are reflected verbally in the verbal du'ā' or actively in the actional du'ā'. Moreover, transmitting the understanding and expression of powerlessness to a higher power can, in turn, give the individual the strength to move on. Therefore, the psychotherapist may encourage the client to first admit in du'ā' weakness and powerlessness and then ask Allah for help to remove these and be strengthened, and finally to support their du'ā's with action. The psychotherapist can also explain that the feeling of weakness and incompetence is not a deficiency but normal human characteristics that can be overcome through verbal and actional du'ā's.

Finally, the person could find the means of self-actualization in this way. In this context, humility plays a crucial role. Du'ā' is also an expression of humility. Today, positive psychology promotes the psychological benefits of humility as a character strength and virtue. Thus, as a virtuous behavior, du'ā' can be integrated into therapy for the client's mental health. Furthermore, feelings of weakness and powerlessness can only be transmitted to Allah through humility. Therefore, a humble du'ā', can be integrated into therapy to enhance self-actualization and self-esteem.

The Search for Meaning

Research suggests (Doğan, 1994) that du'ā' has positive effects on feelings of meaninglessness, withdrawal from life, boredom, desperate crying, and negative thoughts. Güzel (2009) argues that these effects result from the fact that du'ā' contributes to the search for meaning and love of life and, together with tawakkul, eliminates negative thoughts. Although du'ā' itself is not necessarily an answer to the search for meaning, it can be used as a tool in that search.

In counseling or psychotherapy, the questions of why and meaning are frequently asked and usually directed to the counselor or psychotherapist. However, these will not be able to provide a satisfactory answer to these questions. In such cases, they may suggest using du'ā' as an instrument for finding meaning. The psychotherapist, for whom it is almost impossible to answer these questions, can encourage the client to ask these questions to the right addressee, such as Allah, as the creator of life and death (Quran 67:2), good and evil (Quran 4:78).

The search for meaning is especially crucial during traumatic life events or crisis. Research suggests that du'ā' is usually the first reaction in traumatic experiences, contributes to post-traumatic growth, and has positive subjective effects during critical periods of life (Ai et al., 2006; Askay & Magyar-Russel, 2009; Dinç, 2017; Pfeifer, 2018; Schuster et al., 2001). All this indicates that du'ā' is an effective coping mechanism.

Religious Coping

As a particular type of coping, religious coping is the implementation of religious motives in an attempt to cope with stressful life events and occurs either positively or negatively (Pargament, 1997b). Negative religious coping, also referred to as spiritual struggle, involves questioning, guilt, and a perceived distance from or negative attitude toward a higher power. The person has a negative view of the divine in which they blame God for things that have happened or develop a negative image of God. Reappraisals of God's power and feelings of abandonment or punishment by God reflect a strained relationship with God. In contrast, positive religious coping is expressed in benevolent religious appraisals, religious forgiveness, and a secure, close relationship with God (Pargament et al., 1998).

Pargament et al. (1988) propose three types of religious coping: self-directing religious coping, b) deferring religious coping, and c) collaborative religious coping. In self-directing religious coping, people solve their problems by themselves and claim that they do not need God; in deferring religious coping, people remain passive and delegate the responsibility of solving problems to God; in collaborative religious coping, people become active and take responsibility for actions, but trust in God's help and support for the results.

From an Islamic perspective, the first style contradicts the concept of tawakkul and du'ā'. The second style, which relies on God's will, can be seen as Islamically compatible, but the lack of action-based du'ā' and the responsibility to act before making tawakkul is problematic. The latter style, in which verbal and actional du'ā' and tawakkul can be involved, would be the ideal Islamic coping style. As can be seen from their descriptions, these styles are closely related to attribution theory, search for meaning, trust, and tawakkul, mentioned above.

Many studies report a positive relationship between religious coping and physical and mental health (Koenig, et al., 2012), such that collaborative religious coping is associated with positive outcomes such as increased self-esteem and lower levels of depression (Pargament et al., 1988; Wong-McDonald & Gorsuch, 2000; for further outcomes see Phillips, et al., 2004). People especially turn to religious coping methods during times of crisis. During these times, the leading method of positive religious coping is du'ā'.

Research indicates that people tend to pray when facing personal problems, seeking and expecting help, support, and recognition (Janssen et al., 1990; Richards & Bergin, 2005). Even people who do not believe in religion or prayer turn to prayer as a source of strength (Aydın, 1995; Karacoşkun, 1998). Religious coping in general, and prayer in particular, enable people to reframe crises and problems.

Thus, as an active and meaningful cognitive coping and restructuring strategy (Holahan & Mous, 1987), du'ā' can be employed in the psychotherapeutic process. The psychotherapist might encourage clients to make du'ā' or suggest it as an alternative coping and support mechanism and discuss the effects or outcomes rather than the benefits and effects of du'ā' for coping. Sharing āyāt about du'ā', explaining how and for what to make du'ā' could make it an alternative coping method for the client.

Catharsis

Classic and modern names in psychology link catharsis and religious practices, such as confession (Bonelli, 2018b; Ellenberger, 1994; Jung, 1961). Among these religious practices, du'ā' has a particular cathartic effect and can therefore be applied as a psychotherapeutic intervention technique. In du'ā', a special relationship and communication is established between Allah and man. In this communication, there is no one in between, no intermediary and all thoughts and emotions are transferred directly to the Creator.

These thoughts and emotions can include the most intimate secrets, hidden sins, secret hopes, boundless longings, painful regrets, and the deepest fears. When revealed to Allah in du'ā', hidden thoughts and emotions can unfold in the unconscious, just as in free association in psychoanalysis. Vergote (1996) confirms: "In prayer, *everything* is said. Religious people reveal themselves in prayer far more clearly than in questionnaires; therefore, while making use of such documents, psychology must look anew to religion as it is practiced" (p. 289). The belief that there is a higher power from which nothing can be hidden can lead the person to pour out their heart and say everything as it is. Hökelekli (2003) explains this as follows: du'ā' combines two cases. The first case is that du'ā' is as if the self is talking to itself; the second case is that the self is talking to Allah; and when people talk to Allah, they know that they cannot hide anything, as they can when they talk to other people (p. 217).

Consequently, people confront their negative emotions and are enabled to define the issues and problems with which they are struggling (Kara, 2019) and defining problems and confronting them are the phases of psychotherapy. Especially in psychoanalysis, expressing all thoughts and feelings as they are essential to the healing process. The same cathartic effect occurs in prayer.

By motivating the client to pray, the psychotherapist can provide an alternative cathartic experience outside the therapy room. The results, however, would be different. True healing would be the transformation or the elimination of the client's negative emotions and grief. When the client communicates their feelings of guilt, regret, and the like to the psychotherapist, they are relieving emotions, but the feelings are not erased.

However, the remedy for regret would be forgiveness, the remedy for fear would be security, and for a believer, the supplier and source of all these remedies would be Allah. A psychotherapist can treat psychological damage by normalizing certain thoughts, emotions, and behaviors, but for a religious client, it would be more appropriate to bring the client's negative behaviors in line with their religion. Therefore, du'ā' could be a starting point to remove the negative emotions caused by negative behaviors. By applying this tool, the client can open all emotions to Allah and ask Him for help, support, and remedy.

In summary, du'ā' has positive effects on physical and mental health, well-being, and psychological processes such as meaning-making, encouragement, trust, anxiety, and motivation. Whether in person or in community, worship and prayer are linked to each other (Argyle, 2000). Given these benefits, prayer can be used in psychotherapy as an effective intervention technique. The psychotherapist may gain insights from studies in the field of psychology of religion and spirituality or from psychotherapy approaches that integrate religious and spiritual practices. In the Islamic context, āyāt and aḥadīth about du'ā' and related religious literature also suggest specific du'ā's and teach how, when, and for what to make du'ā'.

Tafakkur

Tafakkur, or in Western terms, reflection or contemplation, is seen as a means of training the mind for righteousness. Tafakkur activities include thinking, emotions, perception, imagination, and ideas, which are intended to influence human behavioral development. The ultimate goal of tafakkur is described as the attainment of the highest state of akhlak, or morality (Akhir & Sabjan, 2015).

In psychology literature, tafakkur is also sometimes translated as "meditation". Badri (2018) argues, however, that meditation has its roots in Eastern religions and is aimed at altering states of consciousness. In contrast, Islamic tafakkur is based on the teachings of the Quran and involves a quest for deep knowledge of Allah. While there are numerous psychological studies on meditation, research on Islamic tafakkur and its psychological effects, as well as its integration into psychotherapy, is very scarce. Recently, the growing literature on Islamic psychology is drawing attention to the topic (e.g., Keshavarzi et al., 2021; York Al-Karam, 2018), but still the most extensive work on tafakkur seems to be Malik Badri's *Contemplation—An Islamic Psychospiritual Study* (2018).

The Quran attaches great importance to thinking and makes suggestions about the goals and ways of thinking (Quran 7:185; 3:190-191; 2:164). Based on the Quran's emphasis, instruction, and suggestions on thinking, Kutluer (1994) concludes that thinking is almost a duty of servanthood and worship. In addition to emphasizing the action, the Quran informs us about the subject matter of thinking, in other words: what to think. This includes topics such as the relationship between Allah and the universe, the universe and man, and Allah and man (Akhir & Sabjan, 2015; Al Waleed, 2019; Kutluer, 1994).

Therefore, man is expected to think about the creation, their place and role within it, the relationship with the Creator—Allah—and all the tasks and meanings associated with it and draw conclusions for themselves. These conclusions include that man was created distinctively, was sent to earth as Allah's khalīfah, has responsibilities because of this role, is accountable for his deeds, comes from Allah and will return to Him (Othman & Mohamad, 2019).

Tafakkur is not just observing the surroundings and thinking about the obvious, but looking behind things, focusing on insight and meaning. Finding out the connection between things and the relationship between everything that has been created can contribute to mental health. Especially in times of distress, negative life events, and at the edges of life and death— these are all moments when the need for meaning grows. This search for meaning can be done with the help of tafakkur. Al Waleed (2019) suggests five areas for tafakkur. As in the previous sections, these areas can function with certain psychological concepts and can be fruitful for psychotherapy.

1. Tafakkur about 'īmān and the beauties that lead to love of Allah. This type of tafakkur can be related to attachment. As mentioned earlier, Allah can be an ideal attachment figure, who fulfills needs such as trust, protection, and love. Thus, contemplating this might resolve feelings of loneliness and abandonment and help one realize that there is someone who can be loved and who loves in return, who protects and shelters. 'Imān in Allah can also help in the search for meaning. By reflecting on where one comes from and to where one is going, that man was created distinctively and has special responsibilities, tasks, and goals one can find direction and meaning in life.

2. Tafakkur about the promised rewards for worship ('ibādah). The positive relationship between worship and mental and physical health is well documented (Koenig, et al., 2012; Koenig, 2005). Next to these objective and worldly benefits, religious practices also have spiritual meanings and benefits. Reflecting on the higher meaning of religious practices and that they might be rewarded in a manner not possible in this world can help individuals make sense of their existence and promote self-actualization.

3. Tafakkur about the fear of Allah, obedience to Him, punishments, and abstention from sins.

4. Tafakkur about the inclination to sin and the nafs, despite Allah's blessings. In contrast to the second type, tafakkur types three and four provide an awareness that bad actions will also return. Such tafakkur calls for repentance and leads to tawbah. This can create awareness of confronting the consequences of one's actions and taking responsibility. Confrontation and acceptance of responsibility are important qualities of psychological and spiritual counseling (Ağılkaya Şahin, 2021) and can be an additional resource for expected behavioral changes and personal growth.

5. Tafakkur about Allah's guidance to the right path, wahy (revelation), and prophets. Through this type of tafakkur, people can gain the insight that they are not unattended, that there are guides who direct their lives, facilitate them, and show them the way. Consequently, they can discover that they are not living arbitrarily and without rules, and that they have a guide in their life struggle. Such a view of life could correspond to the human need to live in an appropriate environment, surrounded by boundaries and rules that protect and guide them.

These points can be incorporated into psychotherapy to help the client understand, meaning making, find solutions to, and cope with the situation in which they find themselves. Searching for the meaning of events is a difficult and exhausting psychological process that requires cognitive activities and transformations. According to Vergote (1996), contemplation is a cognitive restructuring; the person is freed from automatic thoughts and gains insight into reflected things. Cognitive behavioral therapy makes it clear how necessary and important cognitive restructuring is.

When people struggle with inescapable thoughts, unbearable feelings, and unavoidable fears, reflecting on where and why they arise (tafakkur), turning to and connecting with Allah (du'ā'), and taking refuge in Allah for their benefit, harm, and meaning (tawakkul) can provide an alternative way of coping. In this way, the psychotherapist can integrate tafakkur into their treatment and offer explanations and descriptions of how to make tafakkur. With this knowledge and awareness, the client can learn a new cognitive method to use in therapy, either alone or with the psychotherapist.

Conclusion

Religious practices in general and Islamic practices in particular can have psychological effects that can make them available as tools or methods for psychotherapy. The psychological concepts and theories that can be associated with tawakkul, du'ā', and tafakkur can provide an idea of how they can be integrated into therapy. Certainly, psychologically effective Islamic practices are not limited to those discussed in this chapter.

Numerous studies have documented the psychological benefits of religious practices such as du'ā', tawbah, dhikr, and meditation (Bonelli, 2018a, b; Çetin, 2017; Goels, 1996; Hamjah et al., 2017; Irfan, 2017; Karim, 1984; Poloma & Pendleton, 1991; Seyhan, 2013; Utsch, 2018a; Vasegh, 2009; Walsh & Shapiro, 2006; Wilson, 2009). However, all psychological and psychotherapeutic effects aside, one should keep in mind that these religious practices are forms of worship and one should not strip them of their spiritual and religious content and meaning and reduce them to psychotherapeutic intervention techniques only.

Perhaps then their effects could be questioned as Welwood (2000) points out, "When people use spiritual practice to try and compensate for low self-esteem, social alienation, or emotional problems, they corrupt the true nature of spiritual practice" (p. 206). Today, mainstream psychotherapy has stripped several religious practices (e.g., meditation, confession) of their sacred character and turned them into psychological techniques (see Ağılkaya Şahin, 2018; Plante, 2008).

The psychotherapist should be aware of this and take Plante's (2008) warning seriously and not fall into the trap of "repackaging" originally religious rituals, practices, or values: "Psychology seems to have taken principles and techniques from religious and spiritual traditions, secularized them, and repackaged them as modern empirically supported positive psychology related interventions" (p. 432). Not only psychology as a science, but also the Internet shows what and how many inappropriate applications of Islamic practices are on the market. The booming 'asmā' al-ḥusnā (Allah's beautiful names) business in Türkiye, and perhaps in other Muslim countries, is just one of them.

The integration of religious/spiritual practices into therapy depends primarily on the client's desire, willingness, and acceptance. On the other hand, scientific research has shown that religious clients do want religious issues to be addressed in therapy (Ağılkaya Şahin, 2018, 2019, 2020a; Genia, 2000; Goh et al., 2014; Frick et al., 2006; Keshavarzi & Haque, 2013; Pfeifer, 2018; Plante, 2008; Post & Wade, 2009). However, because of the psychological benefits of religious practices, they could also be offered to secular clients, certainly within the context of ethical codes.

Second, implementing religious practices also requires the psychotherapist's knowledge. The psychotherapist should have insight into the practices and related religious literature (e.g. Quran and Sunnah). Undoubtedly, it would be much more sincere and convincing if the therapist would also perform the suggested practices privately. Although this would enrich the therapeutic relationship, it is not mandatory for the psychotherapist to use these religious practices in their life, but at least they should know the meaning, uses, types, contents, contexts, and most importantly, the psychological effects of the proposed religious and spiritual practices. Studies in the field of psychology of religion and spirituality in general, and the growing literature on Islamic psychology in particular, provide rich material.

References

Aboul-Enein, B. (2016). Health-promoting verses as mentioned in the holy Quran. *Journal of Religion and Health*, 55(3): 821–829.

Abramowitz, L. (2001). Prayer as Therapy Among the Frail Jewish Elderly. In L. Francis & J. Astley (Eds.) *Psychological Perspectives on Prayer: A Reader* (pp. 368–372). Gracewing.

Ağılkaya Şahin, Z. (2018). Din ve Psikoloji Arasındaki Uçurum Gerçekten Ne Kadar Derin? Psikoterapilerdeki Dini İzler. *Cumhuriyet İlahiyat Dergisi*, 22(3): 1607–1632.

Ağılkaya Şahin, Z. (2019). Müslüman Psikologlar Kertenkele Deliğinden Çıktı Mı? İslami Psikoloji Alanindaki Gelişmeler. *Turkish Studies*, 14(2): 15–47.

Ağılkaya Şahin, Z. (2020a). *Psikoloji ve Psikoterapide Din.* Çamlıca.

Ağılkaya Şahin, Z. (2020b). Das Konzept der Hoffnung und Hoffnungslosigkeit in der islamischen Seelsorge. In M. Abdallah, T. Badawia, G. Erdem (Eds.) *Grundbegriffe der Islamischen Seelsorge* (pp. 257– 282). Grünewald.

Ağılkaya Şahin, Z. (2021). *Manevi Bakım ve Danışmanlık.* Marmara Akademi.

Ahmed, S., & Amer, M. (2012). *Counseling Muslims.* Taylor & Francis.

Ai, A. L., Peterson, C., Bolling, S. F., & Rodgers, W. (2006). Depression, faith-based coping, and short-term postoperative global functioning in adult and older patients undergoing cardiac surgery. *Journal of Psychosomatic Research*, 60(1), 21–28. https://doi.org/10.1016/j.jpsychores.2005.06.082

Ainsworth, M. (1979). Infant–mother attachment. *American Psychologist*, 34(10): 932–937.

Akhir, N., & Sabjan, M. (2015). *Tafakkur* as the Spiritual Mechanism for Environment Conservation. *Journal of Religious & Theological Information*, 14: 1-12.

Al-Krenawi, A., & Graham, J. (1999). Social work and koranic mental health healers. *International Social Work*, 42(1): 53–65.

Al Waleed, A. (2019). *Tafakkur: A Forgotten Talim of the Qur'an.* www.durrenajaf.com (01.01.2020).

Amer, M., & Jalal, B. (2012). Individual psychotherapy/counseling: Psychodynamic, cognitive-behavioral, and humanistic-experiential models. In S. Ahmed and M. M. Amer (Eds.), *Counseling Muslims: Handbook of Mental Health Issues and Interventions.* Routledge.

Argyle, M. (2000). Psychology and Religion: An Introduction. Routledge.

Arıcı, A. (2005). Ergenlerde dinî başaçıkma yöntemi olarak dua. (Unpublished MA thesis), Uludağ University, Bursa.

Arık, A. (1996). *Motivasyon ve Heyecana Giriş*. Çantay Kitapevi.

Askay, S., & Magyar-Russel, G. (2009). Post–traumatic growth and spirituality in burn recovery. *International Review of Psychiatry*, 21(6): 570–579.

Aten, J., O'Grady, K., & Worthington, E. (2012). The psychology of religion and spirituality for clinicians: using research in your practice. Routledge.

Aydın, A. (1995). *Dini inkarın psiko–sosyal nedenleri*. (Unpublished PhD thesis), Ondokuz Mayıs University.

Ayten, A. (2005). Kendini Gerçekleştirme ve Dindarlık: Üniversite Öğrencileri Üzerine Bir Araştırma. *Marmara İlahiyat Fakültesi Dergisi*, 29(2): 185-204.

Badri, M. (2018). *Contemplation—An Islamic Psychospiritual Study*. The International Institute of Islamic Thought.

Bayram, F. (2017). İsteyeni cevapsız bırakmayan: Mucip. *Diyanet Aylık Dergi*, 319: 46–47.

Benassi, V., Sweeney, P., & Dufour, C. (1988). Is there a relation between locus of control orientation and depression? *Journal of Abnormal Psychology*, 97(3): 357–367.

Benson, H. (1996). *Timeless healing: The power and biology of belief.* Scribner.

Bonab, B., Miner, M., & Proctor, M. (2013). Attachment to God in Islamic spirituality. *Journal of Muslim Mental Health*, 7(2): 77–104.

Bonelli, R. (2018a). Verbitterung und Vergebung. In M. Utsch, R. Bonelli, S. Pfeifer (Eds.) *Psychotherapie und Spiritualitaet* (pp. 237–244). Springer.

Bonelli, R. (2018b). Schuldgefühle, Psychotherapie und Beichte. In M. Utsch, R. Bonelli, S. Pfeifer (Eds.) *Psychotherapie und Spiritualitaet* (pp. 119–126). Springer.

Bowlby, J. (1980). Attachment and loss, Vol. 3. Loss, Sadness and Depression. Basic Books.

Byrd, R. (1988). Positive Therapeutic Effects of Intercessory Prayer in a Coronary Care Unit Population. *Southern Medical Journal*, 81: 826–829.

Çağrıcı, M. (2012). Tevekkül. *TDV İslâm Ansiklopedisi.* https://islamansiklopedisi. org.tr/tevekkul#1 (19.01.2020).

Canan, İ. (1995). *Kütüb–ü Sitte Hadis Ansiklopedisi.* Akçağ Yayınları.

Canda, E. (1990). A holistic approach to prayer for social work practice. *Social Thoughts*, 16: 3–13.

Carrel, A. (1981). *Dua.* (Çev. R. Özdek). Yağmur.

Çetin, Ö. (2017). Sufilerce kendini dönüştürme eğitimi olarak uygulanan zikir ritüelinin bilişsel psikoloji açısından analizi. *Hitit Üniversitesi İlahiyat Fakültesi Dergisi*, 16(31): 1–28.

Cilacı, O. (1994). Dua. *TDV İslâm Ansiklopedisi*, https://islamansiklopedisi. org.tr/dua#1 (26.01.2020).

Cohen, C., Wheeler, S., Scott, D., Edwards, B., Lusk, P., & The Anglican Working Group in Bioethics. (2000). Prayer as Therapy: A Challenge to Both Religious Belief and Professional Ethics. *The Hastings Center Report*, 30(3), 40–47.

Dinç, S. (2017). Travma sonrası stres bozukluğunun terapisinde manevi yönelimli teknikler ve uygulamalar. In H. Ekşi (Ed.) *Psikoterapi ve Psikolojik Danışmada Maneviyat* (pp. 283–310). Kaknüs.

Doğan, M. (1994). *Duanın psikolojik ve psikoterapik etkileri* (Unpublished MA thesis). Uludağ University.

Dwairy, M. (2006). Counseling and Psychotherapy with Arabs and Muslims—A Culturally Sensitive Approach. Teachers College.

Ellenberger, H. (1994). The Discovery of the Unconscious: The History and Evolution of Dynamic Psychiatry. Fontana Press.

Emmons, R. (2000). Is spirituality an intelligence? Motivation, cognition, and the psychology of the spirit. *International Journal for the Psychology of Religion*, 10(1), 3-26.

Erikson, E. (1993). *Childhood and Society.* Norton.

Fatemi, S. (2018). Integrating Duaa Arafa and Other Shiite Teachings into Psychotherapy. In C. York Al–Karam (Ed.) *Islamically Integrated Psychotherapy: Uniting Faith and Professional Practice* (pp. 229–242). Templeton Press.

Finney, R., & Malony, H. (2001). An empirical study of contemplative prayer as an adjunct to psychotherapy. In J. Francis & J. Astley (Ed.) *Psychological Perspectives on Prayer: A Reader* (pp. 359–366). Gracewing Press.

Frank, D. (1991). Religious and ethical issues in psychotherapy. *Current Opinion in Psychiatry*, 4: 375–378.

Frankl, V. (2006). *Man's Search for Meaning.* Beacon.

Frick, E., Riedner, C., Fegg, M. J., Hauf, S., & Borasio, G. D. (2006). A clinical interview assessing cancer patients' spiritual needs and preferences. *European Journal of Cancer Care, 15*(3), 238-243.

Genia, V. (2000). Religious Issues in Secularly Based Psychotherapy. *Counseling and Values,* 44(3): 213–221.

Goels, A. (1996). A note on the psychology of Dhikr: The Halveti–Jerrahi order of dervishes in Istanbul. *International Journal for the Psychology of Religion,* 6(4): 229–251.

Goh, A.M.Y., Eagleton, T., Kelleher, R., Yastrubetskaya, O., Taylor, M., Chiu, E., AM, Hamilton, B., Trauer, T. and Lautenschlager, N.T. (2014). Pastoral care in old age psychiatry. *Asia-Pacific Psychiatry,* 6: 127-134. https://doi.org/10.1111/appy.12018

Güldaş, F. (2021). Cognitive-Behavioral-Related Prayer Types and Mental Health Relations among Muslim Samples. *Cumhuriyet İlahiyat Dergisi,* 25(1): 437-454.

Gültekin, M. (2004). Ergenlerde kontrol alanı algısı. *Uludağ Üniversitesi Eğitim Fakültesi Dergisi,* 17(2): 267–279.

Güzel, S. (2009). *Telkin ve terapide duanın önemi.* (Unpublished MA thesis). Selçuk University.

Hamjah, S., & Akhir, N. (2014). Islamic Approach in Counseling. *Journal of Religion and Health,* 53:279–289.

Hamjah, S., Mat Akhir, N. S., Ismail, Z., Ismail, A., & Mohd. Arib, N. (2017). The Application of Ibadah (Worship) in Counseling: Its Importance and Implications to Muslim Clients. *Journal of Religion and Health,* 56, 1302-1310.

Hanbel. (2003). *el-Müsned* (Trans: S. Sarı & R. Oral). Ensar Yayıncılık.

Haque, A. (1997). Seminar on Islamization of Psychology: Petaling Jaya, November–December 1996. *Intellectual Discourse,* 5(1): 88–92.

Haque, A., & Keshavarzi, H. (2014). Integrating Indigenous Healing Methods in Therapy: Muslim Beliefs and Practice. *International Journal of Culture and Mental Health,* 7(3): 297–314.

Haque, A., & Mohamed, Y. (2009). *Psychology of personality: Islamic perspectives.* Cengage Learning Asia.

Haug, E. (1998). Including a spiritual dimension in family therapy: Ethical considerations. *Contemporary Family Therapy,* 20: 181–194.

Hayta, A. (2006). Anneden Allah'a: Bağlanma teorisi ve İslâm'da Allah tasavvuru. *Değerler Eğitimi Dergisi,* 4(12): 29–63.

Heider, F. (1958). *The Psychology of Interpersonal Relations*. Wiley.

Helminiak, D. (2001). Treating Spiritual Issues in Secular Psychotherapy. *Counseling and Values*, 45:163–189.

Henry, H. (2015). Spiritual Energy of Islamic Prayers as a Catalyst for Psychotherapy. *Journal of Religion and Health*, 54(2): 387–398.

Hökelekli, H. (2003). *Din Psikolojisi*. TDV Yayınları.

Holahan, J., & Mous, R. (1987). Personal and contextual determinants of coping strategies. *Journal of Personality and Social Psychology*, 52(5): 946–955.

İbn Mace. (2012). *Sünen* (Trans: H. Hatipoğlu). Karaman.

Irfan, M., Saeed, S., Awan, N. R., Gul, M., Aslam, M., & Naeem, F. (2017). Psychological healing in Pakistan: from Sufism to culturally adapted cognitive behaviour therapy. *Journal of Contemporary Psychotherapy*, *47*, 119-124.

Janssen, J., de Hart, J., & den Draak, C. (1990). Praying as an individualized ritual. In H. Heimbrock & B. Boudewijnse (Eds.) *Current studies on rituals Perspectives for The Psychology of Religion* (pp. 71-87). Rodopi Press.

Jung, C. (1961). *The Theory of Psychoanalysis*. Pantheon Books.

Kara, E. (2019). Dini inancın bilişsel davranışçı terapiye entegresi. *Dini Araştırmalar*, 22(55): 159–180.

Karaca, F., & Acar, M. (2016). Bireysel psikolojik danışma sürecinde danışanın dini kaynaklarının kullanılması üzerine bir vaka örneği. In A. Ayten vd. (Ed.) *Manevi Danışmanlık ve Rehberlik II* (pp. 157–167). DEM.

Karaca, F., & Acar, M. (2019). Psikolojik danışma sürecinde kullanılan dinî/manevi temelli müdahalelerin vaka analizi yöntemi ile incelenmesi üzerine bir araştırma. In A. Ayten vd. (Ed.) *Sağlık Hizmetlerinde Manevi Danışmanlık ve Rehberlik* (pp. 267–281). DEM.

Karacoşkun, M. (1998). *Psiko–sosyal açıdan iman (dini inanç)–amel (dini davranış) ilişkisi*. (Unpublished PhD thesis), Ondokuz Mayıs University.

Karataş, K., & Baloğlu, M. (2019). Tevekkülün Psikolojik Yansımaları. *Çukurova İlahiyat Fakültesi Dergisi*, 19(1): 110–118.

Karim, G. (1984). The Islamization of Knowledge. *Third International Seminar on Islamic Thought*. Kuala Lumpur.

Kelly, E. (1990). Counselor responsiveness to client religiousness. *Counseling and Values*, 35: 69–72.

Keshavarzi, H., & Haque, A. (2013). Outlining a Psychotherapy Model for Enhancing Muslim Mental Health Within an Islamic Context. *The International Journal for the Psychology of Religion*, 23: 230–249.

Keshavarzi, H., Khan, F., Ali, B., & Awaad, R. (2021). *Applying Islamic Principles to Clinical Mental Health Care*. Routledge.

Keshavarzi, K., & Khan, F. (2018). Outlining a Case Illustration of Traditional Islamically Integrated Psychotherapy. C. York Al-Karam (Ed.) *Islamically Integrated Psychotherapy* (pp. 175–207). Templeton Press.

Kirkpatrick, L. (1992). An Attachment Theory Approach to the Psychology of Religion. *The International Journal for the Psychology of Religion*, 2(1): 3–28.

Koenig, H. (2005). *Faith and Mental Health*. Templeton Foundation Press.

Koenig H., Dana E., Verna B. (2012). *Handbook of religion and health*. Oxford University Press.

Köylü, M. (2003). *Psiko–Sosyal Açıdan Dini İletişim*. Ankara Okulu.

Krauss, S. E., Hamzah, A. H., Suandi, T., Noah, S. M., Juhari, R., Manap, J. H., & Mahmood, A. (2006). Exploring regional differences in religiosity among Muslim youth in Malaysia. *Review of Religious Research*, 238-252.

Kutluer, İ. (1994). Düşünme. *TDV İslâm Ansiklopedisi*, https://islamansiklopedisi. org.tr/dusunme (30.01.2020).

Lines, D. (2006). Spirituality in Counselling and Psychotherapy. SAGE Publications.

Lodi, F. (2018). The HEART Method: Healthy Emotions Anchored in RasoolAllah's Teachings: Cognitive Therapy Using Prophet Muhammad as Psycho–Spiritual Exemplar. In C. York Al-Karam (Ed.) *Islamically Integrated Psychotherapy* (pp. 76–102). Templeton Press.

Marzband, R., Hosseini, S., & Hamzehgardeshi, Z. (2016). A Concept Analysis of Spiritual Care Based on Islamic Sources. *Religions*, 7(61): 1-11.

Maslow, A. (1943). A theory of human motivation. *Psychological Review*, 50: 370–396.

Maslow, A. (1970). *Motivation and Personality*. Harper & Row.

Miller, G. (2003). Incorporating Spirituality in Counseling and Psychotherapy. Theory and Technique. John Wiley & Sons, Inc.

Myers, D., & Twenge, M. (2022). *Social Psychology*. McGraw Hill.

Newberg, A., Pourdehnad, M., Alavi, A., & d'Aquili, E. G. (2003). Cerebral blood flow during meditative prayer: preliminary findings and methodological issues. *Perceptual and Motor Skills*, *97*(2), 625–630.

O'Grady, K., & Bartz, J. (2012). Addressing Spiritually Transcendent Experiences in Psychotherapy. In J. Aten, K. O'Grady, E. Worthington (Eds.) *The psychology of religion and spirituality for clinicians: using research in your practice* (pp. 161–188). Routledge.

Othman, N., & Mohamad, K. (2019). Applying the main concepts of Islamic psychology to Islamic counseling. *International Journal of Academic Research in Business and Social Sciences*, 9(5): 383–393.

Pargament, K. (1997a). *Psychology and Religion: The Search for Meaning*. Guilford Press.

Pargament, K. (1997b). *The Psychology of Religion and Coping*. Guilford Press.

Pargament, K. & Hahn, J. (1986). God and the just world: Causal and coping attributions to God in health situations. *Journal for the Scientific Study of Religion*, 25: 193–207.

Pargament, K., Kennell, J., Hathaway, W., Grevengoed, N., Newman, J., & Jones, W. (1988). Religion and the problem-solving process: Three styles of coping. *Journal for the Scientific Study of Religion*, 27(1): 90–104.

Pargament, K., Smith, B., Koenig, H., & Perez L. (1998). Patterns of positive and negative religious coping with major life stressors. *Journal for the Scientific Study of Religion*, 37: 710–724.

Park, C. (2013). Religion and meaning. In R. F. Paloutzian & C. L. Park (Eds.), *Handbook of the psychology of religion and spirituality* (pp. 357–379). The Guilford Press.

Pfeifer, S. (2018). Das Gebet—Psychodinamik, Wirksamkeit, Therapie. In M. Utsch, R. Bonelli, S. Pfeifer (Eds.) *Psychotherapie und Spiritualitaet* (pp. 227–236). Springer.

Phillips, R., & Pargament, K., Lynn, Q., & Crossley, C. (2004). Self-Directing Religious Coping: A Deistic God, Abandoning God, or

No God at All? *Journal for the Scientific Study of Religion*, 43: 409-418.

Plante, T. (2008). What Do the Spiritual and Religious Traditions Offer The Practicing Psychologist? *Pastoral Psychology*, 56: 429–444.

Poloma, M., & Pendleton, B. (1991). The Effects of Prayer and Prayer Experiences on Measures of General Well–Being. *Journal of Psychology and Theology*, 1: 71–83.

Poole, R., & Cook, C. (2011). Praying with a patient constitutes a breach of professional boundaries in psychiatric practice. *British Journal of Psychiatry*, 199: 94–98.

Post, B., & Wade, N. (2009). Religion and Sprituality in Psychotherapy: A Practice Friendly Review of Research. *Journal of Clinical Psychology*, 65: 131–146.

Rassool, H. (2016). *Islamic Counseling*. Routledge.

Richards, P., & Bergin, A. (2004a). *Casebook for a Spiritual Strategy in Counseling and Psychotherapy*. American Psychological Association.

Richards, P., & Bergin, A. (2004b). A Theistic Spiritual Strategy for Psychotherapy. In P. Richards & A. Bergin (Eds.) *Casebook for a Spiritual Strategy in Counseling and Psychotherapy* (pp. 3–32). American Psychological Association.

Richards, P., & Bergin, A. (2005). *A spiritual strategy for counseling and psychotherapy*. American Psychological Association.

Roberts, L., Ahmed, I., & Davison, A. (2009). Intercessory prayer for the alleviation of ill health. *Cochrane Database of Systematic Reviews*, 2.

Rothman, A. (2022). Developing a Model of Islamic Psychology and Psychotherapy. Routledge.

Rotter, J. (1966). Generalized expectancies for internal versus external control of reinforcement. *Psychological Monographs: General and Applied*, 80(1): 1–28.

Şahin, M. (2018). Dini bir değer olarak tevekkül yöneliminin psikolojik sebep ve sonuçları üzerine araştırma. (Unpublished PhD thesis). Uludağ University.

Schuster, M. A., Stein, B. D., Jaycox, L. H., Collins, R. L., Marshall, G. N., Elliott, M. N., & Berry, S. H. (2001). A national survey of stress reactions after the September 11, 2001, terrorist attacks. *New England Journal of Medicine*, 345(20), 1507-1512.

Seligman, M. (2002). *Authentic Happiness: Using the New Positive Psychology to Realize Your Potential for Lasting Fulfillment.* Free Press.

Seyhan, B. (2013). Dua Tutumu ile Psikolojik İyi Olma Hali Arasındaki İlişkiler. *Cumhuriyet İlahiyat Fakültesi Dergisi,* 17(2): 157–183.

Sides, H. (1997). The calibration of belief. *New York Times Magazine,* 92–95.

Sloan, R., Bagiella, E., & Powell, T. (1999). Religion, spirituality, and medicine. *The Lancet,* 353(9153): 664–667.

Surwillo, W., & Hobson, D. (1978). Brain electrical activity during prayer. *Psychological Reports,* 43(1): 135–143.

Suyuti. (2012). *el-Cami'u's-sağîr* (Trans: S. Avcı). Serhat Kitabevi.

Tacey, D. (2004). *The Spirituality Revolution: The Emergence of Contemporary Spirituality.* Brunner-Routledge.

Tan, S.-Y. (2000). Religion and psychotherapy. A. Kazdin (Ed.) *Encyclopedia of psychology.* American Psychological Association/Oxford University Press.

Tan, S.-Y. (2007). Use of Prayer and Scripture in Cognitive-Behavioral Therapy. *Journal of Psychology and Christianity,* 26(2): 101-111.

Tarhan, N. (2012). *Akıldan kalbe yolculuk.* Nesil.

Tekke, M., & Watson, P. (2017). Supplication and the Muslim personality: Psychological nature and functions of prayer as interpreted by Said Nursi, Mental Health, *Religion & Culture,* 20(2): 143-153.

Thompson, C. (1999). Illusions Of Control: How we overestimate our personal influence. *Current Directions in Psychological Science,* 8(6): 187–190.

Utsch, M. (2018a). Achtsamkeit—eine Brücke zwischen Psychotherapie und Spiritualitaet? In M. Utsch, R. Bonelli, S. Pfeifer (Eds.) *Psychotherapie und Spiritualitaet* (pp. 245–252). Springer.

Utsch, M. (2018b). Ausschlus oder Einbeziehung spiritueller Interventionen. In M. Utsch, R. Bonelli, S. Pfeifer (Eds.) *Psychotherapie und Spiritualitaet* (pp. 128–138). Springer.

Utsch, M. (2018c). Herzensgebet als therapeutische Ressource—Kommentar. In E. Frick vd., (Eds.) *Fallbuch Spiritualitaet in Psychotherapie und Psychiatrie* (pp. 126–127). Vandenhoeck & Ruprecht.

Vasegh, S. (2009). Psychiatric treatments involving religion: Psychotherapy from an Islamic perspective. In P. Huguelet & H.

Koenig (Eds.) *Religion and Spirituality in Psychiatry* (pp. 301–316). Cambridge University Press.

Vergote, A. (1996). Religion, belief and unbelief: a psychological study. Leuven University.

Walsh, R., & Shapiro, S. (2006). The Meeting of Meditative Disciplines and Western Psychology: A Mutually Enriching Dialogue. *American Psychologist*, 61(3): 227–239.

Welwood, J. (2000). *Toward a psychology of awakening*. Boston, MA: Shambhala Publications, Inc.

Wilson, W. (2009). Psychiatric Treatments Involving Religion: Psychotherapy from a Christian Perspective. In P. Huguluet & H. Koenig (Eds.) *Religion and Spirituality in Psychiatry* (pp. 283–300). Cambridge University Press.

Wong, P. (2010). Meaning-Centered Living: A New Approach to Life and Well-Being. In P. Wong & P. Fry (Eds.) *The Human Quest for Meaning: A Handbook of Psychological Research and Clinical Applications* (pp. 3–12). Routledge.

Wong-McDonald, A., & Gorsuch, G. (2000). Surrender to God: An additional coping style. *Journal of Psychology and Theology*, 28(2): 149–61.

Yalom, I. (1980). *Existential Psychotherapy*. Basic Books.

Yapıcı, A. (2007). *Ruh Sağlığı ve Din*. Karahan.

York Al-Karam, C. (2018). *Islamically Integrated Psychotherapy*. Templeton Press.

Zinnbauer, B., & Pargament, K. (2005). Religiousness and Spirituality. In B. Weiner & W. Craig (Eds.) *Handbook of Psychology* (Vol. 5, pp. 21-42). Wiley.

CHAPTER 4

Islamic Mindfulness and Recovery from Addiction

Sarah Huxtable Mohr, LCSW

What is Mindfulness?

Buddhist Mindfulness

The establishment of mindfulness as a central part of the Buddhist path led to its significant development as a contemplative practice throughout the history of the religion. In fact, the foundational precepts of the Buddhist path, the Eightfold Path, include Right Mindfulness. Mindfulness generally means paying attention, nonjudgmentally, to the present moment. This attention is not neutral or aggressive, such as a sharpshooter, but kind and gentle, as a mother holding a child.

Mindfulness is a basic part of Buddhist scriptures, such as the *Satipatthana Sutta*, or *The Foundations of Mindfulness*, from the Majjhima Nikāya (Nanamoli & Bodi, 1995). *Satipatthana*, or simply *sati,* translates as mindfulness. This sutta is a dialogue of the Buddha with his disciples, discussing mindfulness's basic components. It is particularly interesting to see how little has changed about mindfulness since its codification as a central Buddhist practice between the 3rd and 2nd centuries BCE.

Some of the ideas discussed in the sutta will be familiar to many of us. The Buddha directs his disciples about mindfulness, saying:

> Bhikkus, this is the direct path for the purification of beings, for the surmounting of sorrow and lamentation, for the disappearance of pain and grief, for the attainment of the true way, for the realization

of Nibbana, namely the four foundations of mindfulness. (Nanamoli & Bodi, 1995, p. 145)

Significant to us is that from its first conception as a practice, it was intended to alleviate suffering, sorrow, lamentation, pain, and grief. Given the huge modern-day movements to use mindfulness as pain relief, for example, in practices like Mindfulness-Based Stress Reduction (Kabat-Zinn, 2013), it is interesting to note that we are using the practice for the exact same purposes as it was originally taught thousands of years ago.

The Buddha stated that the four foundations themselves are mindfulness of the body, mindfulness of feelings, mindfulness of mind, and mindfulness of mind-objects. It is important to note that Buddhism recognizes the mind as a sense along with sight and hearing, which affected its formulation of how the mind was understood.

The actual practices within the sutta include being aware of breath, body posture, feelings, and experiences such as ill-will, doubt, fear, and sensual desire, among others (Nanamoli & Bodi, 1995). The Buddha states that when a bhikkhu (renunciate or monk) breathes a long breath, he will know he is breathing a long breath, and when he breathes a short breath, he will know he is breathing a short breath. He will be aware when standing, sitting, or lying down. As regards feelings, he will be aware of their presence or absence. When experiencing mental states or mental objects, he will be aware of their presence or absence (Nanamoli & Bodi, 1995).

Mindfulness of the breath, like mindfulness in general, can be found in the Majjhima Nikāya, where the Buddha extensively discusses this element of mindfulness in the *Ānāpānasati Sutta* (Nanamoli & Bodi, 1995). This sutta is the basis for much of modern meditation. Mindfulness practices in some schools of Buddhism, like Theravada, emphasize the importance of mindfulness of the breath more than other forms of meditation. At the same time, they still include loving-kindness and other forms of meditation. However, mindfulness of the breath was never the only form of mindfulness in Buddhism.

Although many people associate Buddhism solely with meditation, meditation was combined with highly complex philosophies of mind and conduct that included understanding the universe from macrocosm to microcosm. Meditation included contemplation of the underlying complexities and structures of reality and the foundations of mindfulness, which focused on developing self-awareness.

So, it is important to distinguish meditation from mindfulness per se. Additionally, the use of mindfulness in various schools of Buddhism varied greatly, from Theravada Buddhism, which tended to be more purely focused on mindfulness, to tantric Buddhism, where meditation, though incorporating mindfulness, had a strong emphasis on deities, prayers, and intellectual complexities, to Zen Buddhism, which emphasized a very pure experience of mindfulness through intensive self-awareness.

Modern-day Buddhist schools of thought draw from these respective traditions. At the same time, in places like the United States, they include a renewed understanding of religion and mindfulness in particular. This modern movement in the West began in earnest in the 1960s and 70s when the hippie movement popularized the study of Eastern religions and coincided with the arrival of teachers from Asia to the West who transmitted the teachings to Western students.

Secular Mindfulness

Secular mindfulness grew directly out of the explosion of the study of Eastern religions in the West. Not surprisingly, with the emphasis on secularism particular to Western culture, mindfulness was taken out of its religious context. It became a medical practice, a psychological practice, and a tool for health and wellness rather than a religious practice. Whereas many of the people who started the mindfulness movement in the West were Buddhists by religion, their work to popularize mindfulness distanced the practice from its religious roots. It made it more scientific and, thus, more credible as a medical practice. As a part of this change, there has been a significant amount of research on mindfulness's effectiveness for medical and psychological treatment.

For example, Mindfulness-Based Stress Reduction (MBSR) is an intervention developed by Jon Kabat-Zinn to use the power of mindfulness to treat chronic pain (Kabat-Zinn, 2013). In psychology, Dialectical Behavioral Therapy (DBT) is a prominent evidence-based use of mindfulness. In addition to MBSR and DBT, which are structured manualized interventions, research has shown the efficacy of mindfulness in medicine and behavioral health (Fortney & Taylor, 2010; Ludwig & Kabat-Zinn, 2008).

Islamic Mindfulness

As the scientific basis for mindfulness has become firmly established, many religious practitioners from other world religions have moved to make mindfulness their own. Recognizing the religious roots of the practice in Buddhism, people in the Judeo-Christian-Islamic tradition have been steadily working to develop a clearer understanding of the role of mindfulness from a faith-based perspective grounded in their own traditions (Abdul-Rahman, 2017a). This has been a steadily growing movement in Islam, particularly Islamic psychology (Badri, 2000). There is a significant theological move to claim mindfulness as a practice that relates to the origins of the tradition in the Quran and the practices of the Prophet (PBUH).

Practices that have been identified as mindfulness in Islam include *dhikr* (remembrance, also translated as mindfulness), *muraqaba* (contemplation on the self), *khushoo* (mindfulness or presence, particularly in prayer), and *tafakkur* and *tadabbur* (meditation on Allah, the natural universe, and other realities, such as heaven and hell). Other forms of mindfulness practices identified as significant in the Islamic tradition include *dua* (supplication) and *salaat* (the formal five daily prayers).

Dhikr is the most well-known mindfulness practice in Islam. The concept of *dhikr* is prominent in the Quran, and many English translators translate *dhikr* simply as the word mindfulness. The root of *dhikr* (ذ ك ر) appears 292 times in the Quran in 14 derived forms (Dukes, 2023). Central to Sufism but fully a part of all schools of thought, *dhikr* is a practice of remembrance.

Dhikr is practiced differently by different groups and schools. It can be individual or group chanting, repetition of supplications, prayers, or the 99 Names of Allah. It is also used in the Quran to describe how people should contemplate nature or other manifest evidence of the Creator. Meditation in Sufism through repetition of Islamic phrases and the names of God in Arabic takes up significant parts of daily and community practice (Khan, H., 1991; Khan, P., 1994). In Sufism, dhikr is seen as a way to purify the heart and the practitioner's whole character and life (Angha, 1991).

Another form of mindfulness central to the religion is *muraqaba*. *Muraqaba* means "to watch, observe, regard attentively" (Parrott, 2017). This form of mindfulness is sometimes conceptualized in the literature as the core of Islamic mindfulness practice and is central to many schools of Sufism (Azeemi, 2005; Isgandarova, 2023). It involves considering oneself and cultivating awareness of one's thoughts, words, and deeds, along with one's mental, emotional, and spiritual condition.

Although the word does not appear in the Quran, the highly respected scholar Imam Al-Ghazali (d. 1111), one of the most prominent theologians, mystics, and philosophers of the Sufi tradition specifically, as well as the Islamic tradition as a whole (Davis, 1948; Malik & Hinnells, 2006), stated in his most famous work, *Ihya Ulum Ad-Din* or *The Revival of the Religious Sciences* (Al-Ghazali, 2014), that the concept was a critical part of self-purification. Similarly, in her groundbreaking work on mindfulness in Islam, Isgandarova (2023) discusses muraqaba as a practice that encompasses other forms of mindfulness, such as *dhikr*, *tadabbur*, and *tafakkur,* to name a few, and emphasizes its usefulness in therapeutic practice.

Khushoo means presence or awareness in prayer. The concept is in the Quran, where it is said: "… and truly it is extremely heavy and hard except for al-khaashi'oon…" (2:45) (referring to prayer; Learn-Islam, 2023). Also, scholars cite the verse, "Successful indeed are the believers, those who offer their salaah (prayers) with all solemnity and full submissiveness" (23:1-2). Several hadiths mention *khushoo*, enjoining the believers to focus their minds on the full rewards of prayer. As such, *khushoo* is a form of mindfulness intrinsic to the five daily prayers, one of the central practices of the religion.

Another major form of mindfulness in Islam is tafakkur, or contemplation, which is closely related to the concept of *tadabbur* (Abdul-Rahman, 2017). Kamali (2006) states, "Approximately 750 verses, or nearly one-eighth of the Qur'an, exhort the readers to study nature, history, the Qur'an itself, and humanity at large" (p. 4). Of these verses, they include exhortations to ponder and meditate.

The meaning of *tadabbur* is "concentrated and goal-oriented thinking provoked by the challenge to find something new or to solve a difficult problem" (Kamali, 2006, p. 4). *Tafakkur* is a form of meditation, often used interchangeably with *muraqaba*, and it "encompasses the process of bringing a thought to conscious awareness" (Abdul-Rahman, 2017). The multiple verses in the Quran that encourage people to ponder, meditate, and think deeply about the signs of God use these concepts.

The merits of contemplation in Islam are established in the hadith or sayings of the Prophet (PBUH). There is a story about three people talking to the Prophet (PBUH), and he told them that an hour of contemplation was worth either 1 year, 7 years, or 70 years of worship. When asked about the discrepancy, he continued the conversation with them, and it was revealed that the contemplation's content gave the merit of its length in worship, the most valuable being reflecting on the hellfire (Sadaqaat, 2023).

Comparisons Between Islamic Mindfulness and Other Forms of Mindfulness

There is little research on the similarities and differences between Islamic and other forms of mindfulness. However, anecdotally and through a review of the literature, it is possible to make some comparisons. The major similarities between Islamic mindfulness and other forms of mindfulness include the significance of calming the mind and body, increasing well-being, character development, and improving spiritual connectedness, to name a few.

Mindfulness, in all its forms, can significantly increase mental and physical wellness. The research (cite) on the health benefits of mindfulness is relevant to Islamic mindfulness as much as to any other form. Islamic mindfulness has the potential to improve mental and physical health outcomes as it continues to be developed by the Muslim community, and this book is part of that effort.

Technology has increased the use and availability of mindfulness of all kinds. Buddhist mindfulness has been the foundation of multiple meditation apps, including free ones like Insight Timer and other apps that require a subscription, like HeadSpace. Recently, some Muslims have developed mindfulness apps, and more are forthcoming. Ruh is perhaps the most well-known and explores Islamic mindfulness as a mental health intervention. It includes meditations and other tools to increase the use of Islamic mindfulness in day-to-day life.

Islamic mindfulness differs from other forms in its origins in the Islamic tradition and the fact that it is theistic rather than philosophical or secular. Nothing in Islam can be separated from the centrality of the believers' relationship to God. For this reason, Islamic mindfulness has a goal beyond simply the health benefits of the practice. Although Muslims can and do recognize the concrete effects of mindfulness for health and wellness, the primary goal of mindfulness in Islam is to develop a deeper relationship with God (Mohr, 2022). Thus, it fundamentally differs from Buddhist or secular versions of the practice.

Mindfulness in Addiction Treatment

One of the major commonalities between Islamic mindfulness and other forms emerging in the current literature is the use of mindfulness in treating addiction. There are many perspectives on the nature of addiction. However, one common conception is the disease model. The disease model of addiction goes back to early innovations in treatment that attempted to move away from viewing addicts and alcoholics as people of weak will or poor character (White, 1998). It was an attempt to understand addiction as something that doctors could treat. Thus, it is also known as the medical model. The American Society of Addiction Medicine defines addiction as follows:

> Addiction is a primary, chronic disease of brain reward, motivation, memory, and related circuitry. Dysfunction in these circuits leads to characteristic biological, psychological, social, and spiritual

manifestations. This is reflected in an individual pathologically pursuing reward and/or relief by substance use and other behaviors.

Addiction is characterized by inability to consistently abstain, impairment in behavioral control, craving, diminished recognition of significant problems with one's behaviors and interpersonal relationships, and a dysfunctional emotional response. Like other chronic diseases, addiction often involves cycles of relapse and remission. Without treatment or engagement in recovery activities, addiction is progressive and can result in disability or premature death. (American Society of Addiction Medicine, 2011)

Addiction, according to the disease model, has a physical component, a mental component, and a spiritual component, among others like genetics (Narcotics Anonymous World Service, 2008). The physical component is the biological cravings for drugs driven by biochemical factors. The mental component consists of the obsession and compulsion to use drugs despite adverse consequences, including the inability to sufficiently grasp the impact of addiction due to denial and other cognitive distortions. The spiritual component of the disease of addiction is generally described as a spiritual void or a sense of emptiness, dissatisfaction, and alienation from other people and authentic engagement in life.

Mindfulness can impact all three of these primary areas of addiction. The use of mindfulness has been shown to reduce physical and mental cravings. Additionally, mindfulness as a spiritual practice can impact the sense of emptiness that characterizes addiction and give people a sense of peace, well-being, harmony, and connection that can alleviate the spiritual suffering associated with the disease.

Recovery: Goal of Addiction Treatment

In general, the goal of addiction treatment is called recovery. The Substance Abuse and Mental Health Administration (SAMSHA) defines recovery as "A process of change through which individuals improve their health and wellness, live a self-directed life, and strive to reach their full potential" (SAMSHA, 2014). The SAMSHA concept of recovery drives behavioral health care throughout the US. It includes various elements, including holistic healing, self-redefinition, personal change and transformation, connectedness to the community, peers, allies, empowerment, hope, and gratitude (SAMSHA, 2009). The idea of recovery in Twelve Step programs is freedom from active addiction and being a productive, responsible member of society (Narcotics Anonymous World Service, 2008).

The idea of the recovery model of addiction has been shifting away from a purely disease-based conception of both addiction and recovery itself. Even though the disease model and medical model remain useful in addiction treatment, shifts are happening towards integrated conceptions of addiction treatment that emphasize wellness rather than disease. Whatever the focus, either on the problem or the goal, mindfulness offers interesting and evidence-based solutions for people seeking to address their substance-related challenges.

Mindfulness-Based Addiction Treatment Modalities

According to the above definitions, recovery is marked by people reaching their full potential. Whereas this generally tends to emphasize abstinence or other profound changes in patterns of the use of drugs and other intoxicants, the basic change goes much deeper than that. For people to achieve their full potential in recovery, fundamental changes in coping strategies and the development of new life skills are required. As has been discussed, research has shown the efficacy of spirituality as an intervention for people in recovery to establish sobriety (Priester, 2000, 2009; Warfield & Goldstein, 1996). This is where the use of mindfulness in addiction treatment can help people with a substance use disorder stop using and find new ways of being in the world.

Twelve-Step Recovery

The Twelve-Step approach that began with Alcoholics Anonymous and spread to multiple other self-help groups works for many people who are seeking recovery from alcoholism or addiction. The success stories of people in self-help groups usually involve a profound spiritual transformation where people engage with their families, communities, and the world with more empathy, compassion, and responsibility and become productive members of society after a pattern of dereliction.

In Twelve-Step groups, prayer and meditation are part of a regular recovery program and are integrated into the structure of meetings. Additionally, steps 3, 7, and 11 all center on prayer practices. The Eleventh Step reads: "We sought through prayer and meditation to improve our conscious contact with God as we understood God praying only for knowledge of God's will for us and the power to carry it out" (Narcotics Anonymous World Service, 2008). Meditation is a critical foundation of spiritual change for people in recovery from self-destructive behavior to a productive, responsible life.

Islamic practices offer new possibilities for using meditation in Twelve-Step programs (Adisa & Steiner, 2021; Mohr, 2022). The mindfulness practices already mentioned, specifically *dhikr*, are being explored by Muslims as ways to practice meditation in Twelve-Step Recovery from an Islamic foundation. Muslims have repeatedly mentioned

Dhikr in recovery literature, which is emphasized as a possible spiritual tool for treating addiction (Adisa & Steiner, 2021; Mohr, 2022; Raslan, 2021; Rassool, 2021). However, currently, there is virtually no empirical literature supporting this.

Additionally, *khushoo* in prayer, specifically a strong presence in the five daily prayers, has the potential to significantly improve mental well-being and outcomes for people in recovery. However, anecdotal evidence and reports of practicing Muslims confirm the challenging nature of establishing good habits of intentional presence in the five daily prayers. It is possible that greater development of Buddhist or secular mindfulness and breathing practices, such as attention to the breath, can increase the ability of practitioners to improve in *kushoo* (Ma et al., 2017). Once practitioners have higher levels of *kushoo*, the regular practice of daily prayer can contribute to physical and mental well-being, as supported by the evidence on the benefits of mindfulness generally and for addiction specifically.

Muraqaba has been connected to the stages of change model (Prochaska & DiClemete, 1983) and the Twelve-Steps as a possible intervention in addiction treatment (Mohr & Ahmed, 2023). In addition, the regular inventory associated with step 10 involves self-reflection, a central concept in muraqaba (Isgandarova, 2023). The intensive introspection and self-examination of the steps can be understood as the same practice as muraqaba, and Muslims are beginning to name this in the literature.

Mindfulness-Based Relapse Prevention

One of the most well-developed clinical uses of mindfulness in addiction treatment is Mindfulness-Based Relapse Prevention (MBRP; Bowen et al., 2009). Due to the chronic relapsing nature of the disease of addiction (Connors et al., 1996), helping people with addiction maintain long–term abstinence is a high priority. For people whose spiritual beliefs conflict with the Twelve Steps, relapse prevention is a cognitive behavioral intervention that has shown promise (Marlatt & Gordon, 1985).

Additionally, mindfulness-based cognitive behavioral therapy has been effective in treating depression and other psychological disorders (Teasdale et al., 2000). Researchers and clinicians have effectively integrated mindfulness, cognitive behavioral therapy, and relapse prevention in MBRP, and increasing evidence exists to support its efficacy. For example, in a randomized controlled trial of 168 adults, MBRP showed improved outcomes as an aftercare intervention for people who had recently completed an intensive treatment program (Bowen et al., 2009).

For Muslims, MBRP has interesting possibilities. Research supports that Muslims prefer directive approaches such as cognitive behavioral therapy (CBT) in treatment (Kesharvarzi & Haque, 2013; Mir et al., 2015). Additionally, research on Religiously Integrated Cognitive Behavioral Therapy (RCBT) continues to emerge, supporting the use of Islamically integrated approaches to CBT (Hodge & Nadir, 2008).

There is also theoretical work supporting the use of RCBT with Muslims for the treatment of addiction (Mohr & Ahmed, 2023) as well as other forms of psychological intervention (Salem & Elzamzamy, 2023). A logical conclusion to draw from these connections is that there is great potential for an Islamically integrated MBRP approach to improve outcomes and help Muslims with challenges associated with addiction to maintain abstinence.

Other Islamic Mindfulness Practices for Addiction Treatment

One of the limitations of a presentation of Islamic mindfulness for addiction treatment currently is the emerging nature of the literature, both theoretical and empirical. Nonetheless, it is possible to comment on the potential of Islamic mindfulness practices and the need to develop a better understanding of how people in recovery can use them to improve their coping skills and better establish their sobriety. However, both tafakkur and tadabbur barely appear in the literature on Islamic mindfulness and addiction recovery.

Nevertheless, it is easy to draw speculative conclusions about how contemplation can benefit people's ability to stay sober. In fact, the stages of change model (Prochaska & DiClemente, 1983) that drives the assessment and treatment of people with a substance use disorder in the medical model of the American Society of Addiction Medicine (ASAM) names the first two stages of recovery as pre-contemplation and contemplation (Mee-Lee, 2013). It can only be surmised then that structured contemplation practices that center on an analysis of the self would naturally lead to advancement in motivation for change for people seeking recovery.

Future Directions

Given the scientific basis for mindfulness as a treatment for addiction, further exploration of the topic's connection to Islamic practices and tradition is merited. It is such a recent development to talk about Islamic mindfulness in relation to health in the West that the theoretical and empirical research is limited, hence the importance of books like this.

One area of exploration that would be useful is to delve into older texts in the Islamic tradition in Arabic, Persian, Turkish, or other ancient languages of Muslim-majority countries and see if there is any older literature on the topic that supports the modern research we have seen over the last 50 years. Work of this type would serve multiple purposes. One would further establish mindfulness as a transcultural practice that crosses religious, temporal, and geographic boundaries. Another would be finding older work on mindfulness in Islam that would reveal the Islamic foundations of the practice more clearly, apart from the influence of modern trends.

Aside from seeking out less well-known sources in non-English languages, it might be fruitful to look for any mindfulness practices that may have been present in Islamic societies that had greater contact with Buddhism, like India, Malaysia, and Indonesia. It would be surprising if these contexts have not produced a variety of iterations of Islamic mindfulness based on local indigenous Islamic understandings of mindfulness and Buddhist concepts.

Some of the importance of these types of explorations would be to understand better how to apply Islamic mindfulness to the treatment of pain, emotional distress, psychological problems, and, of course, addiction. It would also be fruitful to understand an Islamic perspective on mindfulness practices apart from Western influences to see new and more precise ways of benefiting people in need of healing and help.

Additionally, apart from research in mindfulness practices that have developed independently of the West, there is a need to continue to research and theorize the post-Western development of mindfulness in Islam. Some of this work needs to be empirical research on the concrete and measurable impact of Islamic mindfulness practices on physical and psychological health, specifically addiction treatment.

Research on the benefits, for example, of meditation on the Quran through listening, has great possibilities. While recent and superficial connections are made in the literature between mindfulness and listening to and reciting the Quran, as shown by the few articles reviewed here, it remains largely undeveloped. However, significant empirical research shows the benefits of listening to the Quran. This research would be easy to develop in relation to the literature on mindfulness generally.

For example, researchers in Iran did a systematic review of articles on the reduction of anxiety through listening to the Quran and, in their review of 28 articles, found that all but one of the studies showed a positive benefit for the reduction of anxiety (Ghiasi & Keramat, 2018). Another group of researchers (Kannan et al., 2022) reviewed 13 articles on electroencephalography (EEG) and magnetoencephalography (MEG) and found evidence that listening to the Quran affects Alpha and theta neuronal oscillation in brain waves in a way that has pleasing and calming effects as a psycho-spiritual form of therapy. Additionally, researchers (Che et al., 2022) have studied the beneficial effects of listening to and memorizing the Quran, including easing depression and anxiety, physiologic parameters, quality of life, quality of sleep, and the intelligence quotient.

This research on the health benefits of listening to the Quran has possible implications for the treatment of addiction, as stress reduction, psycho-spiritual health, and other factors greatly impact rates of recovery. This area is just beginning to be explored, as a recent article on the connection between Quran recitation, mindfulness, and wellness in COVID-19 patients shows (Malek et al., 2022). However, the lack of literature connecting mindfulness generally to simple practices like listening to the Quran indicates the immense amount of further research needed. Additionally, the integration of mindfulness with Islamic practices like listening to the Quran and addiction treatment are woefully underdeveloped. In fact, all of the aforementioned articles in this paragraph state that their work is intended to be the basis for much more research into the topic.

Conclusion

With the crisis of addiction and mental health that is pervasive both in society as a whole and the Muslim community specifically, the proven beneficial effects of mindfulness indicate a need for more research on Islamic mindfulness practices. The possibilities go far beyond just the needs of the Muslim community, just as the use of Buddhist mindfulness techniques has been utilized by innumerable non-Buddhist people seeking their benefits.

It is easy for Muslims to see how people who do not perform the salaat could turn on the Quran in their cars or their homes and derive benefit from it, and with further research, this could be more widely accepted. Additionally, a better understanding of the value of reflection and contemplation on mental well-being could benefit non-Muslims and Muslims alike. For example, more research on the health benefits of simply sitting and calming the mind through reflection on the natural world could encourage people to utilize this as a spiritual practice.

Specifically, for people who have a substance use disorder, especially Muslims, the current development of the literature, at least in English, remains in its beginning stages. Being able to encourage the use of dhikr in Islamic addiction treatment settings, or the practice of reflection for motivation and change, could improve outcomes and alleviate suffering. The increasing research on the parallels between Islamic practices and mainstream medical interventions indicates the extensive possibilities of developing Islamic mindfulness. Further development of these ideas has great potential benefits for society in the short term with the current mental health crisis and in the long term in our understanding of spiritual development and overall wellness.

References

Abdul-Rahman, Z. (2017a). Islamic spirituality and mental well-being. Yaqeen Institute. https://yaqeeninstitute.org/read/paper/islamic-spirituality-and-mental-well-being

Abdul-Rahman, Z. (2017). The lost art of contemplation. Yaqeen Institute. https://yaqeeninstitute.org/read/paper/the-lost-art-of-contemplation - ftnt54

Adisa, A., & Steiner, J.A. (2021). *Overcoming addiction: An Islamic approach to recovery: 12 Steps for the Muslim & the Muslim Addiction Recovery Program.* Tayba Foundation.

Ahmed, S., Abu-Ras., W., & Arfken, C. (2014). Prevalence of risk behaviors among U.S. Muslim college students, *Journal of Muslim Mental Health, 8* (1). https://doi.org/10.3998/jmmh.10381607.0008.101

Ahmed, S., & Doukas, N. (2016). Substance use among Muslims residing in the United States: A literature review. *Journal of Alcoholism Drug Abuse & Substance Dependence, 2*:006. http://10.24966/ADSD-9594/100006

Al-Ghazali. (2014). *Mukthasar: Ihya ulum ad-din.* (Khalaf, M., Ed. and Trans.) Spohr Publishers Limited.

American Society of Addiction Medicine (ASAM). (2011). Public Policy Statement: Definition of Addiction. Chevy Chase, MD: American Society of Addiction Medicine. https://www.asam.org/docs/default-source/public-policy-statements/1definition_of_addiction_long_4-11.pdf

Angha, N. (1991). *Principles of Sufism.* Fremont, CA: Asian Humanities.

Azeemi, K. (2005). *Muraqaba: The art and science of Sufi meditation.* Plato.

Badri, M. (2000). *Contemplation: An Islamic psychospiritual study.* London: IIIT.

Bowen, S., Chawla, N., Collins, S. E., Witkiewitz, K., Hsu, S., Grow, J., Clifasefi, S., Garner, M., Douglass, A., Larimer, M. E., & Marlatt, A. (2009). Mindfulness-Based Relapse Prevention for Substance Use Disorders: A Pilot Efficacy Trial. *Substance Abuse, 30*(4), 295-305. https://doi.org/10.1080/08897070903250084

Che Wan Mohd Rozali, W. N. A., Ishak, I., Mat Ludin, A. F., Ibrahim, F. W., Abd Warif, N. M., & Che Roos, N. A. (2022). The Impact of

Listening to, Reciting, or Memorizing the Quran on Physical and Mental Health of Muslims: Evidence from Systematic Review. *International Journal of Public Health, 67.* https://doi.org/10.3389/ijph.2022.1604998

Connors, G. J., Maisto, S. A., & Donovan, D. M. (1996). Conceptualizations of relapse: a summary of psychological and psychobiological models. *Addiction, 91*: 5–13.

Davis, G. W. (1948) Sufism from its Origins to Al-Ghazali. *The Muslim World (Hartford), 38* (4), 241–256. https://doi.org/10.1111/j.1478-1913.1948.tb00983.x

Dukes, K. (2023). Quran Dictionary - ذ ك ر. *The Quranic Arabic Corpus.* University of Leeds.

Fortney, L., & Taylor, M. (2010). Meditation in medical practice: a review of the evidence and practice. *Primary Care, 37*(1):81–90. https://doi.org/10.1016/j.pop.2009.09.0

Ghiasi, A., & Keramat, A. (2018). The Effect of Listening to Holy Quran Recitation on Anxiety: A Systematic Review. *Iranian journal of nursing and midwifery research, 23*(6), 411–420. https://doi.org/10.4103/ijnmr.IJNMR_173_17

Hodge, D., & Nadir, A. (2008). Moving toward culturally competent practice with Muslims: Modifying cognitive therapy with Islamic tenets. *Social Work, 53* (1), 31–41. https://doi.org/10.1093/sw/53.1.31

Isgandarova, N. (2023). Murāqaba as a Mindfulness-based Therapy in Islamic Psychotherapy. In A. Haque & A. Rothman (Eds.) *Clinical Applications in Islamic Psychology* (pp. 109–134). International Association of Islamic Psychology.

Kabat-Zinn, J. (2013). *Full Catastrophe Living.* Bantam Books.

Kamali, M.H. (2006). Reading the Signs: The Qur'anic Perspective on Thinking. Malta: International Institute of Advanced Science (IAIS).

Kannan, M. A., Ab Aziz, N. A. A., Ab Rani, N. S., Abdullah, M. W., Mohd Rashid, M. H., Shab, M. S., Ismail, N. I., Ab Ghani, M. A., Reza, F., & Muzaimi, M. (2022). A review of the holy Quran listening and its neural correlation for its potential as a psycho-spiritual therapy. *Heliyon, 8*(12), e12308. https://doi.org/10.1016/j.heliyon.2022.e12308

Kesharvarzi, H., & Haque, A. (2013). Outlining a psychotherapy model for enhancing Muslim mental health within an Islamic context. *The International Journal for the Psychology of Religion, 23,* 230-249.

Khan, H. I. (1991). *The mysticism of sound and music.* Boston, MA: Shambhala.

Khan, P. V. I. (1994). *That which transpires behind that which appears: The experience of Sufism.* Omega Publications.

Learn-Islam. (2023). *Tips for attaining kushoo in prayer.* Learn-Islam. https://learn-islam.org/class10-khushoo

Ludwig, D. S., & Kabat-Zinn, J. (2008). Mindfulness in Medicine. *JAMA, 300* (11):1350–1352.

Ma, X., Yue, Z.-Q., Gong, Z.-Q., Zhang, H., Duan, N.-Y., Shi, Y.-T., Wei, G.-X., & Li, Y.-F. (2017). The effect of diaphragmatic breathing on attention, negative affect, and stress in healthy adults. *Frontiers in Psychology,* 8, 874. https://doi.org/10.3389/fpsyg.2017.00874

Malek, J. A., Hasan, A. Z., Rahman, A. Z., Khairuddin, W. H., Muhamad, S. N., Said, S. M., & Tahir, Z. (2022). Significance of mindfulness, Al-Quran recital and prayer factors in coping with COVID 19 symptoms. *International Journal of Health Sciences,* 6380-6400. https://doi.org/10.53730/ijhs.v6ns6.11332

Malik, J., & Hinnells, J. (Eds.). (2006). *Sufism in the West.* Routledge.

Mallik, S., Starrels, J. L., Shannon, C., Edwards, K., & Nahvi, S. (2021). "An undercover problem in the Muslim community": A qualitative study of imams' perspectives on substance use. *Journal of Substance Abuse Treatment, 123,* 108224.

Marlatt, G. A., & Gordon, J. R. (Eds.) (1985). *Relapse Prevention: Maintenance Strategies in the Treatment of Addictive Behaviors.* New York: Guilford Press.

Mee-Lee, D. (Ed.). (2013). *The ASAM criteria: Treatment criteria for addictive, substance-related, and co-occurring conditions* (3rd ed.). The Change Companies.

Mir, G., Meer, S., Cottrell, D., McMillan, D., House, A., & Kanter, J. W. (2015). Adapted behavioural activation for the treatment of depression in Muslims. *Journal of Affective Disorders, 180,* 190–199. https://doi.org/10.1016/j.jad.2015.03.060

Mogahed, D. (2021). Substance abuse and addiction in the Muslim community: Facing Stigma and Seeking Support. *ISPU*. https://www.ispu.org/substance-abuse-and-addiction-in-the-muslim-community

Mohr, S. (2022). *Loving the present: Sufism, mindfulness, and recovery from addiction and mental illness*. Resource Publications.

Mohr, S., & Ahmed, L. (2023). Islamically Integrated Strategies for Addiction Treatment: Al-Ghazali's ʿilm-un-nafs, RCBT, MI, and the Stages of Change. In A. Haque & A. Rothman (Eds.). *Clinical Applications in Islamic Psychology* (pp. 265-282). International Association of Islamic Psychology.

Nanamoli, B. & Bodi, B. (1995). *The Middle Length Discourses of the Buddha: A New Translation of the Majjhima Nikaya*. Wisdom Publications.

Narcotics Anonymous (NA) World Service. (2008). *Narcotics Anonymous: Sixth Edition*. Narcotics Anonymous World Service.

Parrott, J. (2017). How to be a Mindful Muslim: An Exercise in Islamic Meditation. Yaqeen Institute. https://yaqeeninstitute.org/read/paper/how-to-be-a-mindful-muslim-an-exercise-in-islamic-meditation#ftnt4

Priester, P. E. (2000). Varieties of Spiritual Experience in Support of Recovery from Cocaine Dependence. *Counseling & Values*, *44*(2), 107. https://doi.org/10.1007/s11089-009-0196-8

Priester, P. E., Scherer, J., Steinfeldt, J. A., Jana-Masri, A., Jashinsky, T., Jones, J. E., & Vang, C. (2009). The frequency of prayer, meditation and holistic interventions in addictions treatment: A national survey. *Pastoral Psychology*, *58*, 315-322.

Prochaska, J. O., & DiClemente, C. C. (1983). Stages and processes of self-change of smoking: Toward an integrative model of change. *Journal of Consulting and Clinical Psychology, 51*(3), 390–395. https://doi.org/10.1037/0022-006X.51.3.390

Raslan, M. S. (2021). *The danger of personal drug abuse: Addiction and the breakdown of society* (Trans. Imran, A.). Muktabaturlirshad Publications.

Rassool, G. H. (2021). *Mother of all evils: Addictive behaviors from an Islamic perspective*. Islamic Psychology Publishing.

Sadaqaat, S. A. A. (2023). Anecdotes for reflection part 2. Ahlul Bayt Digital Islamic Library Project. https://www.al-islam.org/anecdotes-reflection-part-2-sayyid-ali-akbar-sadaaqat/24-contemplation

Salem, M. O., & Elzamzamy, K. (2023). Spiritually Focused Assistance (SFA) Program: An Islamic Protocol for Religious Cognitive Behavioral Therapy (RCBT). In A. Haque & A. Rothman (Eds.). *Clinical Applications in Islamic Psychology* (pp. 229-264). International Association of Islamic Psychology.

Substance Abuse and Mental Health Administration (SAMSHA). (2009). Recovery: A philosophy of hope and resilience. *SAMSHA News, 5* (17), 1-7. https://taadas.s3.amazonaws.com/files/682584680804252211-aphilosophyofhopeandresilience.pdf

SAMSHA. (2014). Recovery. SAMSHA National and Regional Resources. https://www.samhsa.gov/sites/default/files/samhsa-recovery-5-6-14.pdf

Teasdale, J. D., Segal, Z. V., Williams, J. M. G., Ridgeway, V. A., Soulsby, J. M., & Lau, M. A. (2000). Prevention of relapse/recurrence in major depression by mindfulness-based cognitive therapy. *Journal of Consulting and Clinical Psychology, 68*(4), 615–623. https://doi.org/10.1037//0022-006x.68.4.615

Warfield, & Goldstein, M. B. (1996). Spirituality: The Key to Recovery from Alcoholism. *Counseling and Values, 40*(3), 196–205. https://doi.org/10.1002/j.2161-007X.1996.tb00852.x

White, W. L. (1998). *Slaying the dragon: The history of addiction treatment and recovery in America*. Chestnut Health Systems.

CHAPTER 5

Easing Distress and Increasing Acceptance: Islamic Mindfulness for Patients Diagnosed with Cancer

Fyeqa I. Sheikh, PsyD

Introduction

Mindfulness, deriving from Eastern spiritual traditions, namely Buddhism, has gained recent popularity in the field of psychology. Often synonymous with meditation, mindfulness is the process by which one attends to moment-by-moment experiences. Of late, there has been increasing interest in the secularization of mindfulness practices and integration into Western psychotherapy modalities (Thomas et al., 2018).

Mindfulness-based interventions (MBIs) are currently utilized to improve coping with a variety of psychological and health-related challenges. One widely studied form of mindfulness interventions is Mindfulness-Based Stress Reduction (MBSR), developed by Jon Kabat-Zinn (Kabat-Zinn, 2003), and was initially developed as an intervention for individuals experiencing chronic pain. Its application has expanded, and it is now employed as a treatment strategy for multiple presenting health issues.

The idea of watching one's thoughts, actions, and feelings is central to the concept of mindfulness. Recently, researchers have drawn parallels between the Sufi concept of *muraqaba* and secularized mindfulness. Muraqaba means "to watch, observe, regard attentively" (Wehr et al., 1994, as cited in Parrott, 2017, p. 4). While some scholars (Isgandarova, 2019; Azeemi, 2013) have outlined specific rituals and practices that facilitate the state of muraqaba, other individuals (Parrot, 2017; Saniotis, 2015) have conceptualized the concept more broadly.

Similar to the Western concept of mindfulness, researchers (Parrot, 2017; Saniotis, 2015) have discussed the implications of applying muraqaba in everyday life, to increase one's awareness of the present moment. In contrast to Western mindfulness, however, muraqaba is grounded in Islamic theology, with the core tenet that Allah is always watchful of individuals' actions. This, in turn, encourages individuals to be mindful of their own actions.

Cancer, a chronic health condition, can generate significant distress for an individual diagnosed with the condition. Furthermore, undergoing cancer treatment can contribute to difficulties in adjustment and coping due to the side effects of treatment, existential challenges such as thinking about one's mortality, and changes in role and status (Stark & House; 2000; Ott, Norris, & Bauer, 2006).

Often, individuals diagnosed with cancer can experience difficulty accepting the diagnosis and consequently exhibit symptoms of depression and anxiety (Tsaras, et al., 2018). Additionally, those with end-stage disease, might face despair. Psychotherapeutic interventions can be helpful in reducing the symptoms of distress in patients diagnosed with cancer. One such intervention is MBSR, which has demonstrated efficacy in reducing cancer-related distress in individuals.

In light of the research on the efficacy of mindfulness-based interventions for easing cancer-related distress (Creswell, 2016; Siegel et al., 2009; Secinti et al., 2019; Ahmadiqaragezlou et al., 2019; Al-Jubouri et al., 2020), the current chapter will provide insight on the intersection of secularized mindfulness and muraqaba. The implications for employing Islamic mindfulness to improve coping for individuals diagnosed with cancer will also be discussed.

Mindfulness

Researchers consistently attempt to operationally define the term mindfulness. Mindfulness is described by Parrott (2017) as a metacognition (awareness of one's own awareness) and a self-awareness of what is happening in one's mind. According to Germer (2004), mindfulness can refer to a theoretical construct (mindfulness), a practice to facilitate mindfulness (meditation), or a psychological process (being mindful).

The word mindfulness is derived from the word "sati" in Buddhism. Sati refers to awareness, attention, and remembering (Germer, 2004).

Definitions of mindfulness often include an awareness and attention to the present moment (Creswell, 2016). Other terms considered adjacent to mindfulness are "watchfulness" (Creswell, 2016), non-judgment (Germer, 2004), approaching with curiosity (Bishop et al., 2004), and decentering and disidentification (Didonna, 2009).

Creswell (2016) defined mindfulness as the "process of openly attending, with awareness, to one's present moment experience" (Creswell, 2016, p. 183). Aspects of mindfulness may involve being intentional, present-centered, non-judgmental, exploratory, liberated, and a participant-observer (Germer, 2004). Conceptually, mindfulness is linked to other theoretical notions such as introspection, presence, reflective functioning, deautomization and decentering (Bishop et al., 2004).

The concept of mindfulness is often contrasted with the idea of mindlessness, or acting with little awareness. Kabat-Zinn describes this phenomenon as "automatic pilot" (Kabat-Zinn, 2011). Throughout our day, we might engage in routine activities, such as eating or driving, without awareness or attention to the present moment. For instance, when driving to work, we might arrive with little awareness of the steps involved in reaching the destination. Mindlessness can contribute to carelessness, forgetfulness, inattention, rumination, preoccupation with the past or future, and lack of attunement to inner thoughts, feelings and sensations (Germer, 2004).

In addition to presence of mind, definitions of mindfulness commonly include an attitude of acceptance toward one's present experience. For instance, the following definition is offered by researchers at the Institute for Meditation and Psychotherapy: "Awareness of the present experience, with acceptance" (Germer et al., 2005 as cited in Siegel et al., 2009, p. 18).

Whereas acceptance is implied in the Buddhist understanding of mindfulness, in a psychotherapy context, explicitly turning one's mind towards acceptance can aid in adjustment when faced with difficult experiences and suffering (Germer, 2004). Converging themes in the aforementioned definitions of mindfulness include awareness, presence, non-judgment, and acceptance. Goals of secularized mindfulness practice include turning one's mind to the present, decreasing rumination, untangling oneself from negative thoughts and emotions, and to decrease suffering.

Mindfulness in Islam

Mindfulness in Islam is synonymous with the word "muraqaba." Muraqaba derives from the Arabic word, *raqeeb*, which means to "watch over", "take care of," or "keep an eye on (Isgandarova, 2019). Muraqaba is rooted in Sufism (*tasawwuf* in Arabic) which is Islamic spirituality or mysticism (Isgandarova, 2019). The goal of Sufism is to achieve closeness with Allah while also maintaining an Islamic code of conduct.

Isgandarova (2019) discusses Ibn Aarabi's four levels of understanding in Sufi practice. These include *shari'ah* (religious law), *tariqah* (mystical path), *haqiqah* (truth), and *ma'rifah* (gnosis). Much of the groundwork and underpinnings of Islamic Psychology is paved by Sufism, as this "science of the self" is concerned with knowing oneself (insight) and self-betterment (Mohr, 2022).

Sufi concepts also provide a strong foundation for Islamic psychotherapy (Isgandarova, 2019). For instance, understanding the importance of managing the *nafs* (ego, soul, or self) in emotional and spiritual diseases is translated into reducing symptoms of depressed mood and anxiety in Western psychotherapy terms. There are many definitions of Sufism. One example, according to Al-Daghistani (2016), is that it is:

Purification of the heart from the associating with created beings, separation from natural characteristics, suppression of human qualities, avoiding the temptations of the carnal soul, taking up the qualities of the spirit, attachment to the science of *abadiyya*, counselling all the community, being truly faithful to God, and following the Prophet according to the Law. (p. 16)

While similarities are drawn between muraqaba and mindfulness, there are clear distinctions. Classically, muraqaba is translated as meditation or contemplation (Isgandarova, 2019). During muraqaba, the individual engaging in meditation frees oneself from outward senses and turns inwards (Azeemi, 2013).

Similar to secularized mindfulness, during muraqaba, there is an emphasis on observing one's inner thoughts, reflections, and ideas (Al-Daghistani, 2016). In contrast to secularized mindfulness, the goal of muraqaba is not only to increase one's awareness of the present moment, but also to develop proper character and *ihsan* (realization of good and beautiful; Al-Daghistani, 2016).

When the Prophet (pbuh) asked the angel Jibrael what *ihsan* means, he responded with, "To worship God as if you see Him, for even though you may not see Him, He (always) sees you" (al-Qushayri, 2007). This hadith exemplifies the process of muraqaba. Thus, the core differentiation in Islamic mindfulness is awareness of Allah's presence and to observe one's thoughts, feelings, and actions in service of the Almighty.

104

Azeemi (2013) describes the practice of muraqaba as akin to the practice of mindfulness meditation. He describes the process of muraqaba as becoming "thoughtless in a thought" (Azeemi, 2013, p. 38). He further elucidates the concept as a means of contemplation (*tafakkur*) through which man can gain access to his ego or soul. The basis of muraqaba is that Allah is watching the individual and knows each individual's actions, thoughts, feelings, and inner state of mind (Khalid et al., 2021).

Goals of muraqaba include being near Allah, being conscious of His presence, and spiritual growth. The overarching goal is to be a more integrated individual as opposed to compartmentalizing spiritual and worldly aspects (Abdur Rashid, 2007). Resultant consequences of muraqaba (as opposed to the intended goals in secularized mindfulness) are stillness (*al-sakinah*), calmness, and contentment in this life (Khalid et al., 2021).

Azeemi (2013) further outlines various techniques one can utilize to practice muraqaba. These include muraqaba of colored lights and *tasawur* (imagination), amongst others. The goal of such meditations is to alleviate physiological and psychological disorders. For instance, the author suggests that meditation on blue lights is helpful for mental health challenges, whereas meditation on yellow lights helps with digestive challenges (Azeemi, 2023).

Mindfulness in the Islamic lens involves mindfulness of one's own intentions, thoughts, emotions, and inner states (Parrott, 2017). Azeemi (2013) postulates that the message in most scripture is to contemplate and engage in *salah* (prayer). He suggests the role of contemplation in everyday affairs is emphasized in Islam, citing the Quranic passage:

In the creation of earth and skies and in the daily routine of day and night, there are signs for those wise people who remember God, standing, sitting and resting and those who contemplate on the creation of skies and earth and as a result come to the conclusion that O' Our Lord, Thou has not created these with no purpose. (3:191)

Khalid et al. (2021) agree with Azeemi regarding the importance of contemplation and the centrality of salah in Islam. They assert that salah, *dhikr* (remembrance), and *taddabur* (contemplation) are nearest to the traditional technique of muraqaba. *Tahujjud* (middle of the night prayer) is a means of spiritual connection that can be observed on a daily basis (Khalid et al., 2021). The importance of tahujjud is stressed in many hadiths including the following:

Reported by Abu Hurayra (RA) that the Messenger of Allah, may Allah bless him and grant him peace, said, "Our Lord, the Blessed and

Exalted, descends to the lowest heaven every night when a third of the night remains. He says, Who is calling on Me so that I can answer him? Who is asking Me for something so that I can give to him? Who is asking Me for forgiveness so that I can forgive him?" (Sahih et al., 2003 as cited in Khalid et al., 2021)

Indeed, the remembrance of Allah through many modalities is stressed in the Quran and hadith. Focused worship through the practice of muraqaba can undoubtedly strengthen ones' ability to be present in remembrance.

Mindfulness-Based Interventions

Therapists in healthcare settings find value in the delivery of MBIs to manage aversive symptoms associated with mental health and physical health conditions (Germer, 2004; Bishop et al., 2004). Mindfulness-Based Stress Reduction (MBSR), Mindfulness-Based Cognitive Therapy (MBCT), Dialectical Behavior Therapy (DBT), and Acceptance and Commitment Therapy (ACT) are the MBIs of choice in these settings (Chisea et al., 2014).

A metanalysis demonstrated positive clinical outcomes with the use of MBIs including decreased stress, anxiety, rumination, and automatic thoughts (Chisea et al., 2014). Furthermore, symptoms decreased for individuals coping with physical health issues, including breast cancer, inflammatory bowel disease, and chronic pain (Chisea et al., 2014).

MBSR is regarded as the gold standard intervention for individuals facing health difficulties and is an eight-week program consisting of weekly sessions that are 2–2.5 hours long. In addition, the program includes one all-day session that occurs after 6–7 weeks. MBSR consists of standardized elements including body scan exercises, exercises focused on attending to one's breath, physical exercises involving being attuned to bodily sensations, and practicing being aware in daily activities (Institute for Mindfulness-Based Approaches, n.d.). MBSR and other MBIs have demonstrated efficacy (Carlson, 2012) in relieving both physiological and psychological distress in individuals diagnosed with a number of physical health conditions, including diabetes, pain, fibromyalgia, cardiovascular diseases, HIV, IBS and IBD, and cancer amongst others.

MBSR for Cancer

Cancer is the second leading cause of death in the United States (Ott et al., 2006) and is one of the leading causes of death worldwide (National Cancer Institute, n.d.). In 2019, in the United States, 1,752,735 new cancer cases were reported and 599,589 individuals died of cancer (CDC, 2022). Being diagnosed with cancer is an inherently stressful experience. Many individuals diagnosed meet criteria for anxiety and depressive disorders.

In a study of 152 individuals attending an outpatient oncology clinic who were diagnosed with breast cancer in Greece, researchers found 38.2% qualified for a diagnosis of depression and 32.2% met symptom criteria for an anxiety disorder (Tsaras et al, 2018). Due to the chronicity and high mortality rates associated with certain types of cancer, being diagnosed with cancer is threatening and therefore can be anxiety-provoking (Stark & House, 2000).

Despite the challenges associated with distinguishing pathological anxiety from expected anxiety in light of being diagnosed with cancer, disruptive experiences of anxiety that impact overall functioning can be appropriately classified as anxiety or adjustment disorders (Stark & House, 2000). Often times, the physical symptoms associated with cancer and cancer treatment can also contribute to significant anguish (i.e. nausea, fatigue, vomiting, mouth sores; Ott et al., 2006). Moreover, some physiological symptoms associated with cancer such as nausea and fatigue can also be related to the presence of anxiety (Stark & House, 2000).

Research has consistently demonstrated (Zainal, Booth, & Huppert, 2012; Carlson & Garland, 2005; Lengacher et al., 2016; Zhang, 2015; Birnie, Garland, & Carlson, 2009) MBSR is an efficacious form of treatment to reduce symptoms of depression, anxiety, and distress that accompany being diagnosed with cancer. Individuals diagnosed with cancer can experience a range of trials, from loss of control and helplessness (Ott et al., 2006), difficulties accepting the diagnosis, being faced with one's own mortality (Carlson, 2012), adjusting to changes in identity and role, to fear of disease progression and worrying about recurrence.

In a study conducted to determine the role of mindfulness and hope as an intervention for women with cancer recurrence, Thornton and colleagues (2014) found individuals in the mindfulness group exhibited decreased anxiety-related worry. Additionally, a systematic review of nine published studies demonstrated moderate to large positive effect sizes for MBSR on the mental health of breast cancer patients (Zainal et al., 2012).

Other researchers (Rouleau et al., 2015) observed a reduction in psychological distress, reduction in sleep disruption and fatigue, improvement in quality of life (QOL), and enhancement of positive well-being and spirituality. MBSR is also effective for reducing mood and sleep disturbance (Carlson & Garland, 2005; Garland et al., 2013), decreasing pain severity (Ngamkham et al., 2018), decreasing symptoms of stress

(Garland et al., 2013), mitigating distress (Shennan et al., 2011), reducing symptoms of anxiety and depression (Sarenmalm et al., 2017; Ngamkham et al., 2018; Zhang et al., 2015) and improving mood as well as quality of life (Bränström et al., 2010; Lengacher et al., 2016; Ngamkham et al., 2018).

Ludwig and Kabat-Zinn (2008) outline the mechanisms of action for mindfulness in medicine. They report mindfulness can be effective in decreasing the perception of pain severity, increasing the ability to tolerate pain, reducing symptoms of stress, anxiety or depression, reducing reliance on medications, increasing one's ability to reflect on one's choices, improving adherence, increasing motivation for health-related behaviors, and improving interpersonal relationships.

Others (Carlson, 2012) have also attempted to explain the mechanism of action for the therapeutic effects of mindfulness. The understanding that unpleasant symptoms are temporary and thus tolerable is a gateway to free oneself from suffering. Individuals who are diagnosed with health issues and practice mindfulness ruminate and worry about the future less and do not avoid painful feelings as often.

A key element in mindfulness treatment that is particularly helpful for individuals diagnosed with cancer is acceptance. According to Carlson (2012), the understanding that the only constant in life is change is a means of acceptance of one's current health status. Acceptance in MBSR is described as "letting go and letting be" (Santorelli, 2014). This process denotes acceptance of the situation just as it is without trying to fix or deny the reality.

An individual can engage in acceptance by engaging in an uncomfortable experience and being aware of one's thoughts feelings and actions (Thomas et al., 2017). Research has demonstrated acceptance of illness in cancer is associated with associated with lower anxiety and depressive symptoms (Secinti et al., 2019). Acceptance is described as a nonjudgmental and compassionate way of viewing one's illness.

Further acceptance is regarded as an active process of embracing the reality of one's illness (Secinti et al., 2019). Acceptance is contrasted with resignation, a more passive approach, and is associated with higher anxiety and depressive symptoms. Acceptance of one's illness, prognosis, and the changes that might stem from a cancer diagnosis can certainly contribute to reductions in overall suffering (Chinh et al, 2020).

Integration of Muraqaba into Western Psychotherapy Models

Historically, researchers have attempted to explore the compatibility of Islamic principles and Islamic-oriented psychotherapy with Western psychotherapy approaches (e.g., see York Al-Karam, 2018). In this vein, researchers (Thomas et al., 2017) have studied integrating Islamic principles into MBSR. These authors utilize examples from Islam in each component of MBSR. For instance, to demystify meditation and provide psychoeducation to clients about "automatic pilot" in MBSR, the authors propose using the concept of *khushu*, or humility and presence of mind during salah. During salah, it is essential that the individual fully focus on the actions and recitation to attain full benefit. While the mind can wander during salah, a believer is asked to bring one's attention back to the actions and recitations.

Isgandarova (2019) also asserts the compatibility of muraqaba with Western psychotherapy, namely cognitive therapies including MBSR, DBT, and MBCT. The author outlines how a therapist can facilitate muraqaba in the context of psychotherapy. Specific steps include the preparation stage, in which the Muslim therapist introduces the idea of Islamic mindfulness to the client (akin to the *salik* in traditional muraqaba) and encourages the client to make ablution.

The client is then encouraged to observe thoughts, feelings, and bodily sensations (Isgandarova, 2019). In addition, the client is encouraged to utilize deep breathing coupled with dhikr. This then gives way to *mushahada* (contemplation) corresponding to an improved ability to concentrate and focus. The goal is to control undesired thoughts and be aware of them through witnessing and observing.

Cognitive shifts to reduce rumination can also occur by focusing on God, the Prophet, or the Quran. It is important to note there are thoughts that the person might not be able to control, and thus there is a focus on acceptance and acknowledgement of both positive and unpleasant experiences without judgment. The author further asserts one should be properly trained in Sufi meditation prior to leading the client in these activities (Isgandarova, 2019).

Parallels are drawn between cognitive psychology and Islamic psychology in regards to automatic thoughts (al-Qushayri, 2007). Automatic thoughts, in cognitive psychology, refer to those thoughts that seem to appear in one's mind without willfulness. In Islamic psychology, automatic thoughts are regarded as *khawatir*, or inner speeches (al-Qushayri, 2007).

According to al-Qushayri (2007), khawatir can originate from four different sources: angelic (ilqa malak), satanic (ilqa shaytan), self-suggested (ahadith nafs), or divine (min a-haqq subhanahu). Scholars (Al-Daghistani, 2016) see exploring one's thoughts as a two-step, interdependent process involving both muraqaba and *muhasaba* (self-examination).

The purpose of muraqaba and muhasaba is to purify the heart and facilitate higher levels of knowledge and spiritual insight (Al-Daghistani, 2016). Through these processes, an individual becomes aware of God's presence and is observing God in one's thoughts and actions (Al-Daghistani, 2016). The process of muraqaba is defined by Imam Al-Ghazali as being "vigilant in acts of obedience through sincerity" (Al-Ghazali, 2015, p.29).

Further, Imam Al-Ghazali (2015) stresses the importance of being introspective in every moment and always being God-conscious. Self-examination in this way is seen as a catalyst for purity in intention and truthfulness in actions (Al-Daghistani, 2016). In his important work, *On Vigilance and Self-Examination* (2015), Imam Al-Ghazali writes:

> Said al-Hasan [al-Basri], 'The faithful one manages his soul and calls it to account for the sake of God. The reckoning is lighter for people who examine themselves in this world, but it will be harsher on the Day of Resurrection for those people who deal with this matter without self-examination.' (p. 34)

Thus, both MBSR and Islamic mindfulness underscore the importance of examination of one's automatic thoughts. In MBSR and other MBIs, automatic thoughts are to be acknowledged and seen as simply thoughts rather than facts (Ludwig & Kabat-Zin, 2008; Branstrom, Kvillemo, Brandberg, 2010; Thomas, Grey, and Kinderman, 2017). Similarly, as outlined above, Islamic mindfulness stresses the importance of examining thoughts and the origins of these thoughts. Introspection and self-examination are key elements in psychotherapy, therefore further emphasizing the compatibility between Islamic mindfulness and secularized psychotherapy.

In MBSR and other MBIs, mindfulness can be practiced in daily activities rather than just in a meditative state. In fact, a core component of MBSR is mindfulness in daily activities or routines. Everyday mindfulness can be practiced when eating, brushing one's teeth, making a cup of coffee, or driving (Thomas, Grey, & Kinderman, 2017).

Similarly, in the context of Islamic mindfulness, daily, ritualistic practices can ground one's awareness of Allah and increase one's remembrance of Him. Imam Al-Ghazali as discussed in Parrot (2017) outlined four daily spiritual practices aiding in remembrance of Allah: *dua*, *dhikr*, *qira'at* (recitation of the Quran), and *fikr* (contemplation).

Furthermore, there exist specific prescribed rituals in Islam that are part of one's everyday routines, which facilitate the remembrance of Allah. Examples of such rituals include facing the direction of the *qiblah* when sitting; sleeping on the right hand and facing the qiblah (Al-Ghazali, 2015); duas one engages in before going to the restroom, driving a car, or leaving the house; invoking Allah's blessings and protection before engaging in an act (saying bismillah ar-rahman ar-rahim); wearing the right side of a garment first; and stepping inside the restroom with one's left foot and leaving with one's right foot amongst others (Thomas et al., 2018).

Similarly, certain *duas* are part of one's everyday practice such as recitation of the dua before eating, before driving, and when entering or exiting a bathroom (Thomas et al., 2017). Certainly, the prescription of salah upon a believer is a ritualistic, mindful act facilitating the remembrance of Allah five times daily. The routine nature of salah is exemplified by the following Quranic verse: "Surely the salah at fixed hours (of the day and night) has been enjoined upon the believers" (Quran 4:103).

The purpose of salah, similar to other acts of mindful worship, is to establish reconnection with Allah. It also serves as a means of self-examination of one's behaviors: "Verily, salah restrains (oneself) from shameful and unjust deeds..." (Quran 29:45). These acts of daily remembrance reorient our attention to the present, with the knowledge that Allah is watching us and our actions.

Another spiritual act that can help us achieve the goal of Islamic mindfulness is being in seclusion. It is stated that the Prophet (pbuh) spent time in silence and seclusion (Parrott, 2017). Observing silence and reflection can also be practiced through activities such as *itikaf* or isolation that some take part in during the last ten days of Ramadan (Khalid, et al., 2021; Saniotis, 2015). In certain Sufi orders such as the Khlwatiyya, Shadhiliyya, and Chistiyya, *khalwa* or spiritual seclusion is prescribed during which the individual engages in focused dhikr (Hill, 2019).

These practices hold implications for Islamic psychotherapy. For example, one option could be for psychotherapists to prescribe the invocation of Allah as a means of attending with awareness to one's thoughts, feelings, and actions while reinforcing the intentionality and remembrance of Allah in each deed.

Integration of Islamic Mindfulness for Patients Diagnosed with Cancer

As illustrated above, an individual diagnosed with cancer can exhibit signs of depression, anxiety, and distress. The case for mindfulness-based interventions, specifically MBSR has been well-established in the existing research. Despite apparent distinctions between secularized and Islamic mindfulness, it is hypothesized that the positive benefits achieved from mindfulness interventions would generalize to the applicability of Islamic mindfulness in these contexts.

In fact, research has demonstrated the impact of dhikr therapy for reducing anxiety in cancer patients (Sulistyawati et al., 2019). In that study, dhikr therapy was administered at least once a day for a minimum of ten minutes per day. Significant differences in anxiety levels between the intervention group and control group were observed.

Similarly, a study on the impact of recitation of the Quran on chemotherapy-induced anxiety demonstrated reduced anxiety in patients listening to the recitation of the Quran during chemotherapy (Al-Jubouri et al., 2021). As mentioned previously, researchers have demonstrated the successful integration of Islamic mindfulness into Western mindfulness. There exists a paucity of research, however, on implications of employing Islamic mindfulness as a means of coping with health issues, specifically cancer.

Rumination in patients diagnosed with cancer can undeniably contribute to significant distress. Worry about one's mortality, fear of disease progression, and anxiety about cancer recurrence after remission are concerns routinely faced by individuals diagnosed with cancer. Indeed, the impact of mindfulness interventions, specifically MBSR, for reducing cancer-related worry has been well-documented in the research.

One of the major departures from traditional mindfulness in muraqaba is the connection with spiritual aspects of Islam and the knowledge of Allah's ever-presence. Engagement in traditional Sufi meditation can be practiced as a means of decreasing anxious rumination as demonstrated in the research (Gul & Jehangir, 2019), while other daily Islamic practices can also help bring one's attention back to the present moment.

For instance, Imam Al-Ghazali (2015) has conceptualized muraqaba as vigilance of Allah that is present every waking moment of one's life. Rather than engaging in a specific meditative practice, individuals can be mindful of Allah when they catch themselves ruminating about their illness. Specific Islamic practices can aid in combatting rumination effectively. Dua and salah with sincerity and presence of mind (khushu) can help an individual cope with rumination and can be a mindful practice (Thomas et al., 2018). Focusing on or attending to a specific verse in the Quran can also be helpful in decreasing rumination. For instance, the Qur'anic verse: "For indeed with hardship will be ease" (Quran; 94:5) can be a focal point for meditative practice to decrease anxious rumination.

Often times, distress that accompanies being diagnosed with cancer originates from challenges with acceptance of the diagnosis. One of the core tenets of mindfulness as emphasized previously is acceptance of the present reality, in MBSR termed, "letting go and letting be" (Thomas et al., 2018). *Sabr,* or patience, in Islam can correspond to the notion of acceptance. From the vantage point of sabr, being diagnosed with cancer can be seen as a test or trial from Allah and can lead to acceptance of the situation without attempting to fix or deny reality.

Sabr has also been defined as being able to bear adversity (Aoude, n.d.) and thus trusting in Allah's will. Once individuals accept their fate without denying reality, it enables them to engage in necessary problem-solving such as pursuing further diagnostic testing, engaging in cancer treatment, and coping more effectively with the illness.

The concept of *sabr* can also be effective strategy to manage the distress associated with cancer treatment itself. The importance of patience in the face of adversity has been repeatedly mentioned in the Quran, as exemplified by the verse: "And certainly, We shall test you with something of fear, hunger, loss of wealth, lives and fruits, but give glad tidings to the patient ones" (Quran 2:155).

Tanhan (2019) discusses the compatibility of ACT with Islam. ACT also involves components of mindfulness and similar to MBSR, the goal is acceptance of the present experience. The author draws similarities between the interpretation of pain and unpleasant experiences in ACT and Islam. Both regard suffering and pain as normal life experiences one must accept rather than normalcy being tied to the absence of suffering.

In patients with terminal cancer diagnoses, feelings of despair can be prevalent. Muraqaba can be an antidote to end-of-life despair. Similar to secularized mindfulness, one can witness the gains of muraqaba expand beyond the meditative space and apply to everyday life. In a mindfulness of feelings approach, feelings are viewed as temporary, and the goal is to acknowledge feelings without resigning oneself to them.

Mindfulness of Allah and trust in the path He has laid out for us is central to a Muslim's faith. Trusting in divine will can also help ease distress. Analogous to the theoretical concept of acceptance is the ideology of *rida* (contentment, satisfaction, good pleasure). Rida is seen as an active surrendering to divine will (Khalil, 2014). Islamic scholars have posited that no matter how trying life circumstances might be, one should respond without bitterness and discontentment (Khalil, 2014). In this vein, individuals can accept their terminal illness with understanding that it is Allah's decree. Khalil (2014) points out that more recent scholars such as Makki have clarified that individuals can express their feelings of grief and at the same time, possess the ability to accept Allah's divine will.

While acceptance of one's fate is one way of coping with adversity, engagement in classical muraqaba can also be helpful. One form of muraqaba commonly practiced in the Naqshbandi order is Muraqaba-e-Isme Zaat or the visualization of the sacred name (Kashmir, n.d.). In this meditation, an individual visualizes the name of Allah on his heart and focuses on nothing but Allah. The individual breathes in and says "Allah" and breathes out and says "Hu" either silently or aloud.

During this time, the individual also focuses on the attributes of Allah. The idea that Allah has 99 names and attributes is part of Islamic teachings. The focus on these attributes, such as As-Salam, the one who gives peace, can be particularly helpful. This strategy coupled with dhikr can ease sorrow that arises from the eventuality of one's fate. The focus on one's actions in the present moment can provide respite from projecting into the future.

As mentioned previously, engagement in muraqaba in a meditative way can create calmness and stillness, which can be a psychological buffer for feelings of depression and despair. Studies have consistently demonstrated how spirituality can provide relief from suffering and despair in individuals diagnosed with cancer, specifically those with terminal diagnoses (McClain-Jacobson et al., 2004; Williams, 2006), thus highlighting the significance of spiritual connection as an aid for coping with illness.

Conclusions and Future Directions

Based on the research on the positive impact of MBSR and other mindfulness-based strategies on coping with cancer, conclusions can be drawn about how muraqaba, too, can be a beneficial intervention. While MBSR and other MBIs have been well-studied in the literature, the research on the integration of muraqaba into Western psychotherapies is far more limited. The current chapter attempts to scratch the surface in regards to how muraqaba can be an effective strategy to manage the distress brought on by a cancer diagnosis. Undoubtedly, far more research is needed in this area.

Mindfulness is regarded as an antidote to not only the distress that emerges from physiological health conditions, but as a means of holistically reducing suffering in one's life that comes from attachment to thoughts and feelings. While Muslims invariably invoke Allah in all of their actions, engaging in practices that serve as reminders of Allah's presence strengthens the place of Allah in our lives. Islamic mindfulness encourages not only examination of one's thoughts and feelings, but also one's actions and intentions. Indeed, physical illness, especially cancer, has the potential to contribute to great agony. Employing muraqaba as a therapeutic strategy has the potential to promote an overall reduction in suffering through trust in Allah's will and reliance on Him.

References

Al-Daghistani, R. (2016). Mindfulness and Self-Examination in Sufism. KUD Logos. http://kud-logos.si/2016/mindfulness/

Al-Ghazali, A.H. (2015). On Vigilance and Self-Examination. Islamic Texts Society.

Al-Jubouri, M. B., Isam, S. R., Hussein, S. M., & Machuca-Contreras, F. (2021). Recitation of quran and music to reduce chemotherapy-induced anxiety among adult patients with cancer: A clinical trial. *Nursing Open*, *8*(4), 1606–1614. https://doi.org/10.1002/nop2.781

al-Qushayri, A. (2007). *Al-Qushayri's epistle on Sufism*. Garnett Publishing Limited.

Aoude, S. (n.d.). The Concept of Sabr in Islamic Spiritual Care–Definitions and Contextual Adaptations. Retrieved from: https://www.academia.edu/25631939/The_concept_of_sabr_in_Islamic_spiritual_care_definitions_and_contextual_adaptions

Azeemi, K. S. (2013) Muraqaba: The Art and Science of Sufi Meditation. Azeemi University Press.

Bishop, S. R., Lau, M., Shapiro, S., Carlson, L., Anderson, N. D., Carmody, J., Segal, Z. V., Abbey, S., Speca, M., Velting, D., & Devins, G. (2004). Mindfulness: A proposed operational definition. *Clinical Psychology: Science and Practice*, *11*(3), 230–241. https://doi.org/10.1093/clipsy.bph077

Bränström, R., Kvillemo, P., Brandberg, Y., & Moskowitz, J. T. (2010). Self-report mindfulness as a mediator of psychological well-being in a stress reduction intervention for cancer patients—a randomized study. *Annals of Behavioral Medicine*, *39*(2), 151–161. https://doi.org/10.1007/s12160-010-9168-6

Carlson, L. E. (2012). Mindfulness-based interventions for physical conditions: A narrative review evaluating levels of evidence. *ISRN Psychiatry*, 2012, 1–21. https://doi.org/10.5402/2012/651583

Carlson, L. E., & Garland, S. N. (2005). Impact of mindfulness-based stress reduction (MBSR) on sleep, mood, stress and fatigue symptoms in cancer outpatients. *International Journal of Behavioral Medicine*, *12*(4), 278–285. https://doi.org/10.1207/s15327558ijbm1204_9

Carlson, L. E., Labelle, L. E., Garland, S. N., Hutchins, M. L, & Brinie, K. (2009). Mindfulness-based interventions in oncology. In Didonna, F. (Ed.). *Clinical Handbook of Mindfulness*. Springer.

Centers for Disease Control and Prevention. (2022, June 6). U.S. cancer statistics: Highlights from 2019 incidence. Centers for Disease Control and Prevention. Retrieved August 24, 2022 from https://www.cdc.gov/cancer/uscs/about/data-briefs/no29-USCS-highlights-2019-incidence.htm

Chinh, K., Secinti, E., Johns, S. A., Hirsh, A. T., Miller, K. D., Schneider, B., Storniolo, A. M., Mina, L., Newton, E. V., Champion, V. L., & Mosher, C. E. (2020). Relations of mindfulness and illness acceptance with psychosocial functioning in patients with metastatic breast cancer and caregivers. *Oncology Nursing Forum, 47*(6), 739-752. https://doi.org/10.1188/20.ONF.739-752

Chisea, A., Anselmi, R., & Serretti, A. (2014). Psychological mechanisms of mindfulness-based interventions: What do we know? *Holistic Nursing Practice, 28*(2), 124-148. https://doi.org/10.1097/HNP.0000000000000017

Creswell, J. D. (2016). Mindfulness interventions. *The Annual Review of Psychology, 68*(18), 18.1-18/26. https://doi.org/10.1146/annurev-psych-042716-051139

de Vibe, M., Hammerstrom, K., Kowalski, K., & Bjorndal, A. (2010). *Protocol: Mindfulness*-Based Stress Reduction (MBSR) for Improving Health and Social Functioning in Adults. Campbell Collaboration.

Didonna, F. (2009). Introduction: Where new and old paths to dealing with suffering meet. Clinical Handbook of Mindfulness. Springer. https:// doi.org/10.1007/978-0-387-09593-6

Dobkin, P. L. (2008). Mindfulness-based stress reduction: What processes are at work? *Complementary Therapies in Clinical Practice, 14*, 8-16. https://doi.org/10.1016/j.ctcp.2007.09.004

Garland, S. N., Tamagawa, R., Todd, S. C., Speca, M. & Carlson, L.E. (2013). Increased mindfulness is related to improved stress and mood following participation in mindfulness stress reduction program in individuals with cancer. *Integrative Cancer Therapies, 12*(1), 31-40. https://doi.org/10.1177/1534735412442370

Germer, C. (2004). What is mindfulness? *Insight Journal, Fall 2024*, 27-29.

Germer, C. K., Siegel, R. D., & Fulton, P. R. (2005). *Mindfulness and Psychotherapy*. Guilford Press.

Gul, L. & Jehangir, S.F. (2019). Effects of mindfulness on anxiety and mental health of females. *Pakistan Journal of Psychological Research*, *34*(3), 583-599, https://doi.org/10.33824/PJPR.2019.34.3.32

Hill, J. (2021). Sufism Between Past and Modernity. In: Lukens-Bull, R., Woodward, M. (eds) Handbook of Contemporary Islam and Muslim Lives. Springer, Cham. https://doi.org/10.1007/978-3-030-32626-5_9

Institute for Mindfulness-Based Approaches. (n.d.). *What is MBSR?* Retrieved August 31, 2022, from https://www.institute-for-mindfulness.org/offer/mbsr/what-is-mbsr4o

Kabat-Zinn, J. (2003). Mindfulness-based interventions in context: Past, present, and future. *Clinical Psychology: Science and Practice*, *10*(2), 144-156. https://doi.org/10.1093/clipsy/bpg016

Kabat-Zinn, J. (2011). Some reflections on the origins of MBSR, skillful means, and the trouble with maps. *Contemporary Buddhism*, *12*(1), 281-306. https://doi.org/10.1080/14639947.2011.564844

Kashmir Thunder. (n.d.). *Muraqaba – Dhikr/remembrance of Allah through meditation of the heart*. Kashmir Thunder. Retrieved August 31, 2022, from https://kashmirthunder.com/2017/03/18/muraqaba-dhikrremembrance-of-allah-through-meditation-of-the-heart/

Kenne Sarenmalm, E., Mårtensson, L. B., Andersson, B. A., Karlsson, P., & Bergh, I. (2017). Mindfulness and its efficacy for psychological and biological responses in women with breast cancer. *Cancer Medicine*, *6*(5), 1108–1122. https://doi.org/10.1002/cam4.1052

Khalid, I., Gulzar, S., & Amin, M. (2021). A critical review of Shamsuddin Azeemi's "Muraqabah" through the lens of Quran and Hadith. *Journal of Islamic Thought and Civilization*, *11*(1), 302-317. Doi: https://doi.org/10.32350/jitc.111.16

Khalil, A. (2014). Contentment, satisfaction, and good-pleasure: Rida in early Sufi moral psychology. *Studies in Religion*, 1-19. https://doi.org/10.1177/0008429814538227

Isgandarova, N. (2019). Muraqaba as a mindfulness-based therapy in Islamic Psychotherapy. *Journal of Religion and Health*, *58*, 1146-1160. https//doi.org/10.1007/s10943-018-0695-y(01

Lengacher, C. A., Reich, R. R., Paterson, C. L., Ramesar, S., Park, J. Y., Alinat, C., Johnson-Mallard, V., Moscoso, M., Budhrani-Shani, P., Miladinovic, B., Jacobsen, P. B., Cox, C. E., Goodman, M., & Kip, K. E. (2016). Examination of broad symptom improvement resulting from mindfulness-based stress reduction in breast cancer survivors: A randomized controlled trial. *Clinical Oncology, 34*(24), 2827-2834. https://doi.org/ 10.1200/JCO.2015.65.7874

Ludwig, D. S. & Kabat-Zinn, J. (2008). Mindfulness in medicine. *JAMA, 300*(11), 1350-1352. https://doi.org/10.1001/jama.300.11.1350

McClain-Jacobson, C., Rosenfeld, B., Kosinski, A., Pessin, H., Cimino, J. E., & Breitbart, W. (2004). Belief in afterlife, spiritual well-being and end-of-life despair in patients with advanced cancer. *General Hospital Psychiatry, 26*(2004), 484-486. https://doi.org/10.1016/j.genhosppsych.2004.08.002

Mohr, S. H. (2022). Loving the Present: Sufism, Mindfulness, and Recovery from Addiction. Resource Publications.

National Cancer Institute. (n.d.). Cancer statistics. Retrieved August 15, 2022, from https://www.cancer.gov/about-cancer/understanding/statistics

Ngamkham, S., Holden, J. E., & Smit, E. L. (2018). A systematic review: Mindfulness intervention for cancer-related pain. *Asia-Pacific Journal of Oncology Nursing, 6*(2), 161-169. https://doi.org/10.4103/apjon.apjon_67_18

Ott, M., Norris, R. L, & Bauer-Wu, S. M. (2006). Mindfulness meditation for oncology: A discussion and critical review. *Integrative Cancer Therapies, 5*(2), 98-108. https:// 10.1177/1534735406288083

Parrott, J. (2017). *How to be a mindful Muslim: An exercise in Islamic meditation*. Yaqeen Institute for Islamic Research. Retrieved July 10.1016/j.cpr.2019.05.00114, 2022, from https://yaqeeninstitute.org/read/paper/how-to-be-a-mindful-muslim-an-exercise-in-islamic-meditation

Rouleau, C. R., Garland, S. N., & Carlson, L. E. (2015). The impact of mindfulness-based interventions on symptom burden, positive psychological outcomes, and biomarkers in cancer patients. *Cancer Management and Research, 7*, 121-131.

Saniotis, A. (2015). Understanding mind/body medicine form Muslim religious practices of salat and dhikr. *Journal of Religion and Health, 57*(3), 849-857, https://doi.org/10.1007/s10943-014-9992-2

Santorelli, S.F. (2014). Mindfulness-based stress reduction (MBSR): Standards of practice. Center for Mindfulness in Medicine, Health Care, & Society. Retrieved from: https://mindfulness.au.dk/fileadmin/mindfulness.au.dk/Artikler/Santorelli_mbsr_standards_of_practice_2014.pdf

Secinti, E., Tometich, D.B., Johns, S.A. &Mosher, C.E. (2019). The relationship between acceptance of cancer and distress: A meta-analytic review. *Clinical Psychology Review, 71,* 27-38. https://doi. 10.1016/j.cpr.2019.05.001

Shennan, C., Payne, S., & Fenlon, D. (2010). What is the evidence for the use of mindfulness-based interventions in cancer care? *A Review. Psycho-Oncology,* *20*(7), 681–697. https://doi.org/10.1002/pon.1819

Siegel, R. D., Germer, C. K., & Oldendzki, A. (2009). Mindfulness; What is it? Where did it come from? In Diodonna F. (Ed.). *Clinical Handbook of Mindfulness.* Springer.

Stark, D. P. H., & House, A. (2000). Anxiety in cancer patients. *British Journal of Cancer, 83*(10), 1261-1267. https://doi.org/10.1054/bjoc.2000.1405

Sulistyawati, R. A., Probosuseno, & Setiyarini, S. (2019). Dhikr therapy for reducing anxiety in cancer patients. *Asia-Pacific Journal of Oncology Nursing,* *6*(4), 411–416. https://doi.org/10.4103/apjon.apjon_33_19

Tanhan, A. (2019). Acceptance and commitment therapy with ecological systems theory: Addressing Muslim mental health issues and wellbeing. *Journal of Positive Psychology & Wellbeing, 3*(2), 197-219. https://doi.org/10.47602/jpsp.v312.172

Thomas, J., Furber, S. W., & Grey, I. (2018). The rise of mindfulness and its resonance with the Islamic tradition. *Mental Health, Religion & Culture,* *20*(10), 973-985. https://doi.org/10.1080/13674676.2017.1412410

Thomas, J., Grey, I., & Kinderman, P. (2017). Exploring culturally attuned mindfulness based stress reduction (MBSR) as a means of improving quality of life, emotional well being, and academic performance of Emirati college students. *Working Papers*, 24.

Thornton, L. M., Cheavens, J. S., Heitzmann, C. A., Dorfman, C. S., Wu, S. M., & Andersen, B. L. (2014). Test of mindfulness and hope components in a psychological intervention for women with cancer recurrence. *Journal of Consulting and Clinical Psychology, 82*(6), 1087-1100. https://doi.org/10.1037/a0036959

Tsaras, K., Papathanasiou, I.V., Mitsi, D., Veneti, A., Kelesi, M., Zyga, S., & Fradelos, E.C. (2018). Assessment of depression and anxiety in breast cacner patients: Prevalence and associated factors. *Asian Pacific Journal of Cancer Prevention, 19*(6), 1661-1669. https://doi.10.22034/APJCP.2018.19.6.1661

Williams, A. (2006). Perspective on spirituality at the end of life: A meta-summary. *Palliative and Supportive Care, 4*, 407-417. https://doi.org/10.10170S1478951506060500

York Al-Karam, C. (2018). Islamically Integrated Psychotherapy: Uniting Faith and Professional Practice. Templeton Press.

Zainal, N. Z., Booth, S. & Huppert, F. A. (2012). The efficacy of mindfulness-based stress reduction on mental health of breast cancer patients: a meta-analysis. *Psycho-Oncology, 22*(7), 1457-1465. https://doi.org/10.1002/pon.3171

Zhang, M.-F., Wen, Y.-S., Liu, W.-Y., Peng, L.-F., Wu, X.-D., & Liu, Q.-W. (2015). Effectiveness of mindfulness-based therapy for reducing anxiety and depression in patients with cancer. *Medicine, 94*(45). https://doi.org/10.1097/md.0000000000000897

—————— ◄•►•◄ ——————

Mindfulness Meditation for the Management of Chronic Pain: An Islamic Approach

Dr. Razia Bhatti – Ali

Surely, in this, there is a reminder for one who has a [mindful] heart or lends an ear as a witness. (Quran 50:37)

Here I am, afflicted by pain, and you are the most merciful of all the merciful (Quran 21: 83)

Since the 1990s, mindfulness and meditation have boomed in popularity, promoted through books, talks, documentaries, and instantly available guided meditations. Many studies have evaluated mindfulness meditation's efficacy on health and academic performance with promising results (Keng et al., 2011). Mindfulness is often described as being aware of what is happening in the present moment at any given time. Meditation, conversely, refers to cultivating an awareness of inner processes or a set of skills intended to promote a heightened state of awareness and focused attention. Mindfulness is often used interchangeably with meditation or as mindful meditation (Behan, 2020). The most cited definition of mindfulness is what Jon Kabat-Zinn offers as "the awareness that arises through paying attention in a particular way: on purpose, in the present moment, and nonjudgmentally" (Kabat-Zinn, 2011, p 4).

MINDFULNESS MEDITATION FOR THE MANAGEMENT OF CHRONIC PAIN: AN ISLAMIC APPROACH

Whereas mindfulness itself is deeply rooted in Eastern philosophies, mindfulness meditation, as it is known today, can also be traced to early Buddhist teachings. These teachings were traditionally confined to monks and nuns, who used chanting and breathwork meditation to develop spirituality and insight. Over time, mindfulness began to spring up in the secular world without the chanting and ceremony associated with Buddhist practices and eventually became integrated with Western psychology and psychotherapy.

Further developments commenced with Kabat-Zinn's work, which transformed meditation from a religious Buddhist practice to a therapeutic approach known popularly as Mindfulness-Based Stress Reduction (MBSR), a form of behavioural intervention for treating chronic pain (Kabat-Zinn, 1982). Other mindfulness-based interventions included Mindfulness-Based Cognitive Therapy (MBCT; Segal et al., 2002), Acceptance and Commitment Therapy (ACT; Hayes et al., 1999), and Dialectical Behaviour Therapy (DBT; Linehan, 1993), with the latter two using less meditation-oriented techniques. Contemporary mindfulness practice is promoted in the West to reduce stress, strengthen focus, enhance self-awareness, increase emotional health, and boost the immune system (Zhang et al., 2019).

Steven Hayes (1999), one of the co-developers of ACT, purports that contemplative practice and meditation are spiritual traditions that promote values-based action, compassion for others, and strong moral development, whether it be in the form of Christian contemplative prayer, Sufi Dhikr (remembrance of Allah), or Buddhist techniques. In its secular form, mindful meditation practices have been marketed to alleviate human suffering and control or manage unpleasant thoughts and emotions. However, meditation practised with this aim may produce adverse outcomes by potentiating unpleasant private experiences (Tifft et al., 2022; Hayes, 2006). Research has shown that avoiding negative thoughts and feelings is detrimental to well-being. Instead, having a sense of purpose enables the growth of resilience (Ford et al., 2018).

Tifft et al. (2022) showed that using meditation to manage, control, or avoid difficult experiences would increase psychological distress and negative effects. Participants willing to open up and tolerate difficult internal experiences achieved greater psychological flexibility and acceptance of their difficulties. Regardless of the thoughts and feelings that arose, those willing to accept themselves and not be dominated by their experience gained increased resilience.

Accepting painful experiences is the first step to cultivating compassion for oneself and others and can allow emotional healing and movement towards a value-based life (Ostafin et al., 2014). Hayes argues that the benefits of mindfulness meditation are contingent on intention. If people only practice meditation and mindfulness to relieve stress and fear and to manage unpleasant personal experiences, they gain little benefit. Instead, the more people are willing to open up to their vulnerability, the better they will learn to engage with life by fully experiencing feelings, thoughts, sensations, and memories and be able to see reality with the necessary clarity (Hayes, 2006). Thich Nhat Hạnh, the renowned Buddhist monk, concurs that "Meditation is not evasion; it is a serene encounter with reality" (Thich Nhat Hạnh, 1997, p. 42).

Victor Frankl (1905 - 1997), a renowned Austrian Psychiatrist who spent several years in concentration camps, argued that humans can overcome life's inherent suffering and disappointments by finding meaning and a sense of purpose in every moment. His sole purpose whilst in the concentration camps was to be reunited with his wife. His suffering and his greatest trial were not while imprisoned but when he left and discovered his beloved wife and other close family members had been killed. "Everything can be taken from a man but one thing: the last of the human freedoms—to choose one's attitude in any given set of circumstances, to choose one's own way" (Frankl, 2006, p. 66).

Mindfulness and Islam

As a modern therapeutic technique, mindfulness meditation aims to increase emotional well-being by focusing on the present moment with quiet recognition, observation, and acceptance of one's feelings, thoughts, and sensations. From an Islamic perspective, however, this process is incomplete without a spiritual element. The benefits of spiritual wisdom and contemplative practice are humility and willingness to embrace any difficult external and internal experiences that may emerge. Islamic-based mindfulness should be rooted in the desire to become closer to Allah and elevate one's spirituality.

Imam Abu Hamid Al-Ghazali (1058–1111) was a prominent Islamic scholar and mystic who wrote extensively on various aspects of spirituality, including mindfulness and meditation practices. One of his most outstanding works, the "Ihya Ulum al-Din" (The Revival of the Religious Sciences), is a comprehensive text which highlights amongst other topics, concepts such as self-awareness, contemplation (muraqaba), and the remembrance of Allah (dhikr). The practice of contemplation/mindfulness meditation helps cultivate a spiritual state characterised by the conscious awareness of the Almighty over one's inward states and outward actions and is a means of attaining spiritual insight and closeness to Allah. It is the window that allows Divine light to enter the heart (Al Ghazali, 2021). Mindfulness-based approaches incorporating a spiritual element can be a means to live life fully and purposefully through worshipping Allah (Abdussalam, 2016).

The key is to consider the world as consisting of three moments: the moments that have passed and cannot be changed, the moments in the future that are unknown and may never transpire, and the present moment, which can be fully experienced with gratitude. Practising being present without attachment to the past or the future is a central principle in Islam, as having a present state of mind allows for an appreciation of the Almighty's moment-by-moment creation with gratitude and awe (Thomas et al., 2018).

The Sufi form of meditation called muraqaba is derived from the root word raqib, which in Arabic means watching, observing, or regarding attentively, emphasising the omnipresence of the Almighty where nothing escapes His notice (Al Ghazali, 1992; Quran 50:18, 4:1). Muraqaba is a form of divine mindfulness, or effort, to remain conscious of the Almighty's watchfulness over one's inward states and actions. It was often performed by Prophet Muhammad ﷺ, who meditated in isolation in the cave of Mount Hira.

It was on one of these occasions that, during the Holy month of Ramadan, Angel Jibril descended to give revelation to the Prophet ﷺ. Knowing Allah is always watching facilitates greater attention and mindfulness of our actions, thoughts, feelings, and inner states. The Quran emphasises that Allah Almighty is aware of our actions, emotions, and innermost experiences: "Remember that Allah knows what is in your souls, so be mindful of Him" (Quran 2:235).

Ibn al-Qayyim (1292–1350; n.d.), a well-known Islamic jurist, polymath and commentator on the Quran and the sciences of Hadith and Fiqh, defined muraqabah as: "Continuous awareness of the objective, meaning the continuous presence of heart with Him" (Madārij al-Sālikīn, 1976, Vol 2). Ibn al-Qayyim (n.d.) said that thoughts and ideas are as constant as breathing, but only for a short time. To reach the pinnacle of spiritual perfection (al Ihsan), one must constantly keep Allah in one's mind and heart through worship, adoration, reverence, and awe. Those who are prudent and trust Allah will seek positive and constructive mental states and avoid destructive ones to grow spiritually and develop a stronger relationship with their Lord (Mawjud & Ali, 2006).

Professor Malik Badri (1932-2021) was well-known as the founder of modern Islamic psychology and the author of several pioneering works, including *Contemplation: An Islamic Psychospiritual Study*. Badri's synthesis of traditional Islamic ideas with modern scientific developments in the field of psychology drew on the works of prominent Muslim scholars such as Al Balkhi (850–934), Ibn Sina (980–1037) and Ibn al Qayyim (1292–1350; n.d.). He described mindfulness as seeking insightful knowledge of Allah the Creator through contemplation and worship (Badri, 2000).

Badri regarded Western psychology as neglectful of the spiritual dimension of human existence. He believed the way for the individual to observe and care for their soul and gain a close connection to their Creator was through contemplative practice (tafakkur) using controlled breathing and rhythmic repetition of Allah's names. Furthermore, Badri argued that tafakkur is not a state of altered consciousness but a form of worship that links the mind with the heart and soul, the rational with the emotional, and the sensible with the passionate, allowing the individual the space to respond to challenging experiences in a proportionate way. He considered tafakkur a process of reflection and contemplation akin to mindfulness (Badri, 1993).

Kabat-Zinn (2003) considers three necessary ingredients to mindfulness: having a purpose, a state of presence, and a non-judgmental attitude. From an Islamic perspective, purpose relates to the concept of intention (niyyah), which acts as an anchor to help make decisions and choices. However, within this framework, any action or intention will be lifeless without the inner sincerity to please Allah. Therefore, the spiritual intention of actions is motivated by seeking Allah's pleasure and being mindful of the eternal abode.

Being present before the Creator is a required practice that Muslims engage in five times daily when performing salah (prayer). The Prophet said that in prayer, one is conversing with Allah; therefore, intention, sincerity, and the presence of heart are essential to attaining intimacy with the Almighty. Prostrating during salah entails connecting our frontal lobe (the forehead) to the ground in a symbolic act of harnessing cognitions while elevating the heart physically and spiritually to connect with the Almighty. With each ritual action in prayer, being present or in a state of khushu (when a person's thoughts are humble, and the heart is focused on Allah), one can push aside worldly matters and pay attention to the inner meaning of the salah and "know well that Allah knows what is in your souls, so be mindful of Him" (Quran 2:235).

One way to cultivate presence is to keep Allah in mind wherever possible. According to Al Ghazali (Ihya Ulum al-Din, 1976), dhikr (remembrance) involves both the heart and tongue. When the tongue recites dhikr, the heart will naturally respond in unison with the remembrance of the Almighty rather than drifting into a state of heedlessness.

Ibn al-Qayyim (n.d.) concurs that our actions and deeds can only be righteous if our contemplative thoughts come from a close spiritual bond with Allah based on intention and purpose and without judgment. The development of spiritual perfection (al Ihsan) in remembrance of Allah can only be attained if one pays attention to the human ego, reigns its propensity to stray into the past or the future and connects with the heart.

In muraqaba or mindfulness, it becomes easier to control emotional responses to thoughts and strengthen the connection with the Almighty. Being God-conscious, or cognizant of Allah Almighty's omnipresence, enables individuals to engage in spiritual obligations while accepting Allah's will (qadr). Being aware that Allah is the All-knowing, All-seeing, and the source of success nurtures physical, mental, emotional, and spiritual health, brings the soul closer to Allah, and helps safeguard Iman (faith).

Prophet Muhammed ﷺ taught his followers to cultivate a non-judgmental attitude, which equates to having the best expectation from Allah for any event and situation and being grateful and patient. It means being mindful of Allah and His divine attributes and knowing that no situation is bad for the believer: "And it may be that you dislike a thing which is good for you and that you like a thing which is bad for you. Allah knows, but you do not know" (Quran 2:216). This means that regardless of the adversities one faces in life, whether physical, psychological, social, environmental, or even trivial, knowing that Allah knows best makes it less challenging to manage intrusive ruminations and despair.

According to Al-Ghazali (2010), practising mindfulness meditation in isolation can help silence the mind's invasive ruminations, ephemeral ideas, unproductive self-talk, and trivial concerns. Unhelpful thoughts may arise because of internal biases and experiences or, at other times, from angels or malevolence from Satan. To respond to thoughts in a balanced and effective way, one must learn to observe them without judging them or becoming entangled by them.

As these thoughts develop, examining them objectively allows for a stronger connection and focus on strengthening the relationship with the Divine:

> Let him strive to not think of anything concerning his affair except for Allah Almighty, continuing to sit in seclusion while saying the name of Allah constantly, with presence of heart… Upon that, if his intentions are true, his concerns are in order, and his diligence is improved . . . (Ihya Ulum al-Din 3/19).

The aim of mindfulness is not to dispense with unwanted internal experiences but to have the psychological flexibility to anchor the mind as if amid a storm. Trying to push unwanted inner experiences away causes an increase in turbulence. Regardless of how strong the turbulence is, one needs to be willing to remain present until the storm dies down. Thoughts are like waves coming and going, but when the mind begins to wander, focusing on Allah's remembrance through the heart enables the waves to dissipate.

Anas Ibn Malik (612 - c712) was a prominent companion of the Prophet Muhammad ﷺ who outlived the Prophet ﷺ by 80 years. He narrates the Prophet ﷺ as saying, "Deliberation is from Allah, and recklessness is from Satan" (Sunan al-Tirmidhi 2012). Through mindfulness meditation, it is possible to deliberate before reacting to thoughts or extreme emotions such as anger and grief, reducing the risk of being reckless and impulsive. This ties in with the process of tafakkur described by Badri (1993) and resonates with the quote: "Between stimulus and response, there is a space. In that space is our power to choose our response. In our response lies our growth and our freedom" (Covey, 2010, p. vi).

Al-Aghar al-Muzani, a companion of the Prophet Muhammad ﷺ, narrated that the Prophet's ﷺ default condition was one of conscious awareness of Allah. However, if there were times when the Prophet ﷺ thought he might have become distracted, he would anchor into the present moment and ask forgiveness of his Lord: "There is (at times) some sort of shade upon my heart, and I seek forgiveness from Allah a hundred times a day" (Sahih Muslim, 2702a).

In Sufism, the heart (Qalb) is not just the organ that circulates blood throughout the body but is regarded as the source of experiential knowledge of Allah. Aristotle also recognised the heart as the human body's centre of intelligence and attentive awareness, where insight, contemplation, changes, and direction occur. This view contradicts Western thought, where the brain is the central processor that regulates cognition, judgement, behaviour, and reasoning.

Nevertheless, several scientific studies have found evidence that the heart is cognizant of the body's status even before the conscious mind is aware of any changes (McCraty et al., 2009). Armour (2003) states that in addition to having its own network of neurons that allow it to beat freely, the heart has a sophisticated information processing centre that enables it to process hormonal and electrical inputs to maintain the balance of the body. When there is heart consciousness, the brain's electrical signals coordinate with the heartbeat (Montoya et al., 1993). Therefore, it is conceivable that the communication between the heart and the brain has a significant role in determining physical health.

Sufis assert that it is through the heart that religious truths and divine knowledge can be acquired. The heart is cleansed and purified through mindfulness meditation, opening a window to access knowledge of the Divine. The heart is where Allah speaks to human beings and where humans experience responsibility and accountability. The Quran and hadith refer to the heart as the centre of cognition, religious and human life, and where faith is held.

The verse "Surely in this, there is a reminder for one who has a [mindful] heart or lends an ear as a witness" (Quran 50:37) suggests that people may possess intelligence but lack awareness because they are not fully present in a situation. Those with heart-consciousness possess a deeper awareness and understanding. "Verily in the remembrance of Allah do hearts find rest" (Quran 13:28). A hadith narrates that the Prophet Muhammad ﷺ pointed to his heart when he said: "Taqwa ha-huna-Mindfulness of God is here, and he pointed to his chest three times" (Hadith an-Nawawi 35, 40)

Tawba (repentance) is a process that results in increasing heart consciousness and striving towards a values-based life. It refers to repentance or returning to the correct path. By practising tawba, one puts faith in Allah's capacity to pardon, which enables letting go of past events. To stay present, one must have tawaqqul (trust in Allah), which means to let Allah take care of the future without stressing about what may or may not happen. Accepting qadr (divine decree) and placing problems in Allah's hands frees one to welcome situations in the moment without avoiding them, thereby creating meaning and purpose based on acceptance. "When we are no longer able to change a situation, we are challenged to change ourselves" (Frankl, 2006, p. 112). "Verily, God does not change the condition of a people until they change what is in themselves" (Quran, 13:11).

Mindfulness and Chronic Pain

Pain is a part of the human condition. The struggle with pain depends on whether it is viewed as a severe affliction that challenges coping mechanisms or to recognise it as a blessing that carries promises of higher psychological and spiritual rewards. Acute pain typically acts as a warning signal of injury or illness and resolves as the underlying issue heals, whilst chronic pain is characterised by its persistence over an extended period. Chronic pain has been defined by the International Association for the Study of Pain (IASP) as "an unpleasant sensory and emotional experience linked to, or resembling that associated with, actual or potential tissue damage" (IASP, 2020). This definition highlights the multifaceted nature of chronic pain, encompassing the physical sensations and the emotional dimensions associated with persistent discomfort.

The complex experience of pain involving the interaction of sensory, cognitive, and affective factors makes the treatment of chronic pain challenging and financially burdensome. While international comparisons are difficult to make, chronic pain has a huge human and economic impact, impacting more than 30% of individuals globally (Cohen et al., 2021). Chronic pain has physical and psychological consequences, placing a substantial economic burden on limited healthcare resources and loss of economic productivity for persons unable to work (Phillips, 2009). Low back and neck pain have continuously been the primary causes of disability globally, with additional chronic pain diseases featuring significantly in the top ten causes of disability (Mills et al., 2019).

Furthermore, the effects of chronic pain can become a permanent feature of a person's life and lead to depression, anxiety, sleep disturbance, fatigue, and declined physical and cognitive functioning. This can also lead to poor self-esteem and confidence, loss of social relationships, and an adverse impact on quality of life (Ashburn & Staats, 1999). The National Institute for Health Care and Excellence (NICE, 2021) in the U.K. advocates the importance of psychological interventions such as cognitive behaviour therapy (CBT) and acceptance and commitment therapy (ACT) as effective ways to manage chronic pain. Mindfulness meditation, one of the core processes of ACT, has been found to reduce the pain experienced in experimental and clinical settings (Kabat Zinn, 1985; Cramer et al., 2012).

Kabat-Zinn (1982), a renowned professor of medicine who developed MBSR, argues that the preoccupation with interconnected parts of experience, like feelings, thoughts, images, memories, judgments, and beliefs, can increase stress levels and pain perception. Mindfulness meditation can reduce stress intensity and allow difficulties to be managed calmly and clearly. Kabat-Zinn (1985) trained 90 chronic pain patients using MBSR and found significant reductions in measures of present-moment pain, negative body image, inhibition of activity by pain, mood disturbance, and reduced levels of anxiety and depression. Furthermore, the patients used less pain medication due to the training, and improvements were sustained after a three-year follow-up (Kabat-Zinn et al., 1985).

Kabat-Zinn (1985) attributed pain reduction to the "uncoupling" of the physical sensation of pain from the emotional and cognitive experience of pain. Since then, further research has reported similar findings (Cramer, 2012; Lee et al., 2014). Studies of people with fibromyalgia and chronic lower back pain who received mindfulness training show the same separation of sensory and emotional distress. While the intensity or frequency of pain does not necessarily decrease, people's reduced emotional distress can help them better manage their pain condition (Bawa et al., 2015; Merkes, 2010).

A recent study in Iran looked at the benefits of MBSR on quality of life and pain. They found that breathing exercises and mindful living heightened the participant's awareness of maladaptive coping strategies and effectively reduced the perception of pain severity (Banth & Ardebil, 2015). Further research suggests that mindfulness meditation engages alternative brain pathways to cope with pain compared to other pain treatments.

Although various pain management approaches may target specific neural mechanisms, mindfulness meditation involves unique processes in the brain. A study by Talebkhah (2018) showed that meditation and mindfulness can change the brain structure to better deal with pain. The study found that the change involved cortical thickness in some brain areas, making people less sensitive to pain signals.

Neuroimaging techniques, such as functional magnetic resonance imaging (fMRI), have shown that mindfulness meditation can impact brain regions associated with pain perception and processing. Lutz et al. (2015) used fMRI scans to demonstrate how mindfulness can regulate neural brain processes before (anticipation) and during (attentional) painful stimuli. They found changes in pain signal processing, particularly in relation to pain anticipation and attentional processing. Furthermore, a study by Zeidan and Vargo (2016) found that mindfulness meditation activated the body's opioid system, a set of neurotransmitters produced naturally by the brain to enable communication of several different neural mechanisms, leading to decreased pain perception.

Whereas traditional pain treatments, such as medication or physical therapy, may target more conventional pain pathways, body awareness, mindfulness meditation, and movement in MSBR can raise a person's distress tolerance and alter their pain response (Cosio & Demyan, 2021). Mindfulness meditation's impact on attention, awareness, and emotional regulation suggests a distinctive approach to pain management. By promoting non-judgmental awareness of sensations, thoughts, and emotions, mindfulness may offer a psychological buffer against the experience of pain. Thus, exploring mindfulness as a complementary approach to pain management is highlighted by its potential to address the sensory dimensions of pain and the cognitive and emotional aspects.

Islamic-Based Mindfulness for Chronic Pain Management

Chronic pain gives rise to complexities related to loss and grief and can cause considerable psychological distress and poor quality of life. The biopsychosocial model of pain helps identify the bidirectional link between physical and mental health, but there is also an existential aspect of chronic pain. Living with chronic pain can strip a person of the ordinary and meaningful elements of their life and the state of existence that is considered normal.

A person with chronic pain is often forced to slow down, prompting them to reconsider their moral and spiritual lives. These individuals are also more likely to experience a grief reaction due to the associated losses (Cosio, 2019). Pain has a way of interfering with a person's natural disposition. The responses to chronic pain may not always be constructive as they are often quick, automatic, and habitual. For example, when pain is experienced, the reaction to the stress of the pain may be aversion and avoidance or maladaptive pleasure-seeking such as comfort eating.

The practice of mindfulness offers an opportunity to respond to stressors with awareness, allowing the cultivation of effective coping strategies rather than relying on automatic reactions. This can help manage challenging situations with greater acceptance, resilience, and insight. Examining the emotional roadblocks makes it possible to realign oneself to core values and develop an enhanced spiritual state.

From an Islamic viewpoint, the material world is characterised by strife because trials and tribulations help people realign with their true selves and realise their full potential through the struggle with their nafs (self/ego). The Quran depicts the nafs, or self, as having three states: nafs al-ammara (commanding self), nafs al-lawwama (accusatory self), and nafs al-mutmainna (peaceful self).

These three states govern the mind and control, guide and conquer behaviour. When the nafs al-ammara dominates, the mind is enslaved by worldly desires, sensual pleasures, and passions, and by its very disposition, it directs the individual to actions that are harmful to the soul. The nafs al-lawwama is the aspect of the self that experiences cognitive dissonance, is conscious of its flaws, questions behaviour and actions, and is guided by the heart. The third aspect, nafs al-mutmainna, signifies contentment and tranquillity in obeying Allah and opposing its animalistic desires (Madarij as-Salikin, Vol 1, 1976).

Being in a place of suffering can raise the nafs (ego) from a state of nafs al-ammara to nafs al-mutmainna and give spiritual freedom and meaning to life. The verses frequently cited in the Quran, "We burden not any person, but that which he can bear" (Quran 6:152) and "And certainly We shall test you with something of fear; hunger; loss of wealth, lives and fruits (or crops), but give glad tidings to the patient ones" (Quran, 2:155) can inspire people who struggle to deal with life's challenges to use prayer to cultivate a state of being present in the moment rather than distracted by worldly desires. Prayer and praise of Allah can aid in releasing cognitive entanglement and allowing the nafs to move from a commanding state into a state of acceptance and peace.

From an Islamic perspective, the trials of life are a test from Allah and an opportunity for self-improvement to foster the development of attributes such as being patient, forgiving, and grateful. "Do the people think that they will be left to say, 'We believe', and they will not be tried?" (Quran 29:2). This verse highlights the need for Muslims to embrace suffering as part of Allah's divine decree, goodness, and justice, and find comfort in the belief that trials and tribulations enable emotional and spiritual transformation.

Physical or mental suffering is thus regarded as an essential component of the human experience. With chronic pain, rather than attempting to remove or avoid suffering, it is critical to shift one's relationship with it. Mindfulness meditation, or muraqaba, can be used therapeutically as a spiritual and psychological aid to treat the psychological symptoms linked with pain in the context of pain management.

When coping with poor physical or mental health, it is not remarkable for people to conflate the experience, making the discomfort more challenging to live with. The brain receives information from the five senses, beliefs, sensations, feelings, imagination, judgement, and memory, which warns of danger or not. Some sentiments are pleasant and improve one's well-being, while others are negative.

The Buddha described the experience of physical pain as similar to being pierced by two arrows. The first arrow is due to nociception when pain in the body is felt, and the second occurs immediately after when distressing emotions such as fear, sorrow, anxiety, grief, and lack of acceptance are experienced. Although these are appropriate responses to an adverse situation, if they dominate the mind, they become the source of additional pain rather than the response to pain.

A person with chronic pain may strengthen their sense of responsibility by believing that everything happens for a reason, by divine decree, and that they cannot control everything that happens to them. This acceptance can help people achieve inner healing, even if they know they must live with chronic pain. It can also help them become more present and willing to live a life aligned with their values. Being mindful requires coming out of the "autopilot" mode and focusing on the here and now rather than letting thoughts wander into the regrets of the past or the worries for the future.

An interesting story illustrating the concept of mindful presence is that of a man who approached a wise sage seeking help to overcome his pain and anguish. The sage told him that to be helped, he first needed to complete a specific task. The task was to take a spoon, fill it with oil, and walk through the town without spilling a single drop.

The man agreed, thinking it was easy, and set out into the town with a spoon filled with oil. He tried his best to balance the spoon and focused on not spilling any of the oil. He returned to the sage, pleased that he had successfully completed the task. The sage asked the man what he had noticed while conducting the task, whether he saw any beautiful flowers, noticed the trees, or heard the laughter of children playing in the streets. The man then realised that his attention had been so fixated on the spoon that he had failed to notice anything else.

The story's moral is that people experiencing pain may become so absorbed by their suffering that they overlook the blessings and beauty surrounding them, mirroring the man fixated on the spoon. The story is a reminder that, despite adversity, one can discover meaning and cultivate appreciation for life. By shifting focus from the immediate challenges to the positive aspects of existence, individuals can find resilience and a renewed sense of gratitude even amid hardship. Al-Ghazali (1997) believes that being heedful of Allah is fundamental for developing a state of mindfulness that affects all aspects of one's life. Ibn al-Qayyim (n.d.) also explains that when the heart becomes impure due to heedlessness and deviation from its natural disposition, it can be purified by seeking forgiveness and remembering Allah. Reflecting on Allah's blessings instead of uncontrollable worldly matters is a form of worship and mental activity that promotes contentment and discourages materialism, leading to positive psychological outcomes.

To elevate mindfulness, Al-Ghazali (2016) advocates the incorporation of four distinct daily spiritual practices: supplication (dua), remembrance (dhikr), recitation of the Quran (qiraat), and contemplation (fikr). These practices are intended to nurture the heart and mind, fostering a heightened awareness of God's presence and a deep appreciation of His blessings. All four often overlap and blend while reinforcing a continuous connection with the Divine and a steadfast presence in the here and now.

Mindfulness practice based on Islamic traditions can cultivate present-moment awareness by observing inner thoughts and emotional states. These practices aim to bring awareness to the inception of thoughts, allowing individuals to notice their mental and emotional states before they develop into actions. Islam stresses the importance of being present and having intention and purpose in life regardless of pain or suffering and encourages turning to Allah at these times with a promise that "Indeed, with hardship comes ease. So, when you have finished your duties, stand up for worship" (Quran 94:6-7).

Practical Implementation of Mindfulness Exercises

The following section will describe practical exercises integrating mindfulness with Islamic practices to increase self-awareness and self-efficacy and to help build confidence in managing chronic pain.

Mindful Salah

Salah (prayer) assists in connecting with an inner moral compass (fitrah) that points to the Oneness of the Creator and the formation of taqwa (mindfulness of the Divine). It allows the individual to surrender their worries, concerns, and anguish to the care of the Almighty. Engaging in mindful Salah entails maintaining presence of mind, cultivating awareness, and focusing on the act of worship. By adopting a mindful approach to salah, individuals can elevate their spiritual experience, intensify concentration, and establish a meaningful connection with Allah.

This conscious engagement enhances the significance of the prayer ritual, allowing individuals to fully immerse themselves in the sacred moment of communion with the Divine. It transforms the ritual from a series of physical movements conducted in a state of autopilot into a profound and spiritually enriching experience. Indeed, two key ways to cultivate mindfulness in Islamic worship are paying attention to the five daily prayers and praying with khushu, in other words, being in a state of humility, devotion, and attentiveness during worship. During salah, the worshippers remember Allah not for His benefit, as He does not need their prayers, but for the desire to seek His love and grace to help them through their pain and suffering.

Salah serves as a respite for individuals dealing with chronic pain to set aside the challenges of daily life temporarily. During this sacred practice, chronic pain sufferers can seek solace by immersing themselves fully in prayer, being present in the moment, and creating a much-needed proximity to the Almighty. "The people of Paradise do not regret anything except an hour or moment that passed them in the world without the remembrance of Allah" (Sahih Bukhari, 552).

However, the first and essential step to performing salah is ablution. The ablution ritual signifies entering a state of physical and spiritual purity to free the mind from distractions and worldly impurities. Ablution is the gateway to enhanced concentration and mindfulness. The methodical and precise ritualistic steps require individuals to fully engage in the process, enabling a heightened ability to concentrate on worship. Furthermore, ablution cultivates humility by reminding the worshipper of their dependence on Allah and the importance of praying with reverence.

Ablution has been recommended in times of anger and distress to create a pause between stimulus and response, thereby reducing the intensity of the emotion. The same can be applied to times when the experience of chronic pain is high. There is an emphasis on the importance of performing ablution with dedication. "Performing the Wudu thoroughly despite difficult circumstances, walking with more paces to the mosque, and waiting for the next As-Salat (the prayer) after observing Salat; and that is Ar-Ribat, and that is Ar-Ribat" (Riyad as-Salihin 1030). This hadith teaches that performing ablution with dedication, taking more steps to the mosque, and waiting for the next prayer after completing Salat represent Ar-Ribat, a concept denoting steadfastness in faith in the face of challenging circumstances. Thus, the ablution ritual requires paying attention to the process and cultivating body awareness. It involves being fully present and focused on each step, with an awareness of the spiritual significance of the act.

Performing Ablution. First, set an intention (niyyah) to perform wudhu for worship and purification. Begin with Bismillah (in the name of Allah) and take a deep breath. This simple phrase helps to bring focus to the present moment and reminds us that Allah is All-seeing and All-knowing. Try to remain fully present and aware of each step of ablution. Avoid rushing through the process. Take time to perform each action deliberately and with concentration.

Begin by washing the hands up to the wrists three times. Notice the sensation of the water as it comes into contact with the skin, including the temperature and how it feels against the skin. Be conscious of the water cleansing the hands physically and symbolically.

Next, rinse the mouth three times and again become aware of the sensations of the water swishing around the mouth. Then, sniff water into

136

the nose and blow out three times while fully aware of the sensations against the skin and the internal membrane of the nose. Wash the face three times, from the hairline to the chin and ear to ear. Be aware of the water reaching every part of the face and the sensations it creates, taking time not to rush. When the mind wanders, acknowledge this and gently bring the focus back to the action being performed.

Wash both arms up to the elbow three times and remain mindful that the water reaches every part, knowing the arms are being purified. While wiping the head and passing the fingers through the hair, be aware of the symbolic cleansing of the mind and thoughts that may be flitting in and out of the conscious mind. After wiping the back of the ears, wash the right foot up to the ankle three times, followed by the left foot remaining mindful of the water cleansing the feet, symbolising the purity and preparedness for carrying out the prayer.

Another layer of mindfulness and spirituality that can be added to this ritual is to recite supplications and maintain a sense of humility and presence without becoming distracted. Completing each step attentively and purposefully can help promote relaxation. In addition, each step also prepares one to submit to Allah in prayer while putting aside inner and outer conflicts.

Practicing Mindful Salah. The next step is to begin the salah. Salah is a means of having a personal meeting with Allah. Raising both hands to the ear level and making intention at the beginning of each prayer signifies setting aside worldly matters to engage in a conversation with the Divine. Begin the prayer by making a sincere and conscious intention in the heart while recognising the greatness of Allah with the Takbir (Allah Akbar).

Focus on the purpose of the prayer, which is to worship Allah and to increase the spiritual connection with Him. It is recommended to pray slowly and to pay attention to the meaning of the recited verses throughout the prayer to remain present, centred, and maintain a meaningful interaction with the Almighty without becoming disengaged and distracted.

Achieving a state of khushu is variable because being human means becoming easily distracted by inner and outer experiences, but what matters is the endeavour to perfect humility in salah. If the mind wanders, returning attention to the prayer without judgment or self-condemnation is vital, as it is a constant mental struggle requiring regular practice. When the heart and mind wander, the regular practice of bringing back focus helps increase humility. The Prophet used to tell his companions to renew their faith. He was asked, "O Messenger of Allah, how do we renew our faith?" He said,

"By frequently repeating La ilaha ill-Allah (There is no god, but Allah)" (Riyad as-Salihin 393).

Be aware of the body's positions during each part of the prayer, including standing, bowing (ruku), prostrating (sujud), and sitting. Remember to focus on each position's physical sensations and symbolism while observing the breath during the prayer. Taking slow and deliberate breaths and creating rhythmic breathing helps centre the mind and maintain focus. Perform each movement of the prayer with deliberation, avoiding haste. Allow the beauty of the ritual to unfold slowly and savour each moment with the knowledge that Allah is present and that the salah is a conversation with the Almighty.

For those who cannot perform the ritual movements as prescribed due to lack of mobility or physical pain, whichever manner the prayer is conducted, it is essential to remain present in mind and aware of the symbolic nature of the rhythm of salah. The Prophet Muhammed ﷺ advocated flexibility in the positions of prayer during illness. "Pray while standing, and if you can't, pray while sitting and if you cannot do even that, then pray lying on your side" (Sahih al-Bukhari 1117).

In the position of sujud, regarded as the closest connection point with Allah, one should be aware of the humility and submission inherent in this posture. The focus should be on connecting with Allah and expressing gratitude and supplications. As the prayer concludes with Tasleem (salutation), one should be mindful of the closure of this spiritual act and reflect on the experience of tranquillity and proximity to Allah. Maintain present moment awareness throughout the prayer by consistently bringing attention back when the mind wanders without self-recrimination. The key is striving to be fully present in each movement and recitation while accepting that the human mind can easily be distracted.

The post-salah dhikr provides an opportunity to continue connecting with Allah and can compensate for any lack of concentration during the salah. Practicing being present during prayer will have a cumulative effect on emotional, spiritual, and physical well-being. It will help lessen the mind's sensitivity to pain signals and, as a result, reduce the perception of pain. Regular practice will create space for other worthwhile pursuits and mental experiences, making it easier to accept the experience of pain.

Dhikr

One spiritual practice outlined by Al-Ghazali (2016) involves emptying the heart of concerns and striving to let no thought enter the mind except that of Allah. This practice aims to instil the "presence of the heart," and if done with sincere intentions, it can lead to a heart diligent in remembrance. The Islamic concept of dhikr refers to the remembrance of Allah and is the centre of all worship and rituals. "Those who have faith, their hearts find comfort in the remembrance of God. Verily, in the remembrance of God (dhikr), do hearts find rest" (Quran 13:28). The practice of dhikr is another opportunity to help cultivate mindfulness. Dhikr has been shown to increase the secretion of endorphins to induce a feeling of well-being and comfort (Irhas et al., 2023).

The spiritual heart (qalb), the centre of cognition and feeling, can be purified through the practice of mindful dhikr. Al-Ghazali (2016) uses the analogy of the human soul to a mirror, asserting that mindful contemplation acts as a polish for this mirror, intensifying its brilliance and radiance to reflect truth and reality. Through purification or polishing of the mirror, the heart can perceive Allah and be aware of His watchful presence (Al-Ghazali, 2010). For this reason, those living with chronic pain who practice constant dhikr with each heartbeat and breath can train their minds, hearts, and bodies to cultivate wellness, peace, and contentment: "Surely in the remembrance of Allah do hearts find comfort. Those who believe and do good, for them, will be bliss and an honourable destination" (Quran 13:28-29).

Research on the relationship between spirituality and well-being highlights the importance of spiritual practices in enhancing overall life satisfaction (Omais & dos Santos, 2022). Practising dhikr with present-moment awareness helps anchor the wandering mind. This involves repeatedly reciting Allah's name, a verse, or supplication from the Quran or any of the beautiful names of Allah. These anchors generate a sense of spiritual fulfilment and connection with a higher power, contributing to a sense of purpose and meaning in life. The Prophet ﷺ is reported in a hadith to say: "Two words are beloved to the Most Merciful, light on the tongue but heavy on the scale: Glory and praise to Allah (Subhan Allahi wa bi hamdihi), and glory to Allah Almighty (Subhan Allahi al-'Athim)" (Sahih Bukhari 7563). One of the anchors that the Prophet ﷺ often used was *istighfar,* which means "I seek forgiveness from Allah."

Dhikr Exercise for Connection with the Divine

The following dhikr exercise can be used to establish a deeper connection with the Divine while remaining present in mind:

Find a quiet and peaceful place where the dhikr can take place without distractions, such as a dedicated prayer space or calm environment. Assume a comfortable and relaxed posture. Engage in mindful breathing to bring attention to the present moment. Focus on the sensation of the breath, inhaling and exhaling slowly and intentionally. Begin with the sincere intention to remember and draw closer to Allah, focusing on the spiritual significance of the practice of dhikr.

Choose a specific phrase, name of Allah, or Quranic verse that feels instinctive for the dhikr to anchor wandering thoughts and worries. The words should be recited slowly and deliberately with attention to their pronunciation and meaning. Avoid rushing through the repetitions. Be present with each utterance, feeling the words and their significance.

Reflect on the attributes of Allah associated with the chosen phrase and contemplate Allah's greatness, mercy, and wisdom. When the mind starts to wander, acknowledge any arising thoughts without judgment and redirect the focus back to the dhikr. When using prayer beads (tasbih), mindful attention can be enhanced by paying attention to the sensation of the bead's texture against the skin while reciting. As the mind may still be distracted, redirect attention to the texture of the beads and acknowledge Allah's watchful presence.

Practising dhikr with attention helps turn off the autopilot state of being. Conclude the dhikr with expressions of gratitude and supplication. Thank Allah for the opportunity to engage in His remembrance and ask for His guidance, mercy, and forgiveness. By infusing mindfulness into dhikr, it is possible to transform a traditional act of remembrance into a more contemplative and spiritually enriching practice.

Regular practice helps the mind associate the recitations with a profound sense of connection to Allah and strengthens the ability to remain grounded in the present moment with the understanding that He is *all-knowing and all-seeing*. The Quran emphasises the importance of Allah's remembrance in the verse: "So remember Me; I will remember you" (Quran 2:152).

Mindful Breathing

Breathwork is often incorporated into mindfulness-based interventions, and studies indicate that regular practice may contribute to better management of symptoms of anxiety and depression and increased overall emotional resilience (Bawa et al., 2015; Burch, 2011). Mindfulness breathing exercises accompanied by gratitude have been shown to reduce pain anxiety, pain interference, and pain intensity and have improved pain self-efficacy (Swain et al., 2020).

Practising regular breathing exercises helps harness the wandering mind and interrupt the pain cycle (McCraty et al., 2009). Mindful breathing emphasises the connection between the mind and body. Conscious breathing and being present with each breath can foster a holistic mind-body connection that aligns with a state of khushu.

Breathing is automatic and rhythmic and is subconsciously controlled by a network of neurons in the base of the brain. The rhythmic act of breathing becomes a metaphorical guide, highlighting the importance of embracing the reality that certain aspects of life are subject to conscious influence, yet others lie outside the realm of control. Mindful breathing is known for its calming and centring effects. Deep breathing can lower stress levels, encourage calmness, and reduce pain perception (Toussaint et al., 2021). People with chronic pain often hold their breath or breathe quickly and shallowly during flare-ups, which exacerbates their anxiety and discomfort. For this reason, practising deep breathing techniques can be highly beneficial.

Mindful Breathing Practice. To practice mindful breathing, first find a comfortable position to rest with the intention of connecting with Allah's divine presence. Focus awareness on the natural breathing pattern and slow down the breath. Breathe in through the nose at a count of five, pausing for a few seconds and then gently breathing out at a count of eight, as though blowing out a candle. While breathing in, recite the name *Allah*, and on the slow out-breath, recite an elongated *Hu*. Settle the mind by bringing awareness to the relaxed breathing rhythm and paying attention to the heart and mind at that moment. Notice any thoughts, whether good or unhelpful and gently let them go like releasing a balloon into the sky.

Bring the mind's attention to the gift of life from Allah, and with each in-breath, connect to gratitude for life, knowing that He is present at all times. Every time the mind wanders, bring awareness back to being present in front of Allah. Regular mindfulness breathing practice can train individuals to overcome distractions and intrusive thoughts. This skill becomes a valuable tool to connect with the Almighty during times of forgetfulness or when feeling overwhelmed with the experience of pain and emotional distress. The journey of mastering breath control while connecting with Allah's names enhances the spiritual experience of mindful awareness.

Mindful Walking

Numerous studies have shown that being in nature can revitalise the brain by boosting levels of focus and helping free the mind when it is stuck in a maze of stresses and strains that paralyse focus and attention (Pocock et al., 2023; Gotink et al., (2016). Mindful walking is a powerful tool to bring attention to one's surroundings with a sense of wonderment and appreciation of the magnificence of Allah's creation. It can foster awe and interrupt the flow of unhelpful thoughts and sensations. Making a conscious effort to notice the environment when walking can be enlightening and eye-opening, especially when the same steps have been taken numerous times in a state of autopilot (Gotink et al., 2016).

Islamic Mindful Walking Practice. First, initiate the practice with a sincere intention to dedicate the walk to spiritual reflection and worship. Begin with "Bismillah" to invoke Allah's name and blessings for the mindful journey. While walking, attention can be turned inward to the breath, focusing on each inhalation and exhalation to anchor to the present moment. Walk at a relaxed pace, mindful of each step. Using all five senses, observe the environment, such as the trees, shrubs, flowers, the sky, and people. Throughout the journey, reflect on the beauty of Allah's creations, observing nature's elements while acknowledging the signs of Allah's greatness in every detail.

Remain attuned to bodily sensations, paying close attention to the movements of the legs and arms, the tactile experience of the feet meeting the ground and the fluidity of the body's movement with each step. There may be moments when the mind strays, but that is normal. Acknowledge thoughts, sensations, and feelings as they emerge and redirect attention to using the five senses.

Walking in a state of being present is a form of worship as it entails being God-conscious. The Quran refers to being mindful of Allah's creation of the earth, the creation of flowers, plants and all kinds of trees and fruits: "It is He who has spread out the earth for (His) creatures: Therein is fruit and date palms producing sheathes of dates and grain having husks and scented plants" (Quran 55:10-12), which serve to evoke gratitude towards Him and lead to the rhetorical question: "So, which of the favours of your Lord would you deny?" (Quran 55:13).

Incorporate dhikr or recite Quranic verses to add a spiritual dimension to the mindful walk. Express gratitude to Allah for the gift of movement and the ability to experience His creation. "Therefore remember Me. I will remember you. Be grateful to Me and never show me ingratitude" (Quran 2:152). In the end, express thankfulness with "Alhamdulillah," recognising the experience and the opportunity to connect with Allah through each purposeful step. Gratitude is a familiar concept found in both the Quran and Sunnah and is known to promote positive effects on mental well-being and relationships (Tennen et al., 2002).

Islam promotes expressing gratitude even during challenging times to maintain a positive outlook and recognise blessings amidst discomfort. The Quran says: "And [remember] when your Lord proclaimed: If you give

thanks [by accepting faith], I will surely increase you in favour"
(Quran:14:7). Hence, the experience of walking mindfully with gratitude
for Allah's blessings can be experienced as a harmonious blend of physical
activity and spiritual reflection, fostering a profound connection with Allah
and the present moment.

If mobility is difficult and walking is not an option, this exercise
can also be done from home. Paying attention while looking out of the
window, sitting in the garden, or even using the imagination to visit
memorable places while examining each detail with awe and appreciation
of Allah's world helps increase a connection with creation and creates
perspective beyond pain and suffering.

Introspection and Body Awareness

In Islam, maintaining awareness of the body and introspection is
encouraged as part of a holistic approach to spiritual and physical well-
being. By maintaining awareness of the body and engaging in introspection,
individuals can deepen their spiritual connection and cultivate gratitude to
lead a more mindful and purposeful life according to Islamic principles.

> *"And they ask you, [O Muhammad], about the soul. Say, The soul
> is of the affair of my Lord. And mankind have not been given of
> knowledge except a little" (Quran 17:85).*

> *"Does man think that he will be left neglected? Had he not been a
> sperm from semen emitted?" (Quran 75:14-15).*

These verses encourage believers to engage in introspection, contemplate
the signs of creation, and develop gratitude for the blessings bestowed upon
them by Allah. While Islamic literature does not explicitly discuss body
awareness and pain in the same terms as contemporary psychology or
medicine, some general principles and teachings can be applied in these
contexts. Islam encourages believers to remain hopeful and optimistic,
trusting that Allah's mercy is limitless. Despair is discouraged, and
believers are reminded that Allah's mercy is vast and all-encompassing.

Drawing inspiration from Surah Duha (Quran: 93) that was
revealed to the Prophet Muhammed ﷺ when he was experiencing a period
of great difficulties, it is possible to remain aware of internal experiences
while simultaneously having a deep sense of attachment to the Almighty.
Sura Duha unfolds in several steps, establishing a profound sense of
attachment and connection to Allah and instilling hope. It helps
contextualise individual pain and suffering and negates the "why me"
question.

The first part of the surah begins by emphasising that facing hardships or pain is not an indication of divine disdain, highlighting that Allah is with the Prophet ﷺ, no matter what. This verse provides reassurance that Allah has not forsaken the individual and can alleviate feelings of abandonment and despair.

The second step involves a shift in perspective, urging individuals to recognise that whatever challenges they are currently undergoing are transient with a reminder that the Hereafter holds promises of enduring reward and contentment, far surpassing the fleeting hardships of the present life. The approach introduces a cognitive approach of re-evaluation and reinterpretation of one's current circumstances and helps to build resilience.

The third step encourages action to improve behavioural patterns and mindset. The emphasis on caring for orphans and the needy encourages positive actions, which can enhance one's emotional well-being. Engaging in acts of charity and kindness can provide a sense of fulfilment and reduce feelings of loneliness and despair. Finally, Surah Duha advocates for cultivating gratitude (Quran 93:1-11). Regularly acknowledging and appreciating aspects worthy of gratitude can significantly enhance one's overall well-being (Tennen et al., 2002).

The body and the soul are considered a divine gift from God. Consequently, individuals do not have absolute ownership over their bodies; instead, they are entrusted with caring for them as stewards. Being in a conscious state of profound awareness of Allah and one's inner states, whether pain or emotional strife, represents the highest spiritual attainment. It is common for those in pain to experience fear avoidance, which leads to them being aversive to activities that they believe may cause more pain. The Quran states, "Indeed: everyone who surrenders his whole being unto Allah and is a doer of good, shall have his reward with his Sustainer; and all such need have no fear, and neither shall they grieve" Quran- 2:112.

This verse suggests that Allah is the greatest sustainer and protector for those with tawakkul who are willing to sit with discomfort, patience, and fortitude. Their heart will cultivate the strength to face fear and pain and accept adversity as a test from Allah. This willingness to face the fear of pain fosters gratitude and reflection for the blessings of the body and helps them feel and notice their own physical existence. The Quran mentions the importance of reflecting on oneself and the creation as a means to strengthen faith and increase understanding.

"And on the earth are signs for those who have Faith with certainty, And also in your own selves. Will you not then see?" (Quran 51:20-21).

"(This is) a Book (the Qur'an) which We have sent down to you, full of blessings that they may ponder over its Verses, and that men of understanding may remember" (Quran 38:29).

Practicing Body Awareness. The following exercise can help develop body awareness and teach that changing the relationship with pain is possible instead of ignoring it or struggling with the sensations. To begin this exercise, find the area of the body where the pain or discomfort is concentrated and attend to the core of that area. Identify whether the pain is heavy, light, or neutral. Does it feel cold, hot, or neutral? Is it moving slowly or fast, or is it stationary? Is it dense, loose, or dispersed? By describing these aspects of chronic pain, it is possible to become an objective observer and develop a willingness to stand back from the pain and allow space for other experiences and more realistic cognitive appraisals about the experience.

The verses from Surah Ash-Sharh can be a reminder that pain and suffering are transient and should not be used to define the self. "Indeed, with hardship [will be] ease" (Quran 94-6). Thus, facing discomfort is an opportunity for personal growth and spiritual development. Difficulties can serve as a means of purifying one's soul, increasing one's reliance on Allah, and helping develop resilience.

Maintaining awareness of the body and emotions makes it possible to become accustomed to the sensations instead of fighting or reacting emotionally to them. Rather than suppressing feelings and emotions, present-moment awareness enables gradual acceptance and the willingness to acknowledge that Allah is the one who controls health and illness and is the ultimate healer. According to a hadith narrated in Sahih Muslim, when a companion complained of pain, the Prophet stated: "Place your hand over the part of your body where you feel pain and say three times: In the name of Allah. And say seven times: I seek refuge in Allah and his power from the evil of what I feel and worry" (Sahih Muslim 2202).

The Quranic verse "And when I am ill, it is He [Allah] who cures me" (Quran 26:80) instils hope and a sense of mercy from Allah as the source of healing during illness and implies practising patience and seeking help through prayer and supplication during times of distress. This introspective process allows individuals to assess their actions, intentions, and spiritual growth, leading to personal development and greater consciousness of one's behaviours and attitudes despite pain.

Mindful Daily Activities

Mindfulness practice does not need to be formal, as it can seamlessly be incorporated into daily activities. Mindful living involves transforming routine and mundane tasks into intentional, purposeful moments. By infusing these activities with a present mind and spirituality, individuals can find more profound meaning and connection in their daily lives. This involves bringing focused attention and intention to everyday tasks and transforming routine activities into opportunities to remain centred and spiritually connected.

Several mindful exercises to help manage pain, internal sensations, and experiences during day-to-day activities are included here. For intrusive thoughts, observe each one and acknowledge it as just a thought, regardless of its emotional content. Allow all thoughts to come and go moment by moment, breath by breath. Become more aware of any sounds, noticing them, and then letting them go. Try to engage the senses by noticing colours, smells, sounds, textures, and flavours.

While eating meals, take time to eat slowly and without distraction. Notice the texture, taste, and sensation of the food, listen to physical hunger cues and eat only what the body needs. Focusing on the breath while engaging in daily activities helps anchor the mind to the present moment to promote a sense of calm and awareness. Simultaneously reciting supplications, such as Bismillah (In Allah's name), adds a spiritual dimension to the practice. This integration helps foster a connection between routine tasks and a higher purpose. Using silent supplications during activities like cooking, cleaning, and resting enhances mindfulness. These moments of quiet reflection, forgiveness, praise, and gratitude serve as a means to remain connected with Allah throughout the day.

A strategy to transition from automatic pilot to mindful awareness involves directing attention to key elements such as breathing, emotions, and physical sensations. Individuals can disengage from autopilot mode by intentionally setting a goal to relax, actively listening to others with complete focus, and savouring each moment of family time as if it were their last. During routine activities, it is beneficial to periodically check in to assess whether the mind is wandering and if full attention is being paid to the task at hand. Reflecting on what genuinely holds significance in the present moment further contributes to cultivating mindfulness.

Daily activities can be elevated to become worship through the intentional practice of mindfulness and supplications. With this approach, spirituality can be integrated into every facet of one's existence. This fosters a continuous awareness of the Divine in routine and extraordinary moments.

Finally, despondency is a normal reaction to suffering. In Islam, this emotion can be overcome with the reminder that bad experiences such as chronic pain and illness are an expiation for sins and that Allah knows what is best for His creation. The Quran emphasises that relief is accompanied by hardship: "So, verily, with every difficulty, there is relief: Verily with every difficulty, there is relief" (Quran 94:5-7), "If God helps you, none can overcome you; and if He forsakes you, who is there after Him that can help you? And in God (Alone) let believers put their trust." (Quran 3:160). These verses help guide individuals from hopelessness and helplessness to seeing the bigger picture of what is being experienced and to believe that Allah ultimately knows best and has a Divine plan for everyone, whether in this life or the next.

The theme of all these exercises revolves around the remembrance and mindfulness of Allah. Such practices aim to cleanse the heart of negative sentiments and the mind of detrimental thoughts. Traits deemed praiseworthy, such as gratitude and the remembrance of Allah, contribute to the polishing process, opening the innate virtuous nature of the soul or the fitrah to strive towards achieving *tazkiyah* (the cleansing of one's heart and soul from negative traits, vices, and impurities while nurturing positive qualities and virtues). Individuals can strengthen their spiritual awareness through consistent effort and dedication to stay present in mind, fostering a profound and enduring relationship with the Divine regardless of adversity and physical and spiritual afflictions.

Conclusion

This chapter examined mindfulness within the context of Islamic teachings and the idea that it offers a profound journey towards spiritual well-being. Drawing on the wisdom of scholars like Al-Ghazali (1997, 2010; Abdussalam, 2016) and Ibn al-Qayyim (n.d.), integrating mindfulness practices with Islamic rituals enables the state of heightened awareness of the present moment while remaining aligned with spirituality.

As a bridge between the internal and external dimensions of human experience, mindfulness impacts thoughts and feelings and catalyses meaningful outward action (Hayes et al., 1999). Combining mindfulness and Islamic principles provides a comprehensive framework for navigating life's challenges, fostering resilience, gratitude, and a deeper connection with the Divine. This practice enables a recalibration of purpose and values, even in the face of suffering caused by pain and illness. Maintaining present-moment awareness and making dua (prayer) to Allah for the strength to manage the difficulties is an excellent source of comfort. A life of purpose and khushu can only be achieved by maintaining a state of God consciousness and emptying the mind from the troubles of the past and worries about the future to focus on the here and now instead.

As individuals connect with their inner world through mindfulness, they gain awareness of barriers hindering action and recognise their deepest values and goals that are often neglected due to the experience of chronic pain. Thus, mindfulness practice emerges as a potent force capable of shaping both the internal and external dimensions of human experience, offering a journey towards well-being and spiritual connection in the knowledge that life in this world has fleeting moments which are sometimes overflowing with joy and at other times filled with sorrow and despair. This is the nature of life, and this is the human condition. Maintaining consistent engagement in daily practices and seeking guidance from scholars and mental health professionals is recommended to benefit from the holistic nature of this transformative journey.

Looking ahead, future directions in the synthesis of Islamic and secular perspectives on mindfulness present promising opportunities for research and exploration. Further literature and resources are needed to deepen the understanding of how these two perspectives can harmoniously coexist, providing fresh insights into the seamless incorporation of mindfulness practices into daily life within an Islamic context. Scholars and spiritual leaders, with their wealth of knowledge, can play a pivotal role in guiding individuals toward a nuanced understanding of mindful meditation that remains true to Islamic teachings.

For those living with chronic pain, integrating reflective moments into daily routines emerges as a necessary aspect of mindfulness. This practice allows for introspection and self-awareness, offering a valuable tool for tracking progress, identifying challenges, and setting intentions for personal growth. Incorporating gratitude practices rooted in Islamic teachings contributes to a positive mindset and is a transformative path toward well-being, spiritual growth, and a more profound connection with Allah.

Finally, seeking guidance from mental health professionals who are well-versed in mindfulness and Islamic perspectives holds great potential. Such professionals can provide tailored strategies for coping with the unique challenges associated with chronic pain, offering personalised approaches that enhance overall well-being. A collaborative approach, combining spiritual insights with psychological expertise, reflects a holistic and inclusive strategy for individuals navigating the complexities of living with pain.

References

Abdussalam, N. (2016). Al-Ghazali's Adapted Summary of Ihya Ulum al-Din - The Forty Principles of the Religion (Translated). Turath Publishing.

Al-Ghazali. (1981). Sermon to the Faithful, Revival of the Religious Sciences. Beirut, Lebanon: Dar al Nafa'is Publishing House.

Al-Ghazali on the Ninety-nine Beautiful Names of God: Al-Maqsad al-Asna fi Sharh Asma' Allah al-Husna Translated by David Burrell (The Islamic Texts Society's al-Ghazali Series) Paperback – 1 Jan. 1992

Al-Ghazali. The Alchemy of Happiness. Translated by Claud Field. M.E. Sharpe, 1997

Al-Ghazali. The Marvels of the Heart: Science of the Spirit (*Ihya Ulum Al-Din/ The Revival of the Religious Sciences, 21*) Translated by Walter James Skellie Fons Vitae (1 April 2010)

Al-Ghazali. (2021). Kitab al-Tafakkur: The Book of Reflection (Book 39 of The Revival of the Religious Sciences, Ihya Ulum al-Din). In The Revival of the Religious Sciences (Ihya Ulum al-Din). Islamic Texts Society. (Translation: Various translators). Cambridge, UK: Islamic Texts Society.

Armour, J. A. (2003). *Neurocardiology: Anatomical and functional principles*. Institute of HeartMath.

Ashburn, M. A., & Staats, P. S. (1999). Management of chronic pain. *Lancet, 353*(9167), 1865–1869.

Badri, M. (1993). Al-Tafakkur min al-Mushahadah ila al-shuhud. Herndon, VA: IIIT.

Badri, M. (2000). Contemplation: An Islamic psychospiritual study. Kuala Lumpur: Shelbourne Enterprise Sdn. Bhd.

Banth, S., & Ardebil, M. D. (2015). Effectiveness of mindfulness meditation on pain and quality of life of patients with chronic low back pain. *International Journal of Yoga, 8*(2), 128-133. https://doi.org/10.4103/0973-6131.158476

Bawa, F. L. M., Mercer, S. W., Atherton, R. J., Clague, F., Keen, A., Scott, N. W., & Bond, C. M. (2015). Does mindfulness improve outcomes in patients with chronic pain? Systematic review and meta-analysis. *British Journal of General Practice, 65*(635), e387–e400. https://doi.org/10.3399/bjgp15X685297

Behan, C. (2020). The benefits of meditation and mindfulness practices during times of crisis such as COVID-19. *Irish Journal of Psychological Medicine*, *37*(4), 256–258. doi:10.1017/ipm.2020.38

Burch, V. (2011). Living Well with Pain and Illness. ReadHowYouWant.com.

Cohen, S. P., Vase, L., & Hooten, W. M. (2021). Chronic pain: An update on burden, best practices, and new advances. *The Lancet*, *397*(10289), 2082–2097. https://doi.org/10.1016/S0140-6736(21)00393-7

Cosio, D. (2019). Chronic pain and the psychological stages of grief. *Practical Pain Management, 19*(3).

Cosio, D., & Demyan, A. (2021). Behavioral medicine: Applying mindfulness-based stress reduction for comorbid pain and PTSD. *Practical Pain Management, 21*(4).

Covey, S. R. (2010). Foreword. In A. Pattakos, Prisoners of Our Thoughts: Viktor Frankl's Principles for Discovering Meaning in Life and Work (2nd ed., pp. xiii–xvii). Berrett-Koehler Publishers.

Cramer, H., Haller, H., Lauche, R., & Dobos, G. (2012). Mindfulness-based stress reduction for low back pain. A systematic review. *BMC complementary and alternative medicine,* 12, 162. https://doi.org/10.1186/1472-6882-12-162

Ford, B. Q., Lam, P., John, O. P., & Mauss, I. B. (2018). The psychological health benefits of accepting negative emotions and thoughts: Laboratory, diary, and longitudinal evidence. *Journal of Personality and Social Psychology*, 115(6), 1075–1092.

Frankl, V. E. (2006). Man's Search for Meaning. Beacon Press.

Gotink, R. A., Hermans, K. S. F. M., Geschwind, N., De Nooij, R., De Groot, W. T., & Speckens, A. E. M. (2016). Mindfulness and mood stimulate each other in an upward spiral: A mindful walking intervention using experience sampling. *Mindfulness, 7*(5), 1114–1122.

Hadith an-Nawawi Hadith 35, 40 Retrieved from https://sunnah.com/nawawi40/35

Hanh, T. N. (1997). The Miracle of Mindfulness: An Introduction to the Practice of Meditation. Beacon Press,

Hayes, S. C., Strosahl, K. D., & Wilson, K. G. (1999). An experiential approach to behaviour change. Guilford Press.

Hayes, S. C., & Wilson, K. (2006). Mindfulness: Method and process. *Clinical Psychology: Science and Practice, 10*(2), 161–165. https://doi.org/10.1093/clipsy.bpg018

Ibn al-Qayyim al-Jawziyya. (n.d.) Ranks of the Divine Seekers *Al Madaarij as-Saalikeen* Volume 1 & 2. Translated, Annotated and Introduced by Ovamir Anjum 1976 Retrieved from https://ia601707.us.archive.org/21/items/madarij-as-salikin-english-vol-1/Mada%CC%84rij%20as-Saliki%CC%84n%20%5BEnglish%5D%20Vol%202.pdf

International Association for the Study of Pain (IASP). (2020). IASP Announces Revised Definition of Pain. Retrieved from https://www.iasp-pain.org/PublicationsNews/NewsDetail.aspx?ItemNumber=10475

Irhas, I., Aziz, A., & Satriawan, L. (2023). The power of dhikr: Elevating intellectual, emotional, and spiritual quotients. *AL-HAYAT Journal of Islamic Education, 7*(2), 601.

Kabat-Zinn, J. (1982). An outpatient program in behavioural medicine for chronic pain patients based on the practice of mindfulness meditation: Theoretical considerations and preliminary results. *General Hospital Psychiatry, 4*(1), 33–47.

Kabat-Zinn, J. (2003). Mindfulness-based interventions in context: Past, present, and future. Clinical Psychology: Science and Practice, 10(2), 144–156. https://doi.org/10.1093/clipsy.bpg016

Kabat-Zinn, J. (2011). Mindfulness for Beginners: Reclaiming the Present Moment and Your Life. Sounds True.

Kabat-Zinn, J., Lipworth, L., & Burney, R. (1985). The clinical use of mindfulness meditation to self-regulate chronic pain. *Journal of Behavioral Medicine, 8*(2), 163–190.

Keng, S. L., Smoski, M. J., & Robins, C. J. (2011). Effects of mindfulness on psychological health: A review of empirical studies. *Clinical Psychology Review, 31*(6), 1041–1056.

Lee, C., Crawford, C., & Hickey, A. (2014). Mind-body therapies for the self-management of chronic pain symptoms. *Pain Medicine,* 15(Suppl 1), S21–39. https://doi.org/10.1111/pme.12383

Linehan, M. (1993). Cognitive-Behavioral treatment of borderline personality disorder (Diagnosis and Treatment of Mental Disorders). The Guilford Press.

Lutz, A., Jha, A. P., Dunne, J., & Saron, C. D. (2015). Investigating the phenomenological matrix of mindfulness-related practices from a neurocognitive perspective. *American Psychologist,* 70(7), 632-658. https://doi.org/10.1037/a0039585

Mawjud, A., & Ali, S. (2006). The Biography of Imam ibn al-Qaayim. Maktaba Dar us Salam. Retrieved from https://kalamullah.com/Books/The%20Biography%20Of%2 0Imam%20Ibn%20Al-Qayyim%20by%20Salahud-Din%20Ali%20Abdul-Mawjud.pdf

McCraty, R., Atkinson, M., Tomasino, D., & Bradley, R. T. (2009). The coherent heart: Heart-brain interactions, psychophysiological coherence, and the emergence of system-wide order. *Integral Review: A Transdisciplinary & Transcultural Journal for New Thought, Research, & Praxis,* 5(2), 10–115.

Merkes, M. (2010). Mindfulness-based stress reduction for people with chronic diseases. *Australian Journal of Primary Health,* 16(3), 200–210. https://doi.org/10.1071/PY09063

Mills, S. E. E., Nicolson, K. P., & Smith, B. H. (2019). Chronic pain: a review of its epidemiology and associated factors in population-based studies. *British Journal of Anaesthesia,* 123(2), e273–e283. https://doi.org/10.1016/j.bja.2019.03.023

Montoya, P., Schandry, R., & Muller, A. (1993). Heartbeat evoked potentials (HEP): Topography and influence of cardiac awareness and focus of attention. *Electroencephalography and Clinical Neurophysiology,* 88(3), 163–172.

NICE guideline NG193. Evidence review for psychological therapy for chronic primary pain https://www.nice.org.uk/guidance/ng193/evidence/f-psychological-therapy-for-chronic-primary-pain-pdf-9071987011

Omais, S., & dos Santos, M. A. (2022). Happiness in Islam: The role of religion and spirituality in Muslims' well-being. In Shariff, N. N. M., Yakob, M. A., Hamidi, Z. S., Aghwan, Z. A. A., & Lateh, N. (Eds.), *Selected proceedings from the 1st International Conference* on Contemporary Islamic Studies (ICIS 2021). Springer, Singapore. https://doi.org/10.1007/978-981-19-2390-6_19

Ostafin, B. D., Brooks, J., & Laitem, M. (2014). Affective reactivity mediates an inverse relation between mindfulness and anxiety. *Mindfulness,* *5*(5), 520–528. https://doi.org/10.1007/s12671-013-0206-X

Phillips, C. J. (2009). The cost and burden of chronic pain. *Reviews in Pain,* *3*(1), 2–5. https://doi.org/10.1177/204946370900300102

Pocock, M., Hamlin, I., Christelow, J., Passmore, H., & Richardson, M. (2023). The benefits of citizen science and nature-noticing activities for well-being, nature connectedness and pro-nature conservation behaviours. *People and Nature, 5*(2), 591–606. https://doi.org/10.1002/pan3.10432

Riyad as-Salihin 393 Retrieved from: https://sunnah.com/riyadussalihin:393

Riyad as-Salihin 1030: Retrieved from https://sunnah.com/riyadussalihin:1030

Sahih al-Bukhari 7563, Book 97, Hadith 188. Retrieved from https://sunnah.com/bukhari:7563

Sahih al-Bukhari 1117, Book 18, Hadith 37. Retrieved from https://sunnah.com/bukhari:1117

Sahih al-Bukhari Volume 8, Book 76, Number 552. Retrieved from https://sahih-bukhari.com/Pages/results.php

Sahih Muslim 2702a, Book 48, Hadith 52. Retrieved from https://sunnah.com/muslim:2702a

Sahih Muslim 2202, Book 39, Hadith 91. Retrieved from https://sunnah.com/muslim:2202

Segal, Z. V., Williams, J. M. G., & Teasdale, J. D. (2002). Mindfulness-based cognitive therapy for depression: A new approach to preventing relapse. Guilford Press.

Sunan al-Tirmidhi 2012 Book 27, Hadith 118 Retrieved from https://sunnah.com/search?q=Sunan+al-Tirmidhi%2C+Hadith+2012

Swain, N., Lennox Thompson, B., Gallagher, S., Paddison, J., & Mercer, S. (2020). Gratitude enhanced mindfulness (GEM): A pilot study of an internet-delivered programme for self-management of pain and disability in people with arthritis. *The Journal of Positive Psychology, 15*(3), 420–426. https://doi.org/10.1080/17439760.2019.1627397

Talebkhah, K. S. (2018). Neurological evidence of a mind-body connection: Mindfulness and pain control. *Raymond St. Marie and American Journal of Psychiatry Residents' Journal, 13*(4), 2–5.

Tennen, H., Affleck, G., & Tennen, R. (2002). Clipped feathers: The theory and measurement of hope. *Psychological Inquiry, 13*(4), 311–317.

Thich Nhat Hạnh. (1997). The Miracle of Mindfulness: An Introduction to the Practice of Meditation. Beacon Press.

Thomas, J., Furber, S. W., & Grey, I. (2018). The rise of mindfulness and its resonance with the Islamic tradition. *Mental Health, Religion & Culture*. https://doi.org/10.1080/13674676.2017.1412410

Tifft, E. D., Underwood, S. B., Roberts, M. Z., & Forsyth, J. P. (2022). Using meditation in a control vs. acceptance context: A preliminary evaluation of relations with anxiety, depression, and indices of well-being. *Journal of Clinical Psychology, 78*(7), 1407–1421. https://doi.org/10.1002/jclp.23313

Toussaint L, Nguyen QA, Roettger C, Dixon K, Offenbächer M, Kohls N, Hirsch J, Sirois F. Effectiveness of Progressive Muscle Relaxation, Deep Breathing, and Guided Imagery in Promoting Psychological and Physiological States of Relaxation. *Evid Based Complement Alternat Med.* 2021 Jul 2; 2021:5924040. doi: 10.1155/2021/5924040. PMID: 34306146; PMCID: PMC8272667.

Zeidan, F., & Vago, D. R. (2016). Mindfulness meditation-based pain relief: A mechanistic account. *Annals of the New York Academy of Sciences, 1373*(1), 114–127. https://doi.org/10.1111/nyas.13153

Zhang, Q., Wang, Z., Wang, X., Liu, L., Zhang, J., & Zhou, R. (2019). The effects of different stages of mindfulness meditation training on emotion regulation. *Frontiers in Human Neuroscience, 13*, 208. https://doi.org/10.3389/fnhum.2019.00208

CHAPTER 7

Heart-Centered Mindfulness as a Tool for Self-Knowledge
and Self-Improvement

Wadud Hassan & Maneeza Dawood, PhD

Introduction

Mindfulness, of late, has become a buzzword among the general public.
Popular culture has co-opted mindfulness as a wellness trend, emphasizing
its practical benefits for everyday stress and personal growth. Mindfulness
practices have also been recognized in academic literature for their benefits
in developing emotional awareness, regulation, and well-being (Hölzel et
al., 2011). However, contemporary psychological literature often focuses
on practical aspects of mindfulness, devoid of spiritual context.

In contrast, Islamically-integrated mindfulness, *muraqaba*, centers
the heart and offers a spiritual approach to emotional well-being and self-
improvement that prioritizes the remembrance of God. While both forms of
mindfulness emphasize the importance of present-moment purpose and
awareness, Islamically–integrated mindfulness integrates this awareness
with a continuous consciousness of God's presence, aiming to cultivate a
deeper spiritual connection and submission to the Divine will (Rothman &
Coyle, 2018). This integration not only enriches the practitioner's spiritual
life but also aligns them in presence, purpose, and practice. Consequently,
Islamically–integrated mindfulness extends beyond the individualistic
focus of contemporary psychological practices, embedding individual well-
being within the broader context of God-consciousness and spiritual
fulfillment.

This chapter aims to bridge the gap in contemporary psychology literature on mindfulness by reviewing the theological foundations of muraqaba. It explores the development of a heart-centered mindfulness program drawing from contemporary mindfulness literature, as well as the theological foundations of Islamically–integrated mindfulness outlined by Imam Al-Ghazali (d. 1111 AH) and inspired by a Prophetic framework. Lastly, it outlines two specific Islamically–integrated mindfulness practices used in the program: Presence of God (*hudhur*) for cultivating the best-self, and the Spiritual Body Scan (*muhasaba*), for developing deeper self-awareness, self-regulation, and connection with God.

Mindfulness in Contemporary Psychological Literature

Mindfulness meditation in Western psychology encompasses both focused attention and open-monitoring meditations (Kabat-Zinn, 2011). Focused attention involves intensive and sustained single-point focused meditation that explicitly trains the acuity, flexibility, and stability of attention. Open monitoring involves non-reactive, non-elaborative, non-goal directed responses to all sensations and perceptions (both internally and externally), and is explicitly rooted in the body and basic somatic awareness (Lutz et al., 2008). Both practices are often combined in Western mindfulness–based interventions, and the most common definition of mindfulness in contemporary psychology is "paying attention, in a particular way, on purpose, in the present-moment, and non-judgmentally" (Kabat-Zinn, 2011). The general benefits of mindfulness practice described by practitioners are enhanced emotional awareness and emotion regulation (Gross, 1998; Lane et al., 1990).

Kabat-Zinn (1994) integrated mindfulness with Western psychology by developing the Mindfulness-Based Stress Reduction (MBSR) program, highlighting its potential to reduce stress and improve health outcomes. Subsequent research expanded on these foundations, demonstrating the positive impact of mindfulness on anxiety, depression, and attention regulation (Chiesa & Serretti, 2009; Hofmann et al., 2010). Mindfulness practices have also been linked to structural and functional brain changes, suggesting a biological basis for its therapeutic effects (Fox et al., 2014; Hölzel et al., 2011).

A meta-analysis of 47 studies found that clinical mindfulness methods led to decreases in depression, anxiety, and pain. Mindfulness methods were nearly as effective as medication, and without side effects (Bamber & Morpeth, 2019; Goleman & Davidson, 2017; Hilton et al., 2017; Reangsing et al., 2022; Ren et al., 2018; Weilgosz et al., 2022). Additional meta-analyses have examined the efficacy of mindfulness meditation and MBSR for improving sleep quality (Rusch et al., 2019), workplace stress

(Heckenberg et al., 2018), smoking cessation (Maglione et al., 2017), weight loss (Rogers et al., 2017), general psychological well-being (Eberth & Sedlmeier, 2012), and even increased teacher compassion and classroom prosocial engagement (Floman, 2018). This research highlights mindfulness as a powerful tool in psychological interventions, with a growing consensus on its utility across various mental health and behavioral contexts. Consequently, mindfulness meditation is rapidly being integrated with many different forms in clinical, therapeutic, and educational practice.

Islamically–Integrated Mindfulness

The roots of mindfulness meditation in contemporary psychological literature derive from Buddhist tradition. However, mindfulness has been practiced for thousands of years by many cultures and faith traditions (Koenig, 2023; Lutz et al., 2008). Whereas contemporary mindfulness practice focuses on enhancing emotional awareness and regulation, Islamically–integrated mindfulness underpins this through the lens of Divine remembrance. This emphasizes the incomplete nature of popular mindfulness practices from an Islamic perspective, which seeks a God-centered approach in all aspects of life, including emotional and mental well-being. Thus, Islamically–integrated mindfulness is not merely about focused attention and open monitoring, but about anchoring everything in the awareness of God.

Within Islamic tradition, the essence of mindfulness, *taqwa* (God-consciousness), is rooted in the heart. The Prophet (peace be upon him) emphasized the heart's centrality by stating, "Verily, in the body is a piece of flesh which, if sound, the entire body is sound, and if corrupt, the entire body is corrupt. Truly, it is the heart" (Bukhari, n.d.). The Quran states: "Those who honor God's rites show the taqwa of their hearts" (Quran, 22:32). The development of a sound heart involves cultivating emotional awareness and emotion regulation through engagement with one's internal states and motivations.

Two extremely important and influential scholars from the Islamic tradition - Imam Abu Hamid Al-Ghazali, a Persian theologian, jurist, and mystic, and Ibn Qayyim al-Jawziyya, a Syrian jurist and theologian (d. 1350 CE) emphasized the importance of being cognizant of one's mind and body to activate the heart's capacity for ethical discernment and Divine orientation. This process involves recognizing the transient nature of thoughts and emotions and their progression from fleeting ideas to deliberate actions, thereby fostering a heart-centered approach.

Another important classical Islamic figure, Imam Jalal ad-Din al-Suyuti, an Egyptian scholar who made significant contributions to Hadith, tafsir, and jurisprudence (n.d., d. 911 CE), outlined the various stages of thought that lead to mindful action. The first stage, *al-hajis*, is a fleeting thought that comes and goes; it may be implicit. The second stage, *al-khatir*, is a conscious thought that we can choose to act upon or ignore. The third stage, *Hadith al-nafs*, involves the inner dialogue as we consider the explicit actions to take, which may be expanded on or ignored. The final stages, *al-ham* and *al-'azm*, involve the decision itself and the resulting explicit actions and behavior taken as a result (Al-Suyuti, n.d.; Parrot, 2017).

Rooted in Islamic spirituality, Islamic mindfulness (muraqaba) emphasizes the heart's role as the spiritual center, advocating for a consciousness permeated by the awareness of God in every aspect of life. The practices of *dhikr* (remembrance of God) and *fikr* (God-centered contemplation or meditation) serve not only as a method for centering the heart and mind but also as a way to cultivate a deeper connection and submission to God. A primary objective of Islamic mindfulness is spiritual enhancement and ethical self-improvement, aiming for a state of *ihsaan* (spiritual excellence fueled by spiritual presence) as if one sees God, or at least, being mindful that God sees them. In practice, *salah* (the five daily prayers), for example, involves mindfulness in preparation (ablution), movements, and recitations, fostering a state of spiritual attentiveness and connection with God. Fasting, another of the five pillars of Islam, emphasizes spiritual enhancement, reflecting a transformation of the spiritual heart toward greater self-discipline and empathy.

The integration of God-centered and cognitive dimensions of mindfulness represents a unique contribution of Islamic psychology. Drawing from the wisdom of classical Islamic scholars based on the principles found within the Quran and Hadith, Islamic psychology offers a holistic approach to emotional well-being that encompasses not only cognitive restructuring but also spiritual purification and ethical living. This perspective aligns with contemporary psychological practices such as cognitive-behavioral therapy by recognizing the interplay between thought, emotion, and behavior.

However, it goes further by situating emotional regulation within the context of attaining heart-centered and God-conscious excellence. Such an approach not only addresses the symptoms of emotional distress but also nurtures the soul's inherent disposition (*fitrah*) towards tranquility, resilience, and connection with the Divine. By exploring the therapeutic potential of patience, remembrance of God, and repentance, Islamic psychology offers valuable insights into the cultivation of emotional intelligence and spiritual well-being, underscoring the importance of an integrated approach to mental health that honors both the mind and the spirit.

Development of the HEART Model

The HEART Model aims to fill a gap in Western mindfulness meditation programs by integrating the theoretical foundations laid by Imam Al-Ghazali and the Prophetic framework, alongside contemporary psychological research. The theoretical foundation of the model is rooted in the Islamic concept of *hikma*, or wisdom, exemplified by Prophet Luqman. Hikma is the ability to see the beauty and purpose in everything we go through in life. One of Allah's Names is *Al Hakeem*- the All-Wise. When we trust His Wisdom and process everything through the wisdom revealed in His Book, we can gain more clarity and positivity in life.

The Quran states: "The Most Compassionate... Taught the Quran... He created human beings... And taught him speech" (Quran, 55:1-4). Importantly, Allah "taught the Quran" even before the mention of the creation or the intelligent speech of human beings. The Quran provides knowledge and guidance, and Quranic knowledge is not limited to *'aql* (intelligence of the mind), but also spiritual intelligence rooted in the heart. One of the words used to describe the Quran is *Al Hakeem*: the wise book: "By the Quran, rich in wisdom" (Quran, 36:2).

Allah revealed ultimate wisdom or intelligence through Divine revelations to His chosen messengers whom He instructed to teach and reflect. Allah commanded Prophet Muhammad (peace be upon him): "Invite to the way of your Lord with Hikma and kind teaching" (Quran, 16:125). To revive dead hearts, guide lost people, and bring certainty during the uncertainties of life, the quality Allah asked the Prophet to use was hikma. Prophet Muhammad was also the best example of using hikma in his life in addressing challenges and uncertainties he faced when calling others to Islam (Hassan, 2020).

The Quran also teaches wisdom through Prophet Luqman. An entire chapter of the Quran is dedicated to Luqman: "Indeed, We endowed Luqman with wisdom" (Quran, 31:12). Surah Luqman captures his beautiful wisdom in the form of advice to his son. The Quran narrates the advice of Luqman to his son in six verses, reminding him to worship God alone, to be mindful of God, be excellent in worship, give thanks to God and parents, bear challenges with patience, avoid arrogance, lower one's voice, enjoin good and forbid evil, and that God is the final destination (Quran, 31:13-19). These verses highlight several key principles of hikma, including establishing a connection with God through prayer, developing moral responsibility, and having patience in adversity. Hikma is not merely intellectual knowledge but a deeper understanding that integrates both the mind and the heart. It involves applying knowledge in a way that is beneficial and aligned with Divine wisdom (Hassan, 2020).

Another foundation of the HEART Model is the Prophetic response to the overwhelming adversity faced during the incident of Taif. Prophet Muhammad (peace be upon him) faced severe rejection and physical assault in Taif when he went there to invite the town's people to Islam. After being chased out of Taif and pelted with stones, the Prophet sought refuge in an orchard, where he made a heartfelt supplication to God, expressing his vulnerability and seeking Divine support. This moment highlighted his unwavering trust in God's wisdom and mercy, even in the face of severe adversity. Despite the intense hardship, his response was a model of Mindfulness of God and Compassion. His response teaches us that resilience is rooted in a deep spiritual connection and trust in God's plan (Hassan, 2021). These principles also align with Kabat-Zinn's three dimensions of mindfulness: purpose, presence, and absence of judgment (Kabat-Zinn, 2011).

Purpose: The Spiritual Mindfulness of Intention

Intention, a purposeful act of mindfulness, requires focused awareness. In Islamic scholarship, making an intention is foundational, as actions depend on intentions. This principle is rooted in the saying of Prophet Muhammad (peace be upon him), "Every action depends on the intention" (Bukhari, n.d.; Muslim, n.d.). This spiritual process fuels our drive, motivation, and excellence. Ibn Ata'illah al-Iskandari (n.d.; d. 1309 CE) was an Egyptian Sufi scholar and a key figure in the Shadhili Sufi order. He is best known for his work "Al-Hikam" (The Book of Wisdom), which consists of aphorisms on spiritual wisdom and guidance, emphasizing the importance of reliance on God and the inner dimensions of faith. In his Hikam, Ibn Ata'illah (n.d.) emphasized that "actions are lifeless forms, but the presence of an inner sincerity is what endows us with life-giving spirit".

Prophet Muhammad (peace be upon him) said:

> *Whoever makes an intention for the sake of the world, Allah, the exalted, brings poverty before him and leaves him desiring it. Whoever makes the afterlife his intention, Allah, the exalted, makes his heart rich and gathers him with what he lost. (Ibn Majah, n.d.)*

This highlights the importance of intentions aligned with higher purposes, which drives us to serve with our best selves in all areas of life.

Presence: The Spiritual Mindfulness of Hudhur

The concept of Hudhur, or being present with God, was recommended as the most important prerequisite of *khushu* or a mindful salah by Imam Al-Ghazali in his Mysteries of Prayer in *Ihya Ulum Al-Din* (Revival of the Religious Sciences). The Quran states: "And know that Allah knows what is in your souls, so be mindful of Him" (2:235). Presence of mind is crucial for our service to God and for achieving success and satisfaction in our work. Hudhur, in this verse, means being deeply conscious of God (and all that this consciousness entails from doing what He pleases and abandoning what He's displeased with).

Harvard psychologists Daniel Gilbert and Matthew Killingsworth found that our minds wander about 47% of the time, leading to decreased happiness and satisfaction (Killingsworth & Gilbert, 2010). This aligns with the Islamic guidelines of interaction (*muamalat*), in which work is considered a form of worship with the right intention and effort. The Prophet (peace be upon him) exemplified presence through his interactions, where he listened with his heart, turning his entire attention to the speaker. This level of engagement and presence is essential for effective leadership and meaningful relationships at work and home.

Absence of Judgment

The Prophet (peace be upon him) said:

> *How wonderful is the case of a believer, there is good for him in
> everything and this applies only to a believer. If prosperity attends
> him, he expresses gratitude to Allah and that is good for him; and
> if adversity befalls him, he endures it patiently and that is better for
> him (Muslim).*

This Prophetic teaching emphasizes the importance of not judging any situation or circumstance in life as good or bad just by its mere outward appearance.

In Islamic tradition, the concept of not judging any situation as inherently negative is best linked to the notion of *Husn al-Dhann* (having a good opinion of God). This principle encourages believers to trust in God's wisdom and mercy, even when facing seemingly adverse circumstances. The Quran states, "But perhaps you hate a thing and it is good for you; and perhaps you love a thing and it is bad for you. And Allah knows, while you know not" (2:216). This verse highlights the importance of avoiding judgment and recognizing that human understanding is limited compared to Divine knowledge. Through these Prophetic principles of a productive

162

mindset, Muslims are guided to be grateful and patient in every situation, thereby attracting God's pleasure and assistance. This mindset is not just about enduring hardships passively but actively engaging in spiritual practices that promote emotional well-being and resilience (Hassan, 2021).

Components of the HEART Model

The HEART Model offers a comprehensive framework for integrating Islamic principles with contemporary mindfulness practices. Each component of the HEART acronym addresses a unique aspect of personal and spiritual development, combining the wisdom of Islamic teachings with insights from modern psychology and neuroscience. It consists of 6 weeks of training, each session lasting 3 hours. The program includes daily mindfulness practices and weekly homework, correlating the theme of each week with Islamic spiritual practices such as dhikr (remembrance), Salah (prayer), *Du'aa* (supplication), and Prophetic affirmations.

Each week focuses on a specific aspect of the HEART Model, aiming to train the heart and mind through guided practices. The model begins with healing in the Presence of God (H), transitioning from an autopilot lifestyle to one of awareness & intentionality. Engaging with Purpose (E) transitions awareness to an actualization of one's purpose. Achieving with Gratitude (A) focuses on shifting from a mindset of scarcity to one of abundance. Rising with patience and humility (R) involves embracing and regulating challenging emotions through developing emotional awareness. The final module is Thriving with compassion (T) as a foundation for developing interpersonal relationships and leadership. It extends mindfulness, awareness, and compassion in interactions, from family to broader societal roles.

Two Timeless Al-Ghazali Tools for Self-Knowledge and Self-Improvement

Below, we describe two heart-centered mindfulness practices used in the program, drawn from Imam Al-Ghazali's teachings.

Presence of God (Hudhur Al-Qalb)

Islamic teachings emphasize salah (the five daily prayers) as a Divine gift and a fundamental practice for nurturing the heart and soul. This practice, bestowed during the Prophet's (peace be upon him) celestial journey (*Isra wal M'iraj*), serves as a vital tool for enhancing focus, awareness, and Divine connection. The Quran highlights salah as a means of self-regulation, deterring believers from indecency and wrongdoing, and enhancing remembrance of Allah. God mentions in the Quran:

> Recite what has been revealed to you of the Book and establish prayer. Indeed, genuine prayer should deter one from indecency and wickedness. The remembrance of Allah is an even greater deterrent. And Allah fully knows what you all do. (Quran, 29:45)

Prayer and dhikr (remembrance of Allah) act as instruments of mindful heart regulation, steering the self away from the immorality associated with our lower desires. The essence of heartfelt prayer lies in *Hudhur Al-Qalb* (Presence of Heart), a concept detailed by Imam Ghazali in his seminal work, *Ihya Ulum Al-Din*. He outlines that genuine prayer involves more than physical motions; it requires a heart fully engaged in Divine contemplation.

To cultivate Hudhur, practitioners are encouraged to:

1. Sit in Seclusion
2. Empty One's Heart of All Concerns
3. Strive to Let No Thought Enter One's Mind Besides Allah
4. Instill "Presence of the Heart"
5. Train One's Heart to be Diligent in Remembrance

Hudhur, akin to dhikr of the heart, is a meditation for transcending external and internal distractions and achieving a state of complete immersion in Divine presence. It is recommended to begin with brief daily sessions and gradually incorporate this practice into the preparation for salah.

Spiritual Body Scan

The "Spiritual Body Scan," offers a guided meditation technique for enhancing self-awareness and spiritual regulation, inspired by Imam Ghazali's teachings. Similar in concept to the Body Scan in MBSR (Kabat-Zinn, 1994), this mindfulness practice examines the actions of seven bodily limbs in light of *Munjiyat* (actions bringing one closer to Allah) versus *Muhlikat* (actions distancing one from Allah).

The Spiritual Body Scan involves the following steps (as developed in the heart-centered masterclass):

1. Start with a few moments of breathing to activate calm and focus
2. Practice Hudhur or presence of heart,
3. Scan the seven limbs specified by Imam Al-Ghazali one by one for Muhlikat or all actions that one might be committing through that limb that would take one away from God and one's best self:
   - eyes,
   - ears,

- tongue,
- stomach,
- genitals,
- hands, and
- feet.

4. For each limb, stop and reflect on it for a moment. For every undesirable action, ask God for forgiveness and cleansing. Repent and return to Him with this phrase: *"Astagfirullah, Allahumma Atubu 'Ilayk."* Visualize cleansing through God's forgiveness and mercy with a heartful resolve not to return to that action.

5. Once scanning and reflecting on the seven limbs in relation to Muhlikat is completed, do the same for each limb reflecting on Munjiyat or Desirable actions that take one closer to God and one's best self. This time, express heartful gratitude to God for the facilitation of each of these good deeds, ask for His acceptance, and continued presence.

6. After completing the seven limbs, if time permits, add the heart and repeat all the above steps for the actions of the heart including:

7. *Munjiyat* such as *Iman* (faith), *Yaqeen* (certainty), *Taqwa* (God consciousness), *Ihsaan* (Spiritual Excellence fueled by God-centered Presence), *Ikhlaas* (Sincerity*)*, *Shukr (*Gratitude), *Sabr (*Patience), *Rahma (*Compassion).

8. *Muhlikat* such as *Shirk* (*associating partners with God*)*, *Kufr* (*disbelief*)*, *Ghaflah* (heedlessness), *Riya* (showing off), *Hasad* (envy), *Kibr* (superiority), *Bugz* (spite), *Shahwa* (desire).

Engaging in this practice weekly synergizes the principles of muraqaba (mindful meditation on God) and *muhasaba* (self-audit), fostering profound spiritual awareness and self-regulation. This approach embodies the Hadith, "The one who strives in the way of Allah is the one who strives against their own soul" (Ahmad, n.d.; Tirmidhi, n.d.), underscoring the inner journey towards achieving one's highest spiritual potential.

Conclusion

Islamic spiritual tradition and scholarship have a rich history and practice of heart-centered mindfulness as a tool for increased self-knowledge and self-improvement; combined with contemporary psychological approaches, they can become powerful tools for transformation. The HEART Model represents an integrative approach to mindfulness that combines Islamic tradition with contemporary psychological practices. By centering the heart and embedding mindfulness within the remembrance of God, this model moves beyond the individualistic focus of conventional mindfulness practices. The HEART Model's emphasis on purpose, presence, and

absence of judgment aligns deeply with both the teachings of Imam Al-
Ghazali and modern psychological principles, offering a holistic path for
emotional well-being and self-improvement.

Further research on heart-centered mindfulness and its integration
into clinical practice holds significant promise. Future studies can expand
our understanding of how these practices can be effectively utilized in
diverse therapeutic settings. Such research will not only contribute to the
field of Islamic psychology but also enrich the broader landscape of
mindfulness-based interventions. As the field of mindfulness continues to
evolve, the HEART Model provides a compelling framework for
incorporating the Islamic tradition into contemporary practices, fostering a
more inclusive and spiritually enriched approach to mental health and
personal growth.

References

Ahmad, A. H. (n.d.). *Musnad Ahmad*. Noor Foundation, Inc.

Al-Suyuti, J. (n.d.). *Al-Ashbah Wal-Naza'ir Fi Qawa'id Wa Furu' Fiqh Al-Shafi'iyah*. Bayrūt: Dar al-Kutub al-'Ilmiyah.

Bamber, M. D., & Morpeth, E. (2019). Effects of mindfulness meditation on college student anxiety: A meta-analysis. *Mindfulness, 10*(2), 203-214.

Bukhari. (n.d.). *Sahih Bukhari*. Dar Ibn Kathir, Beirut-Damasqus.

Chiesa, A., & Serretti, A. (2009). Mindfulness-based stress reduction for stress management in healthy people: A review and meta-analysis. *The Journal of Alternative and Complementary Medicine, 15*(5), 593–600.

Eberth, J., & Sedlmeier, P. (2012). The effects of mindfulness meditation: A meta-analysis. *Mindfulness, 3*(3), 174–189.

Floman, J. L. (2018). Mindfulness in education: The effect of mindfulness practice on teacher stress and teacher-student relationships. *Educational Psychology Review, 30*(1), 83–110.

Fox, K. C. R., Nijeboer, S., Dixon, M. L., Floman, J. L., Ellamil, M., Rumak, S. P., . . . Christoff, K. (2014). Is meditation associated with altered brain structure? A systematic review and meta-analysis of morphometric neuroimaging in meditation practitioners. *Neuroscience & Biobehavioral Reviews, 43*, 48–73.

Ghazali, A. H. M. (n.d.). *Ihya Ulum al-Din* (Revival of Religious Sciences). Mesir: Matba'ah Mustafa al-Bab al-Halabi.

Goleman, D., & Davidson, R. J. (2017). *Altered traits: Science reveals how meditation changes your mind, brain, and body*. Penguin.

Gross, J. J. (1998). The emerging field of emotion regulation: An integrative review. *Review of General Psychology, 2*(3), 271–299.

Hassan, W. (2020, July 22). The HEART of spiritual intelligence: How to cultivate hikma (wisdom) during uncertain times. *Islamic Insights*. https://www.islamicinsights.com/heart-spiritual-intelligence

Hassan, W. (2021, September 28). Addressing overwhelm with a prophetic H.E.A.R.T. *Islamic Mindfulness*. https://www.islamicmindfulness.com/prophetic-heart

Heckenberg, R. A., Eddy, P., Kent, S., & Wright, B. J. (2018). Do workplace-based mindfulness meditation programs improve

physiological indices of stress? A systematic review and meta-
analysis. *Journal of psychosomatic research, 114*, 62-71.

Hilton, L., Hempel, S., Ewing, B. A., Apaydin, E., Xenakis, L., Newberry, S., ... & Maglione, M. A. (2017). Mindfulness meditation for chronic pain: systematic review and meta-analysis. *Annals of Behavioral Medicine, 51*(2), 199-213.

Hofmann, S. G., Sawyer, A. T., Witt, A. A., & Oh, D. (2010). The effect of mindfulness-based therapy on anxiety and depression: A meta-analytic review. *Journal of Consulting and Clinical Psychology, 78*(2), 169–183.

Hölzel, B. K., Carmody, J., Vangel, M., Congleton, C., Yerramsetti, S. M., Gard, T., & Lazar, S. W. (2011). Mindfulness practice leads to increases in regional brain gray matter density. *Psychiatry Research: Neuroimaging, 191*(1), 36–43.

Ibn Ata'illah. (n.d.). *Al-Hikam.* Trans. Victor Danner (1973). Leiden: EJ Brill.

Ibn Majah. (n.d.). *Sunan Ibn Majah.* Darul Kutub Al Ilmiyyah.

Kabat-Zinn, J. (1994). *Wherever you go, there you are: Mindfulness meditation in everyday life.* Hyperion.

Kabat-Zinn, J. (2011). *Mindfulness for beginners: Reclaiming the present moment—and your life.* Sounds True.

Killingsworth, M. A., & Gilbert, D. T. (2010). A wandering mind is an unhappy mind. *Science, 330*(6006), 932.

Koenig, H. G. (2023). Religion, spirituality, and mental health: The research and clinical implications. *Frontiers in Psychiatry, 14*, 669.

Lane, R. D., Reiman, E. M., Axelrod, B., Yun, L. S., Holmes, A., Schwarz, G. E., & Bearn, J. (1990). Neural correlates of levels of emotional awareness. *Evidence of an interaction between emotion and attention in the anterior cingulate cortex. Journal of Cognitive Neuroscience, 10*(4), 525–535.

Lutz, A., Slagter, H. A., Dunne, J. D., & Davidson, R. J. (2008). Attention regulation and monitoring in meditation. *Trends in Cognitive Sciences, 12*(4), 163-169.

Maglione, M. A., Maher, A. R., Ewing, B., Colaiaco, B., Newberry, S., Kandrack, R., ... & Hempel, S. (2017). Efficacy of mindfulness meditation for smoking cessation: A systematic review and meta-analysis. *Addictive Behaviors, 69*, 27-34.

Muslim. (n.d.). *Sahih Muslim.* Dar-us-Salam Publications Inc; First Edition (June 1, 2007).

Parrott, J. (2017, November 21). How to be a mindful Muslim: An exercise in Islamic meditation. Hassan, W. (2021, September 28). *Yaqeen Institute.* https://yaqeeninstitute.org/read/paper/how-to-be-a-mindful-muslim-an-exercise-in-islamic-meditation

The Qur'an (M.A.S Abdel Haleem, Trans.). (2004). Oxford University Press.

Reangsing, C., Punsuwun, S., & Schneider, J. K. (2022). Effects of mindfulness interventions on depressive symptoms in adolescents: A meta-analysis. *International Journal of Nursing Studies, 123*, 104051.

Ren, X., Li, X., Zhang, X., & Li, J. (2018). Effects of mindfulness meditation on anxiety, depression, stress, and mindfulness in college students: A meta-analysis. *Frontiers in Psychology, 9*, 1037.

Rogers, J. M., Ferrari, M., Mosely, K., Lang, C. P., & Brennan, L. (2017). Mindfulness-based interventions for adults who are overweight or obese: A meta-analysis of physical and psychological health outcomes. *Obesity Reviews, 18*(1), 51–67.

Rothman, A. J., & Coyle, K. K. (2018). Integrating religious and spiritual practices into psychotherapy: A new domain for cross-cultural competence. *Professional Psychology: Research and Practice, 49*(3), 189–195.

Rusch, H. L., Rosario, M., Levison, L. M., Olivera, A., Luberto, C. M., Whitlock, K., & Rothbaum, B. (2019). The effect of mindfulness meditation on sleep quality: A systematic review and meta-analysis of randomized controlled trials. *Annals of the New York Academy of Sciences, 1445*(1), 5–16.

Tirmidhi, M. I. (n.d.). *Jami` at-Tirmidhi* (Sunan at-Tirmidhi).

Weilgosz, J. A., Hofmann, S. G., & Petrocchi, N. (2022). Mindfulness-based interventions for anxiety disorders: A meta-analysis. *Journal of Anxiety Disorders, 85*, 102491.

CHAPTER 8

The Centered Healing: Navigating Psychological Pain and
Peace Through Attachment and Detachment

Mahrukh Mustansar, PhD

Introduction

This chapter guides individuals navigating the depths of their inner turmoil. It transcends the boundaries of a mere self-help guide, delving into the essence of the human soul and its journey through the tumultuous sea of life. It also illuminates the path to safeguarding the heart (qalb) from sinking into despair and offers insights on how to resurface when it does. In addition, this chapter emphasizes the inherent capacity of every heart to heal and the transformative potential embedded within each moment of adversity.

The overarching goal of this chapter is to extend a lifeline of support to those grappling with their darkest hours, offering a roadmap towards healing, awakening, and rediscovering one's authentic self. The chapter serves as a guiding light for individuals going through tough times. Islam is a religion of peace and provides immense teachings for finding peace by adopting its esoteric principles to gain "Heartfulness". However, rates of depression have considerably increased in the last two decades (Wang et al., 2021). The use of antidepressants has increased by 400 percent in recent times (Larura et al., 2011). Spirituality can be essential for exploring emotional stability and managing anxiety (Sakellari et al., 2018).

Many spiritual practices, such as mindfulness meditation, prayer, and seeking guidance through the Qur'an, are effective in reducing stress and anxiety and promoting emotional well-being. The chapter consists of lessons learned from my own profound experience, the science of attachment and detachment, and navigating through life's complexities. There is a need to fill the inner void and create a pathway to purification. Therefore, we need help to psychologically navigate through the complexities of life in the light of the Qur'an and connect with divine wisdom.

This chapter also incorporates my poetic rendition of the soul's quest to find peace within. The mentioned poems reveal the significance of attachment and detachment and how to navigate through these intricate aspects of life. This is not just a chapter but a guiding light for many individuals who are silently suffering from emotional pain.

From a psychological perspective, Islam emphasizes the importance of mental wellness and the connection between the mind, body, and spirit (Isgandarova, 2019). The teachings encourage people to focus on maintaining a healthy balance among themselves by following the right path, doing good deeds, and being kind to others. Islamic spirituality is inseparable from the apprehension of Tawhid, or oneness. Islamic spirituality traces the in-depth impacts of Tawhid in one's life, thoughts, actions, and practices, and these distinguish the human as an ummah capable of leading.

This chapter is a reflection of my own life. It holds academic and personal significance for me. I am a PhD with a specialization in peace psychology, a certified advanced hypnotherapist, and a master NLP (Neuro-linguistic programming) practitioner. A couple of years ago, my life collapsed. While I was practicing psychology-based NLP on my clients, I decided to apply these inner dynamics to myself to heal my pain. As soon as I applied it, I experienced a vision unlike any other. In the recesses of my subconscious mind, I found myself standing before a mysterious cave, bathed in the ethereal glow of a full moon. An old man, cloaked in the radiance of the night sky, beckoned me forward with a knowing smile.

Intrigued and drawn by his presence, I approached the wise figure and posed a question that had long afflicted my soul: "What does this light represent"? His response resonated deep within me, echoing the wisdom of ages past. "This light signifies guidance in the dark moments," he intoned. "You just have to open your heart within."

With those words, the old man disappeared into the shadows, leaving me to contemplate his enigmatic message. Stepping into the cavernous depths of the cave, I was enveloped by an otherworldly glow, casting intricate patterns of light upon the walls. It was then that the old man reappeared, bearing a humble clay bowl filled with water. As I reached out to accept his offering, he imparted a truth that would resonate within my soul for eternity. "Water is needed for the body," he began, his voice a gentle whisper amidst the silence of the cave. "And so are the dark moments needed for the soul. Darkness holds a profound light within; you just need to see through the eyes within. Let your heart bathe in this light. Let your heart grow."

With each word, my understanding deepened, and my heart expanded with newfound clarity. The veils of darkness that had shrouded my perception began to lift, revealing the resplendent truth that had escaped me for so long. In that sacred moment of disclosure, I realized that darkness was not an adversary to be feared but an indication of growth and transformation.

As I emerged from the depths of the cave, bathed in the radiance of newfound understanding, I embraced the profound truth that had been revealed to me. Pain and darkness were not to be shunned or avoided but embraced as integral aspects of the soul's journey toward enlightenment. With each passing moment, I realized darkness is not real darkness. Instead, it holds a guiding light for us.

The apparent darkness becomes real darkness when our hearts become blind. We label the events happening in our lives as darkness because they cause us pain. However, pain is needed for our hearts to grow and our souls to evolve. It is the light in the darkness that makes our sight clearer. We just need to connect with divine wisdom. This chapter holds that secret of life that we all are seeking, but many of us are seeking it from false attachments and the world. Instead, it demands to be sought from the source of the world itself.

Soul Healing

Wake up!!!

A sleeping modern man, Wake up!

Life is changing,

Wake up

There's a lot to do, wake up nature is calling you.

Wisdom says nothing, yet it speaks loudly, like a silent prayer

that influences life paths, profoundly.

Wake up!

HEARTFULNESS

In the hour of loneliness, contemplate and find yourself,

collecting all the broken pieces and begin healing yourself.

Only a thirsty man can tell the worth of water or

ask its meaning from a fighting soldier,

when his breath dies and heartbeat skips,

on the battlefield with parched lips.

fill your soul with content and swim your heart in a divine sea.

else you will be drowned in the thirst of your plea.

Running fast at a lively pace, a restless modern man is so tired,

what a predicament has he brought with his soul on fire,

killing with swords or providing harm,

this is not the meaning of life,

contemplate yourself and make your soul calm.

wake up before it's too late!!!

and when the injuries of your soul get so profound,

it's when you connect yourself with all the hurting,

that is when you will reach for the balm.

The spring of your life which was lost,

where your good deeds were the cost.

The garden of your being was afflicted with crisis,

you found your soul crying and unrighteous.

And that time, you would need medicine for your soul healing:

Kindness, love, and prayer are the utmost medicine; just believe in.

Wake up!!!!

There is so much to do. The nature is calling you, wake up; there is a lot to do!!

Mahrukh Mustansar, Ph.D. (The Center, January 21, 2021)

Attachment and Detachment: Exploring the Reasons Behind Departures

At the beginning of my PhD, I had a dream that I was walking on a path and got a beautiful green bottle with rubies in my hand. As soon as I held that bottle with rubies, I saw my guiding mentor whose existence vanished like dust into a sprinkling star before my eyes. Surprisingly, after I finished my PhD, my mentor passed away. At that very moment, I could not comprehend, but now I realize that dream was very personal to me and a reminder of this mortal life: "Every soul shall taste death." Surah Al-Imran (3:185). That dream was a reminder of this world (dunya).

We, as human beings, have a tremendous ability to attach ourselves to this world. People, places, events, photographs, and moments become objects of attachment. If things do not work out the way we want or imagine, we feel devastated and disappointed, and therefore, some of us never fully recover. The glass lamp at the edge of the counter, when broken, can never be in the same shape as it was. The problem is not the glass lamp but rather putting it at the counter's edge. The same applies to us; the problem is not the people leaving us, passing away, or breaking up, but instead, the problem is our attachments and dependency. This is because when such a situation happens, we set ourselves up for disappointment.

Often, we allow those relationships to control us; therefore, our emotional, psychological, and mental health and well-being become dependent on them. However, within those dark moments lies profound illumination, where Allah (SWT) awaits to extend His assistance and grant tranquility to our hearts. Therefore, I strongly believe that when you are on your knees, you are in the perfect position to pray.

Allah mentions in the Qur'an: "Whoever rejects evil and believes in Allah hath grasped the most trustworthy handhold that never breaks and Allah hears and knows all-things" (Qur'an 2:256). This verse holds deep significance, as it reassures us that there is one constant source of support that never forsakes us—Allah. By placing our trust in Him, we find solace, contentment, and happiness, nurturing a profound connection with the divine.

However, often, we find ourselves entangled in the trappings of the world; we seek solace in various pursuits—some turn to their careers, others chase after wealth, and many seek fulfillment in relationships. Yet, in our quest to fill the inner void within us, we often seek external validation. It is like trying to fit a circle into a triangle, or vice versa—inevitably leading to frustration and discontent. Our souls yearn for belonging, support, and love from the divine, yet we mistakenly seek these in the material world (dunya), exacerbating our wounds instead of healing them. The pain we experience stems from our worldly attachments, each false connection amplifying our suffering and leading us further away from true contentment and peace.

Our lives often resemble a turbulent roller-coaster ride driven by our relentless pursuit of worldly attachments. However, this quest for fulfillment in transient things only leads to inner turmoil. We are left pondering: how can we ever find lasting peace when what we cling to is ever-changing and perishable?

The profound words of Abu Bakr offer a poignant insight into this truth. In the aftermath of Prophet Muhammad's passing, when shock gripped the hearts of many, Abu Bakr stood as a beacon of wisdom. His love for the Prophet was unparalleled, yet he understood where true dependency should lie. With profound clarity, he declared, "If you worshipped Muhammad, know that Muhammad has passed away. But if you worship Allah, know that Allah never dies" (Al-Bukhari, 9th century/1997, Volume 5, Book 59, Number 733). These words contain a profound lesson: our ultimate reliance should be on the eternal, unchanging source of all things, Allah, rather than on transient entities of this world.

Remembering the dream I had at the start of my PhD journey brings back memories that make me think deeply about life. Sometimes, the flashback of that dream comes unexpectedly; I often wonder why. And my heart responds like a reminder from Allah about what is important. It is when Allah is teaching us about the way of life. I've realized it is best to rely on Allah because everything in this world is temporary. People, things, even our own lives—they all come to an end eventually. Only change is constant; nothing stays the same forever. Life is a journey of healing, especially healing from this world. I realized that true healing cannot be found in this world alone, it is a continuous process. One cannot achieve complete healing from the earthly realm. When the continuum stops, entropy destroys, disrupting balance.

This universe and this realm all require balance akin to Taoist philosophy's Yin-Yang. In spiritual terms, this ideal of balance brings out a corresponding balance in human beings. Whether emotional or mystical, it binds us all together—it is the driving force sustaining our connection with ourselves and Allah (SWT).

Healing from this world comes from connecting to the Divine. Knowing this truth aids in maintaining calmness amidst uncertain circumstances or when confronted with challenges. Acknowledging that regardless of the situation, Allah is ever-present provides solace. Rather

than becoming overly attached to transient matters, the focus shifts towards
nurturing a lasting connection with Allah. This approach fosters a sense of
tranquility and equips one to confront adversities with readiness.

Whispers of Healing

In the depths of twilight's sigh,

Where shadows dance and whispers lie,

There blooms a rose with thorns concealed,

Its petals soft, its beauty revealed.

Each delicate touch brings a sweet pain,

A bittersweet melody, a haunting refrain,

For within its fragrance, secrets reside,

Of love lost, of hearts that cried.

With every gentle breeze that blows,

The rose sways, its sorrow grows,

Yet in its tears, there lies a grace,

A silent longing, an eternal embrace.

Oh, how the heartache sings,

In the silence where the night brings,

A symphony of memories, both bitter and sweet,

As we dance with shadows, our souls to meet.

So let us embrace this tender ache,

For in its depths, our souls awake,

To love's exquisite agony, we surrender our fears,

And find solace in the sweetness of our tears.

Mahrukh Mustansar Ph.D.

A pain and peace between leaving and staying and between losing and gaining: His guidance.

Since I was 13, I have wondered why people leave—relationships, life, and
sometimes without any excuse. And if they are gone, do they ever think of
the relationship lost? Do they ever come back? Why do people stay in a

relationship in which they do not belong? What do we gain from the lost relationship?

Between losing and gaining and between staying and leaving, a part of us remains unheard. It is during these uncertain times that we can draw closer to the divine and find peace within ourselves. Allah's guidance is always available, we just need to open our hearts. I remember when I was going through the dark moments of my life, and nothing made sense, I cried to Allah. Putting my trust in Him, I slept and how beautifully I received guidance through a dream, where I saw a verse from the Qur'an:

إنَّ مَعَ العُسر يُسرا

"Verily, with hardship, comes ease."

When I woke up, I realized nothing is permanent; after every night comes morning, the breathtaking roses in my vase will wither away, my youth will leave me, pain will end, and everyone living in this world is growing and evolving from one phase to another, be they plants, trees, animals, or humans. That is the dynamic of nature. Finding the delicate balance in life is the beauty of it. Life is not perfect, and it never was. Life is not perfectly best, nor it is perfectly worst.

Often in life, when we are experiencing happiness, everything around us becomes happiness: our existence, the air, our surroundings—our entire vision of the world becomes happiness, and if we are experiencing sadness, everything becomes dark, and it often replaces our entire vision of the world. In our experiences, some of us may be susceptible to this. Perhaps that is why we sometimes fall into the trap of thinking, "The physical realm has nothing to share but pain—be it emotional, psychological, spiritual, or physical."

Past and present blend into one moment of experience. However, realizing that nothing in life is ever complete changes our perspective. We stop being overwhelmed by negative thoughts. Understanding that nothing lasts forever, and change is the only constant in this process, we begin to see moments for what they truly are—temporary. They are not the entire universe or reality, just singular moments in an infinite string of time. And as always, this too shall pass. This is a life of tests and tribulations. We will lose our dear relationships; some people struggle with hunger, and some struggle with suffering. Every one of us is fighting a battle within that no one else knows. Our Prophets are the example for our lives. They were also tested.

وَلَنَبْلُوَنَّكُم بِشَيْءٍ مِّنَ الْخَوْفِ وَالْجُوعِ وَنَقْصٍ مِّنَ الْأَمْوَالِ وَالْأَنفُسِ وَالثَّمَرَاتِ ۗ وَبَشِّرِ الصَّابِرِينَ

*"And We will surely test you with something of fear and hunger and a loss
of wealth and lives and fruits, but give good tidings to the patient"*
(Qur'an 2:155).

An example of lost relationships followed by gain in the Qur'an can be
found in the story of Prophet Ayub AS (Job). Job endured immense
suffering, including the loss of his health, wealth, and family. Despite his
hardships, Job remained patient and steadfast in his faith in Allah.
Eventually, Allah rewarded Job's patience and perseverance by restoring
his health, wealth, and family, and blessing him with even greater prosperity
than before.

Another example is when Prophet Younus was cast into the sea, he
found himself swallowed by a giant fish, where he remained in the darkness
of its belly, humbly seeking Allah's forgiveness. In his darkest hour,
Prophet Younus called upon Allah, admitting his mistake, and seeking His
mercy. Allah, in His infinite compassion, responded to Prophet Younus's
repentance and forgave him. Eventually, the fish cast Prophet Younus onto
the shore, and he returned to the people of Nineveh. The story of Prophet
Younus in the Qur'an serves as a powerful reminder of the virtues of
patience, repentance, and trust in Allah, even in the face of adversity. It
exemplifies Allah's boundless mercy and forgiveness for those who
sincerely seek His guidance and forgiveness.

Sometimes, Allah takes away something from us to give us
something better, but it is imperative to understand that other times, His
giving is not always how and what we want. But Allah says in the Qur'an:
"It may be that you dislike something good for you and that you love
something bad for you. Allah knows, and you do not know" (2:216).

In the process of losing, we often face profound lessons that
illuminate our path forward. Through loss, we gain invaluable wisdom, a
deeper capacity for repentance, and the opportunity for self-reflection and
contemplation. It is through the trials of loss that we truly discover our
resilience and inner strength. We learn to appreciate the transient nature of
worldly possessions and relationships, prioritizing what truly matters in life.
Moreover, loss teaches us empathy and compassion, as we empathize with
others who are experiencing similar hardships.

Each loss becomes a stepping stone towards personal growth and
spiritual development. It prompts us to reassess our priorities, values, and
goals, leading to a greater sense of clarity and purpose. Loss challenges us
to confront our fears and limitations, pushing us to transcend our comfort

zones. It fosters humility and gratitude, reminding us to cherish the blessings we still possess. Ultimately, through the process of losing, we emerge stronger, wiser, and more resilient individuals.

Ibn al-Qayyim (may Allah be pleased with him examines the phenomenon of gaining and losing, offering profound insights into its spiritual dimensions. He emphasizes that loss is not merely a setback but a catalyst for spiritual growth and development. Ibn al-Qayyim highlights the transformative power of loss, stating that through it, individuals can gain deeper wisdom, strengthen their faith, and cultivate resilience. He underscores the importance of embracing loss as a means of drawing closer to Allah and surrendering to His divine wisdom (Mogahed, 2015).

Ibn al-Qayyim also emphasizes the need for patience and trust in Allah's decree, recognizing that loss is ultimately a test of faith and an opportunity for spiritual elevation. Moreover, the impermanence of worldly attachments and the futility of placing excessive value on material possessions will end. Instead, he advocates for prioritizing spiritual wealth and inner contentment, which transcend the transient nature of worldly gains and losses. Ibn al-Qayyim's teachings serve as a timeless reminder of the profound lessons inherent in the cycles of gain and loss, guiding individuals towards a deeper understanding of themselves and their relationship with the Divine (Mogahed, 2015).

Indeed, Allah's gifts often exceed our expectations, as He has the power to restore lost relationships to us, sometimes even better than before.

So, the question arises: Do we get back our lost relationships? The answer is: YES. Through His infinite wisdom and mercy, Allah may reunite us with loved ones in ways we could not have imagined. Whether relationships are restored exactly as they were or in an improved form, or Allah (SWT) blesses us with someone better for us, it is a testament to Allah's benevolence and care for His servants. Trusting in Allah's plan, we find solace in knowing that He always has our best interests at heart. This verse reminds us to celebrate Allah's blessings. Indeed, Allah is the best planner.

In the Qur'an, Allah reminds us: "In Allah's blessings and mercy, let them find joy. It is far better than what they accumulate" (20:58). Finding solace in Allah's decree purifies the ego and helps us heal. However, modern man often suffers from spiritual crises. Instead of turning to Allah, we expand our inner wounds by filling the void of our lives through societal sedatives.

On Filling the Inner Hole and Light That Guides Us Home

Often, when adversity afflicts us, modern man tends to go towards societal sedatives, be it alcohol, drugs, girlfriends, or boyfriends, using pleasure to manage pain instead of curing it. Therefore, we keep on expanding the wound without knowing what we are doing to ourselves. So, with each passing day, the void increases. Curing pain requires us to get back to the center of the soul and connect with the Divine. Everything happening in our lives holds a deeper meaning—returning to Him. The pain is never for us, it is for HIM. He gives us pain so we connect with HIM. To find HIM is to understand the purpose of pain. For example, some people do not recognize beauty unless it is right in front of them. They can walk by a seashore or a beautiful sunset and not even notice it.

Some individuals possess the remarkable ability to recognize and bask in the splendor of beauty. They pause, allowing themselves to be enveloped by its essence. Yet, for others, this appreciation remains surface-level, akin to admiring a masterpiece without delving into its creator's narrative. Art, in its essence, serves as a conduit for the artist's message. When an admirer becomes lost in the aesthetics, neglecting to decipher the underlying meaning, the artwork fails to fulfill its intended purpose. Within the intricate tapestry of the universe, every element conveys a divine message, imploring us to explore its profound significance.

"Surely, in the creation of the heavens and the earth, and in the alternation of night and day, there are signs for those who reflect" (Qur'an, 3:190). Even the sunset imparts a profound message: Change is inevitable. It reminds us that everything has its conclusion. Just as the day yields to night, hardships, too, shall pass.

When faced with pain or hardship in life, it is important to approach it with a mindful and spiritually attuned perspective. Rather than allowing ourselves to become consumed by the illusion of suffering, we can strive to see beyond it. Every trial and tribulation holds within it a hidden message, a divine purpose waiting to be discovered. Through introspection and spiritual reflection, we can uncover the deeper meaning behind our challenges and use them as opportunities for growth and self-discovery.

In Islam, the concept of "sabr" (patience) at the time of adversity plays a crucial role in navigating difficult times. It is through patience and perseverance that we can endure trials with grace and dignity. By exercising patience, we demonstrate our trust in Allah's wisdom and plan for us. We understand that every hardship we face is a test from Allah, designed to strengthen our faith and character.

The importance of turning to Allah in times of distress, through prayer, supplication, and remembrance of Allah (dhikr), allows us to find solace and comfort in His presence. Connecting with Allah allows us to transcend our earthly concerns and find peace in His divine presence. Islamic teachings remind us of the transient nature of this world and the inevitability of suffering. The Qur'an states, "Verily, with hardship comes ease" (Qur'an 94:6), reassuring us that our trials are temporary and will ultimately be followed by relief and blessings from Allah.

Finding purpose and meaning in our suffering is essential for our spiritual well-being. By viewing our challenges as opportunities for spiritual growth and drawing closer to Allah, we can transform pain into a pathway to divine enlightenment. Through patience, faith, and reliance on Allah, we can navigate life's trials with resilience and grace, emerging stronger and more spiritually aligned than before.

Letting Go and Embracing Change: A Pathway to Purification of Heart

Avoid conflating attachment with love. Attachment stems from fear and dependency, often reflecting self-love more than love for another. Love devoid of attachment embodies purity, as it is not contingent on receiving anything from others because of one's emptiness of the heart. Rather, it focuses on giving to others from a place of inner fulfillment—Heartfulness.

Heartfulness

Love's true essence lies in giving,

Not in the fear of what we're living.

Attachment masks the self's desire,

but pure love sets the soul on fire.

Mahrukh Mustansar, Ph.D.

One of the main reasons that we are unable to see the meaning and the purpose behind our pain or to connect with the Divine is that our hearts are already cluttered by many worldly attachments. To Feel His presence, to connect with the center of the soul, requires emptying the heart of all false attachments, and that is when the heart will be "full" because then comes awakening. When the heart is full and free from all the false attachments, then it experiences the purest form of love. To empty the heart does not mean to avoid love. On contrary, true love flows in, as God intended.

The purification of the heart commences with the shahada (declaration of faith). It is noteworthy that this declaration initiates with a critical negation, signifying a vital emptying process. Before affirming tawhid (the belief in the oneness of Allah), we proclaim: "La ilaha" (there is no deity). An "ilah" is an object of worship, yet it is crucial to grasp that it is not merely something we pray to. Rather, an "ilah" is what forms the core of our existence, what we obediently adhere to, and what holds utmost significance in our lives, above all else (Mogahed, 2015).

Purifying the heart through the shahada, or declaration of faith, is a profound and essential aspect of Islamic spirituality. In Islam, the heart is considered the seat of one's faith, consciousness, and innermost intentions. Therefore, purifying the heart is crucial for cultivating a strong and sincere relationship with Allah and living a righteous life. The shahada consists of two parts: "La ilaha illallah" (There is no deity worthy of worship except Allah) and "Muhammadur rasulullah" (Muhammad is the Messenger of Allah). Each part plays a significant role in affirming one's faith and commitment to Islam.

The first part, "La ilaha illallah," emphasizes the concept of tawhid, or the oneness of Allah. This declaration negates the worship of any other deity besides Allah and affirms His sole right to be worshipped. By uttering these words, a person acknowledges the supremacy of Allah and submits their will to Him alone. This act of surrendering to Allah is the foundation of Islamic monotheism and serves as a powerful means of purifying the heart from the worship of false gods or idols.

The second part of the shahada, "Muhammadur rasulullah," acknowledges the prophethood of Muhammad (peace be upon him) and the importance of following his teachings. Muhammad (peace be upon him) is considered the final messenger sent by Allah to guide humanity to the straight path. By accepting him as the messenger of Allah, Muslims commit to following his example and adhering to the teachings of the Qur'an and Sunnah (traditions of the Prophet). This part of the shahada reinforces the importance of obedience to Allah and His messenger in purifying the heart and living a righteous life.

Purifying the heart through the shahada involves more than just reciting the words; it requires a deep internal transformation of one's beliefs, attitudes, and behaviors. It entails striving to align one's thoughts, intentions, and actions with the teachings of Islam and seeking forgiveness for past transgressions. It also involves cultivating virtues such as sincerity, humility, gratitude, and compassion while striving to overcome vices such as arrogance, envy, and greed.

One of the key concepts in purifying the heart is the notion of "tazkiyah," or spiritual purification. Tazkiyah involves cleansing the heart from impurities such as sins, doubts, and negative emotions, and filling it with virtues such as faith, love, and piety. It is a continuous process of self-examination, repentance, and spiritual growth aimed at attaining nearness to Allah and achieving spiritual excellence.

The journey of purifying the heart through the shahada requires sincere effort, patience, and perseverance. It involves seeking knowledge of Islam, performing acts of worship such as prayer, fasting, and charity, and engaging in acts of kindness and service to others. It also involves fostering a deep connection with Allah through constant remembrance (dhikr), supplication (dua), and reflection on His signs and attributes. The rewards of purifying the heart through the shahada are immense and far-reaching. A purified heart is characterized by inner peace, contentment, and tranquility, as it is free from the burdens of sin and worldly attachments. It is also receptive to guidance from Allah and His messenger, enabling the individual to navigate life's challenges with wisdom and resilience.

A purified heart is a source of light and guidance for others, inspiring them to embrace the path of righteousness and seek closeness to Allah. It serves as a beacon of hope and inspiration in a world filled with darkness and despair, offering solace and guidance to those who are lost or struggling. My mentor once said and I quote: "Every person, whether Atheist, Muslim, Christian, or Jew, has an Illah. Everyone is devoted to something. For many, this object of devotion is tied to the worldly life, the Dunya. Some are devoted to their careers, intellect, relationships, wealth, or fame. And many, as the Qur'an so eloquently states, worship themselves and desires."

"Have you seen he who has taken as his god his [own] desire, and Allah has sent him astray due to knowledge and has set a seal upon his hearing and his heart and put over his vision a veil? So, who will guide him after Allah? Then will you not be reminded?" (Qur'an 45:23). These objects of worship are often the things we become deeply attached to. However, it is important to recognize that an object of attachment is not a necessity, but rather a desire. When we lose such an object of attachment, it can lead to profound devastation, pain, and suffering. False attachments can lead to pain and suffering.

The struggle to purify and clean one's heart from all avarice, reprehensible attributes, and false attachment is real. It is the greatest struggle in earthly life. And this struggle is the essence of tawhid. If we look deeply at the five pillars of Islam, we will realize they are spiritual in nature, as these five pillars actually work to clean our hearts and help us make a connection with Allah for the sake of His love.

Everyone of has intense moments of life—hardships, pain, suffering, and sometimes uncertainty. However, seeing through the illusions of hardships, pain and suffering can only happen when we do not allow our heart to focus. Focus can only happen if we are not operating from cognitive distortions. When we like something or someone dearly, we tend to exaggerate our thoughts and feelings about them, and often, we become blind to the miseries they cause us, and if we dislike something or someone, our mind operates in exaggeration, as it tends to amplify the negative attributes of another person. Exaggerations often lead to cognitive distortion and clutter the heart with false attachments. In both examples, we become falsely attached to our mindset. Therefore, each behavior, thought, and decision stems from that cognitive distortion. To make a heart focus, it is important to clean it from all these exaggerations caused by false attachments. This is why seeing through illusion becomes one of the biggest struggles for mankind.

Seeing through the illusions is through tawhid. The concept of Tawhid provides solace and direction. It reminds us that we are not alone in our struggles but are united with all of creation in reliance upon Allah. This sense of unity instills resilience and fortitude, enabling individuals to confront challenges with unwavering faith. The essence of Islam resonates with th principle of Tawhid, emphasizing the oneness of God. Tawhid transcends mere recognition of Allah's unity; it encompasses a profound unity of purpose, fear, worship, and love for God.

By seeking refuge in Allah's mercy and guidance, individuals embark on a journey towards inner healing, personal growth, and spiritual fulfillment, even amidst the darkest of times. When people find themselves trapped in hardships, struggles, unknown fear, heartbreak, and pain, all they need to do is turn to Allah, and He always makes a way for them in the most unexpected ways. This is not a feel-happy theory. It is a promise from Allah (SWT) Himself. As He says in Qura'n:

وَمَن يَتَّقِ اللَّهَ يَجْعَل لَّهُ مَخْرَجًا (٢) وَيَرْزُقْهُ مِنْ حَيْثُ لَا يَحْتَسِبُ ۚ وَمَن يَتَوَكَّلْ عَلَى اللَّهِ فَهُوَ حَسْبُهُ ۚ
إِنَّ اللَّهَ بَالِغُ أَمْرِهِ ۚ قَدْ جَعَلَ اللَّهُ لِكُلِّ شَيْءٍ قَدْرًا

"And whoever fears Allah - He will make for him a way out (from every difficulty) and will provide for him from where he does not expect. And whoever relies upon Allah - then He is sufficient for him. Indeed, Allah will accomplish His purpose. Allah has already set for everything a [decreed] extent." (Qur'an, 65:2-3)

I cried for every heartache, I cried for every pain.

But then my heart found YOU,

And never I cried again.

Mahrukh Mustansar, Ph.D. (The Center, January 21, 2021)

Breaking the shackles of this world:

Compassion

Love, a silent ache within,

A bittersweet melody, pure and thin,

Untouched by worldly woes and fears,

It whispers softly, wiping tears.

In its depths, a boundless sea,

Where hearts find solace, wild and free,

With every beat, a tender sigh,

it's a touch of Divine, we can't deny.

Mahrukh Mustansar, Ph.D.

Love and desire are two different concepts. We often mix love with our desire to get someone or something. We often name our attachments to our desires as "Love." If our heart has desires, it is enslaved by worldly attachment, and the heart is never going to be full. However, true love is free from all desires, it is pure and sweet as the true essence of purity is love. To demonstrate this I mention the story of Amna and Zayn. Amna and Zayn were good friends. Amna, a talented artist, lived a life of luxury, and her affection for Zayn knew no bounds. She made his sculpture, and his presence felt like a refreshing breeze to Amna on a scorching day. Zayn, on the other hand, possessed charm and mystery, and his allure captivated Amna like a warm winter sunshine.

However, Amna's desire for Zayn soon turned into an obsession, and her greatest fear was losing him. Consumed by her desire to marry him, Amna thought she was in Love, but she was enslaved by her emotions, desires, and obsessions. She was unaware that her affection had turned into captivity. She wed Zayn, hoping to secure their love forever.

Yet, as time passed, cracks began to appear in their relationship. Zayn, ever the enigmatic figure, found himself drawn to another woman whom he believed to be his soulmate. This revelation shattered Amna, her heart breaking at the realization that her love had been one-sided all along. Her pain was intense because she enslaved herself with her obsessions and desires for getting Zayn. She struggled hard to win him, but she lost him over and over again. "The one who is (truly) imprisoned is the one whose heart is imprisoned from Allah and the captivated one is the one whose desires have enslaved him" Ibn Taymiyyah (1263–1328).

Amna's story holds a profound lesson for us because it demonstrates the truth of existence. As human beings, we are created with a particular nature (fitrah). That fitrah is to recognize the oneness of God and making it full of His divine presence, because people will leave us, but Allah never leaves. Therefore, no heartbreak, no loss. Nothing will cause more pain than putting someone equal to God in our lives—and in our hearts. Amna story tells us all love, except for love for God, eventually fades. The pain demands to be felt but navigating through those intricacies of life is through the guidance of Allah. We try to find happiness and solace in this world and worldly attachments, but the fact of the matter is, our pain becomes our strength when we turn to the source of the world—the Creator, Allah

Allah mentions in Qur'an Surah Ar-Ra'd (13:28): "Those who believe and find comfort in remembering Allah. Surely, hearts find peace through the remembrance of Allah." We are travelers, traveling this earth. And it is this very concept that Prophet (SAW) spoke about so eloquently: "What relationship do I have with this world? It's like a traveler resting briefly under a shade of tree before continuing the journey, leaving the tree behind" (Sahih al-Bukhari, Book 76, Hadith 425). Take a moment to ponder the analogy of a traveler. When you are on a journey, do you become deeply attached to your temporary stopovers? Imagine passing through a city for just one night—you may find comfort in staying at a motel, but would you yearn to settle there permanently? Likely not. This is the mindset of a traveler: a natural detachment arises from the awareness that something is only transient.

In his profound wisdom, the Prophet Muhammad (SAW) recognized the peril of becoming overly attached to this fleeting world. Indeed, there was nothing he feared more for us than this very attachment. He likened our existence in this world to that of a traveler passing through, reminding us of the impermanence of our stay. Just as a traveler does not cling to their temporary lodgings, we too should not become overly attached to the passing pleasures and possessions of this world.

Consider the fleeting nature of life itself. Our time on this earth is but a brief sojourn, a temporary stop in the grand journey of existence. Like the passing clouds in the sky, our days drift by swiftly, leaving behind only memories and echoes of moments gone by. The Prophet (SAW) urged us to reflect on the transient nature of our worldly pursuits, cautioning against investing too deeply in that which is ephemeral. Yet, despite the ephemeral nature of this world, it is all too easy to become ensnared by its fleeting allure. We chase after wealth, status, and material comforts, believing them to be the keys to happiness and fulfillment. Yet, the Prophet (SAW) reminded us that true contentment lies not in the accumulation of worldly possessions, but in the richness of our spiritual connection to the Divine.

In the face of life's transient nature, the Prophet (SAW) encouraged us to cultivate a mindset of detachment, to hold onto the world with a gentle grasp, knowing that it is but a passing shadow. Just as a traveler carries only the essentials for their journey, we too should travel lightly through life, unburdened by the weight of excessive attachments. Let us heed the Prophet's (SAW) timeless wisdom and strive to emulate his example of detachment and humility. By anchoring our hearts in the eternal truths of faith and righteousness, we can find true peace and fulfillment, even amidst the fleeting pleasures of this world. He (SAW) said: "By Allah I don't fear for you poverty, but I feel that the world will be abundant for you, as it has been for those before you, so you compete for it as they competed for it, so it destroys you as it destroyed them." The Prophet Muhammad (SAW) understood the reality of this world. He navigated the same journey that we all embark upon. However, his vessel was guided by the knowledge of its origins and destination. He recognized that although the ocean may gleam in the sunlight, it ultimately becomes a graveyard for ships that venture into it.

The crux of this chapter is that when we are faced with hard times, we need to open our hearts and let the light pass through them instead of becoming blind and finding peace in false attachments and societal sedatives. Pain brings a lot of lessons with it. If our hearts are open, our vision becomes clearer, and pain no longer appears like pain but a pathway to the divine light that connects us with the source of this world—the Creator.

Purify Your Soul

Look up to the sky

and spread your wings to fly.

Break the chain of procrastination, and make your aims high, one day you will fly high with no sighs.

Re-live the moments you read, Embrace the happy and sad days, Have faith in Divine

and lead. You will see, your fears will fade away.

Dance in the imaginative endeavor, and belief that you will touch the heaven, hold your

faith with all the care, each day teaches us a lifelong lesson.

Live the up and down rhythms of life, Faith sets the spirit free, everything will get better.

Just believe Aim high, and you will see.

But, trust the Divine,

Who lives in your heart and shines, Only He can satisfy your begging bowl,

But remember, a shady heart can never purify a soul.

Mahrukh Mustansar, Ph.D. (The Center, January 21, 2021)

References

Larura, A. P., Debra, J. B., & Gu, Q. (2011). *Antidepressant use in persons aged 12 and over: United States, 2005–2008*. (NCHS Data Brief No. 76). National Center for Health Statistics.

Wang, H., Tian, X., Wang, X., & Wang, Y. (2021). Evolution and emerging trends in depression research from 2004 to 2019: A literature visualization analysis. *Frontiers in Psychiatry, 12*, 705749. https://doi.org/10.3389/fpsyt.2021.705749

Isgandarova, N. (2019). Muraqaba as a mindfulness-based therapy in Islamic psychotherapy. *Journal of Religion and Health, 58(4), 1146–1160.*

Mogahed, Y. (2015). *Reclaim your heart* (2nd ed.). FB Publishing.

Sakellari, E., Psychogiou, M., Georgiou, A., Papanidi, M., Vlachou, V., & Sapountzi-Krepia, D. (2018). Exploring religiosity, self-esteem, stress, and depression among students of a Cypriot University. *Journal of Religion and Health, 57, 136–145.*

Khan, M. M. (Trans.). (1997). *The Translation of the Meanings of Sahih Al-Bukhari: Arabic-English* (Volume 5, Book 59, Number 733). Darussalam. (Original work published 9th century).

About the Editor

Carrie M. York, PhD is founder and president of the Alkaram Institute, a 501c3 non-profit research and educational institution dedicated to advancing Islamic psychology to benefit society and improve lives and whose vision is to become the first Muslim graduate school of psychology in the United States. She is also publisher of Alkaram Press. She has a PhD in transpersonal psychology from Sofia University, a Master's degree in Middle East Studies from the American University of Beirut, and is currently pursuing a graduate certificate in non-profit management at Harvard University. Dr. York's areas of expertise include Islamic psychology, spiritually integrated psychotherapy, Islamic spirituality, and virtue and character development. Over the past twenty years has taught, researched, and published extensively on these and related topics at the intersection of psychology and religion. She was also an associate editor of the American Psychological Association's journal *Spirituality in Clinical Practice* ® for four years. Her books include *Mental Health and Psychological Practice in the United Arab Emirates* (2015), *Islamically Integrated Psychotherapy: Uniting Faith and Professional Practice* (2018), a children's character development book *Maya and the Seven Limbs* (2020), *The Way of Love: Towards an Islamic Psychology of Virtues and Character Development* (2023), and *Heartfulness: Islamic Spiritual Practices for Health and Wellbeing* (2024). Having lived outside her native United States in various countries for nearly 17 years, she now lives in Great Falls, Virginia. In her free time, she enjoys jogging, traveling, and spending time with loved ones. She also enjoys real estate investment and development as a side hobby.

About the Contributors

Zuhal Ağılkaya-Şahin, PhD completed her master's and doctorate degrees in the field of psychology of religion at Marmara University. In 2015, she started to work as an Assistant Professor at Izmir Katip Çelebi University, Department of Psychology of Religion. In 2018, she started to work as an assistant professor at Istanbul Medeniyet University, Department of Psychological Counseling and Guidance. She received various trainings in the fields of spiritual, psychological and Islamic counseling from Turkey and abroad. She is one of the founding members of the Turkish Association for the Psychology of Religion and serves as a member of the board of directors and vice president. She also co-founded ISIP Turkey (International Students of Islamic Psychology) and serves as a member of the advisory board. She authored books such as *Manevi Bakım ve Danışmanlık* (Spiritual Care and Counseling, 2nd Edition, Marmara Akademi) and *Psikoloji ve Psikoterapide Din* (Religion in Psychology and Psychotherapy, 2nd Edition, Çamlıca). She co-edited books such as *Psychology of Religion in Turkey* (Brill), Din Psikolojisi (Psychology of Religion, Lisans), and *Sociology of Religion in Turkey* (Çamlıca). She has numerous papers, publications, and presentations in English, German, Turkish, national and international in the fields of psychology of religion, spiritual/pastoral care and counseling, and Islamic psychology and psychotherapy. She is currently working as an Associate Professor at Istanbul Medeniyet University, Department of Psychological Counseling and Guidance. zuhal.agilkayasahin@medeniyet.edu.tr

Razia Bhatti-Ali, DClin, Psych is a UK based and trained Consultant Clinical Psychologist with over 30 years' experience in adult mental health. She has worked in both NHS and private healthcare settings and is a skilled practitioner trained in a variety of evidence-based therapeutic approaches including Cognitive Behavioural Therapy (CBT), third wave CBT approaches such as Acceptance and Commitment Therapy (ACT), Dialectical Behaviour Therapy, Compassion Focused Therapy (CFT) and Mindfulness. In recent years, she completed level two training in Islamic Psychology anPsychotherapy endorsed by the International Association of Islamic Psychology (IAIP). Dr. Bhatti-Ali is a published author. Her publications include: Integrating Acceptance and Commitment Therapy with Islamic Psychotherapy for Managing Chronic Pain (Routledge, 2024), Culturally Adapted Pain Management Services in Dogra, S.A. (Ed.), British Muslims, Ethnicity and Health Inequalities. Edinburgh University Press (2023) and several children's books (Halima's Miracle, The Woodcutter & the Bird, Edge of The World, and Musa and the Wise Pigeon).

Maneeza Dawood, Ph.D., is a Research Scientist at Stanford SPARQ and an Islamic Psychology Research Fellow at the Alkaram Institute. She completed her doctoral degree in Psychology from Columbia University and did her postdoctoral work at the Yale Center for Emotional Intelligence. Her research broadly centers on understanding the social psychological processes that lead to social change, with a focus on education inequality, religious identity, and race in the media. Her work as a fellow at the Alkaram Institute is aimed at developing a framework of Islamic social psychology.

Wadud Hassan is the founder of Muraqaba - a global community dedicated to cultivating spiritual and emotional wellness at the intersection of faith and science, reviving the traditions of experiential dhikr (remembrance of God), tafakkur (contemplation), tadabbur (Quranic deep reflection), muraqaba (God-centered meditation), and muhasaba (self-examination) through an app, the signature HEART-centered Mindfulness Masterclass, and a series of courses and programs with Muslim mindfulness educators, psychologists, and counselors. Wadud and his wife Leiya are also the founders of The Muraqaba School, a K-12 school of Prophetic Tarbiyah in the greater Dallas area committed to reviving an Islamic pedagogy and Islamic worldview-based education. They also incorporate Muraqaba's work of Prophetic Wellness at their school. Wadud is a student of Imam Dr. Yusuf Ziya Kavakci, the former Imam of Dallas Central Mosque and member of the ISNA Fiqh Council, Sh. Abdul Nasir Jangda at the Qalam Seminary, and Sh. Khalil A. Rasheed at Harvard. Wadud, Leiya, their parents, and twin daughters live in the Dallas metropolitan area. For more on his work visit https://www.muraqabaschool.org and https://muraqaba.app

Ghena Ismail, PsyD is an Assistant Professor in the Psychology Department at the American University of Beirut. She is also a Clinical Associate in the Department of Psychiatry, Faculty of Medicine where she sees patients presenting with a wide range of issues including complex trauma, eating disorders, grief and loss, depression, anxiety, self-growth, relationships, and interpersonal problems. From 2014-2017, she served as the psychosocial director of the inpatient psychiatric services at AUBMC and subsequently as the founding director of the AUBMC Treatment and Outreach Program for Eating Disorders (TOP-ED). Dr. Ismail is registered with the College of Psychologists of Ontario as a Clinical and Forensic Psychologist. She earned her doctoral degree in Clinical Psychology at James Madison University and completed graduate level courses in Qur'anic studies at the University of Toronto. Her work centers on promoting an integrative and interdisciplinary discourse to wellness. She has published articles and book chapters on the topics of trauma, the psychology of religion and spirituality, mindfulness and ethics, and served as a reviewer in peer-reviewed scientific journals. She supervises medical residents and psychology interns and teaches undergraduate and graduate courses in Abnormal Psychology, Professional Ethics and Cognitive and Behavioral Interventions. Dr. Ismail served on several committees within AUB including the Palliative Care committee, the Medical Education committee, the Salim El-Hoss Bioethics & Professionalism Program, and the Advisory Committee for the Islamic Studies Program. She also provides ongoing consultation to varied segments within the community including training programs, wellness centers and the corporate sector.

Sarah Huxtable Mohr, LCSW was born and raised in the San Francisco Bay Area, the traditional territory of the Ohlone people, and is passionate about serving her community. She is a certified drug and alcohol counselor and Licensed Clinical Social Worker. She earned her MSW from California State University, East Bay (2017). She has a BA in Religion from Dominican University, with minors in Women and Gender Studies and Philosophy and a Masters in Religion and Psychology from the Graduate Theological Union (GTU) with a Certificate in Islamic Studies (2009). She is a visiting scholar at the GTU and is on faculty at the Alkaram Institute. She has published in a variety of formats on various topics including liberation psychology, conversion, addiction treatment, mindfulness, and more. Her most recent book is *Islamic Liberation Psychology: The Transformational Force of Self-Development, Community Empowerment, and Revolutionary Change.*

Mahrukh Mustansar, PhD is the CEO and co-founder of Mintlife Health, Virginia, and a leading expert in psychology, executive mental health coaching, master neuro-linguistic programming (NLP), well-being consulting, and hypnotherapy. She is a certified advanced professional hypnosis practitioner from the National Guild of Hypnotists (NGH) and ICBCH. As one of the few Peace Psychologists globally, Dr. Mustansar serves as a board member of APA Division 48 (Society for the Study of Peace, Conflict, and Violence) and APA Division 9 (Society for the Psychological Study of Social Issues). She is also a member of the American Psychological Association and the International Network of Peace Psychologists (INPP). Dr. Mustansar holds a Bachelor's and Master's degree in behavioral analysis and applied psychology, as well as a second Master of Philosophy and Doctorate of Philosophy research focusing on behavioral analysis, Peace Psychology, and Mental Health Rehabilitation. She has also authored two poetry books: *Resonance of the Souls* and *The Center*, and has written numerous research and web articles on peace and social psychology.

Fyeqa Sheikh, PsyD is a clinical psychologist who specializes in working with individuals with acute and chronic health challenges. She is currently practicing within a hospital system in the Chicagoland area. Her clinical and research interests include traumatic stress, Islamic psychology and faith-based approaches, management of depression and anxiety secondary to medical challenges, and psycho-oncology.

Farah Zahir, PhD is a genomics scientist of nearly 20 years and an authorized Islamic spiritual guide. She completed her doctoral training at the University of British Columbia (Canada). During her doctorate and post-doctorate she identified nine new Intellectual Disability syndromes, including Zahir Friedman Syndrome (ZFS, OMIM#6134571). To date she has published approximately 35 scientific papers in top-tier journals for her field, with over 2000 citations. Dr. Zahir is also a trained scholar in tasawwuf or what she terms 'the science of Ihsan'. She has studied with prominent masters of tazkiyah ul nafs of our time, completing her training under the guidance of Imam Fode Drame of the Jahanke scholars of West Africa - spiritual masters with over 11 centuries of recorded scholarship. To date she has published seven books in advanced Islamic spirituality and actively teaches and counsels as a spiritual guide. She currently serves as the Founding President of Irfa'a Foundation, which is dedicated to reviving the science of Ihsan, and as faculty at the Alkaram Institute. Her present academic work is focused on how spirituality impacts genes via epigenomic regulation, thus causing distinct biological impacts that can also be hereditary.